PRIVACY AND HEALTHCARE DATA

The question of how to balance individual privacy interests and community interests in the exploitation of healthcare data is one of the most vexing issues facing privacy scholars. In this important contribution Munns and Basu, by putting patient choice and technology at the centre of the debate, make a key contribution that must be read by all interested parties.

Andrew Murray, London School of Economics, UK

I found this study of health informatics to be an invaluable addition to the literature on technology regulation and the disruptive capacity of technological innovation, demonstrating our need to re-evaluate core concepts of privacy and data ownership under the forces of information technology.

Robert Lee, University of Birmingham, UK

This book provides a very important contribution to the debate about consent and the use of health information that we should be having increasingly with the public. Transparency is not only ethically correct but also incredibly empowering, breaking down barriers to information sharing which so often jeopardise safe care. This novel proposal unites traditional privacy theory with innovation, offering mechanisms to make such empowerment a reality.

Dame Fiona Caldicott, FRCPsych, FRCP; National Data Guardian;
Chair, Independent Information Governance Oversight Panel (IIGOP)

Writing in the shadow of care.data, the authors suggest that, by an imaginative use of online portals and platforms, the collective interest in sharing healthcare data can be reconciled with the individual interest in controlling access to one's personal health records. The proposal in this timely book merits serious consideration.

Roger Brownsword, King's College London, UK

'I have been impressed with the urgency of doing.
Knowing is not enough; we must apply.
Being willing is not enough; we must do.'

Leonardo da Vinci (1452–1519)

Privacy and Healthcare Data

'Choice of Control' to 'Choice' and 'Control'

CHRISTINA MUNNS

SUBHAJIT BASU
University of Leeds, UK

Routledge
Taylor & Francis Group
LONDON AND NEW YORK

First published 2015 by Ashgate Publishing

2 Park Square, Milton Park, Abingdon, Oxfordshire OX14 4RN
52 Vanderbilt Avenue, New York, NY 10017

Routledge is an imprint of the Taylor & Francis Group, an informa business

First issued in paperback 2020

British Library Cataloguing in Publication Data
A catalogue record for this book is available from the British Library.

The Library of Congress has cataloged the printed edition as follows:
Munns, Christina, author.
Privacy and healthcare data : 'choice of control' to 'choice' and 'control' / by Christina Munns and Subhajit Basu.
pages cm
Includes bibliographical references and index.
ISBN 978-1-4724-2686-4 (hardback : alk. paper) 1. Medical records–Law and legislation–Great Britain. 2. Medical informatics–Law and legislation–Great Britain. 3. Data processing–Law and legislation–Great Britain. I. Basu, Subhajit, 1973– author. II. Title.
KD3410.R43M86 2015
344.4104'19–dc23

2015019280

ISBN: 978-1-4724-2686-4 (hbk)
ISBN: 978-0-367-59731-3 (pbk)

Contents

List of Figures and Tables

Figures

Tables

Foreword

As a privacy sceptic it seems to me that there are no more diverse views on medical privacy than between the academic and the citizen. The academic typically espouses the sanctity of the informational relationship between patient and doctor, asserting it as a fundamental right. The citizen, in practical reality, seems never to be happier than when talking about their own and other's health issues. Simply stand in any town centre and you can hear intimate details of personal health being discussed by those entering or past middle age. We all know individuals who insist on talking about their health when we have long lost interest. I have been offered a view of a photograph of scar tissue from a terminally ill friend. That reality does not fit the typical academic article. Certainly there are issues of privacy around health, but these are set in a more complex framework than is often enunciated.

It is into this gap between an idealistic view of medical privacy and citizens interested in discussing health that Munns and Basu enter with their concept of 'control' as mediating concept, and – as they say – it will help develop better discussion than putting up the barrier of 'privacy' to terminate sensible discussion.

There are two forces at work which Munns and Basu outline. The most obvious one is the change in the world around us brought about by new technology and the Information Society project. A hugely positive force in many ways, information technology offers means of improving the health of the populations at large through the collection and analysis of patient data whether by national health systems or through private/academic research. But it is also a force for destruction, as Veblen noted: 'Technology marches in seven-league boots from one ruthless, revolutionary conquest to another, tearing down old factories and industries, flinging up new processes with terrifying rapidity.' Perhaps hospitals are not yet being torn down (the medical factories and industries) but certainly a medical revolution is about to happen and the lawyer needs to understand the issues which the authors highlight so well.

The second force is the changing relationship between the citizen and the medical professional. In the UK it was only in the 1990 Access to Health Records Act that a patient gained access to their own medical records and a paternalistic attitude towards giving patients knowledge about their own condition was the norm. The sceptic might suggest that – like medical privacy generally – one of the problems with the prior relationship was that it protected the medical profession more than it educated the patient (an essential if 'consent' is to have any real meaning). The new technological framework is certainly tearing through this paternalism as citizens seek knowledge about their and others' conditions (for example, the online world is full of forums discussing the most intimate details) and try to educate themselves on health issues. This is the control, it seems to me, that Munns and Basu are focusing upon.

And law is beginning to recognise this new world as in *Montgomery v Lanarkshire Health Board*,[1] where the Supreme Court overturned *Sidaway* ('the provision of too much information may prejudice the attainment of the objective of restoring the patient's health' [Montgomery, para. 74]) and initiated a new balancing of the duty of a doctor towards a patient in relation to advice about treatment:

> It would therefore be a mistake to view patients as uninformed, incapable of understanding medical matters, or wholly dependent upon a flow of information from doctors. The idea that patients were medically uninformed and incapable of understanding medical matters was always a questionable generalisation, as Lord Diplock implicitly acknowledged by making an exception for highly educated men of experience. To make it the default assumption on which the law is to be based is now manifestly untenable. (Para. 76)

If the Information Society is about anything, it is about having a knowledgeable citizen who can participate fully through access to relevant information. Without knowledge and education we live in darkness. Munns and Basu are thus to be commended for working towards enabling light.

This is not just a subject of academic interest to me, but is also a personal one. Lack of information about medical issues – indeed a failure to seek the information myself – affected my family with the most serious consequences. I hope, therefore, that Munns and Basu can move the argument from sterile discussion of the nature of medical privacy, towards a better health system to serve a much better educated citizen.

Philip Leith

1 [2015] UKSC 11.

Acknowledgments

It is our profound admiration for the NHS that has inspired us to write this book, together with our heartfelt belief that the appropriate use of information saves and improves lives. It is our hope that patients will soon be fully empowered by the choice of control to make information sharing choices that will undoubtedly affect them and society at large.

This book summarises more than four years of research that has been painstakingly carried out with the aim of generating arguments, to provoke and stimulate new visions for the sharing of healthcare data. As with any project of this scale, duration and complexity, there are too many influences to name individually and the influences are too extensive to fully acknowledge. Nevertheless an attempt needs to be made. This book would not have been completed without the continued guidance and inspiration of Philip Leith. We particularly valued his readiness to read and critically comment on our work whenever we needed feedback. The book has greatly benefited from stimulating discussions and debates we had at different international conferences – particularly they helped us to develop the balance between 'individual privacy' and our concept of 'collective transparency'. We appreciate the people who offered suggestions for ways to expand or improve our collective thinking, in particular, Joseph A. Cannataci.

We would like to gratefully acknowledge the support of Katherine Pearson and Ryan Givens, Dickinson School of Law, Penn State University, USA, who have read and commented on every single chapter in this book.

We greatly appreciate that we were able to conduct this research in the intellectually stimulating, demanding and yet supportive environment of the School of Law, University of Leeds. We would like to gratefully acknowledge the support of Alastair Mullis and would like to thank many of our colleagues and friends for their support, advice, and encouragement, including Graham Dutfield, Amrita Mukherjee and César J. Ramírez-Montes. We express our sincere gratitude to Richard Jones for his invaluable advice as the work progressed, which provided us with much needed confidence. We also wish to express our appreciation and gratitude to two anonymous reviewers for their excellent suggestions and comments, which have definitely made the book much stronger. Finally, this book would not have been completed without the continued guidance and support of Alison Kirk, Publisher at Ashgate.

Perhaps most importantly, we would like to thank our respective families and friends for their patience and unconditional support. We wouldn't be in the position of writing a book of this scope without them.

Part I

INTRODUCTION AND BACKGROUND

Chapter 1
Individual Privacy versus Collective Transparency

INTRODUCTION AND OVERVIEW

Aims and Rationale

In order to realise the full potential of an information society, personal and confidential data must sometimes be shared. On face value that statement should not create alarm.[1] However, when extending that concept to apply to the information many of us classify as the most personal of all – our health data – its credibility is tested to the limit. It is natural to entertain all forms of suspicions – identity theft and confidential health data being exposed to the world are those the media often cite. That is the negative concept of 'privacy', which we assert is a construct of the here and now. This is because when you think about why you should feel alarmed, there is actually more reason to feel alarmed if your data is not shared; as it is, this has such truly adverse consequences as avoidable deaths.

The aim of this book is to generate debate and to provoke new visions for the sharing of personal and confidential medical data. Such discussion is framed through an exploration of the changing concept of 'privacy' and 'patient control' in healthcare information management. Best practices from Europe and the USA are combined to form a suggested vision for the UK as an early adopter of change. We argue that the UK has established a solid foundation upon which to build, but we also suggest that in today's global society, which is no longer bound by geography, best practices from one part of the world can and should be replicated in other parts of the world. This model is therefore intended as an exploration of 'the art of the possible' in the management of healthcare data. All are invited and encouraged to build upon what we present herein.

This argument is hardly surprising as currently the question of 'what is possible' rests solely with the National Health Service (NHS); its artistic licence may well be exercised at will but we as the public know next to nothing about it. The onset

1 The views expressed in this article are the authors' own, as an academic pursuit, and do not reflect those of the NHS or any other organisation.

of the Information Revolution[2] created a dilemma for the NHS in terms of how it addresses its obligation to use information to improve best practice (termed 'collective transparency') whilst also keeping personal information confidential (termed 'individual privacy'). Unfortunately, to use a contradiction in terms, there is 'limited transparency' for the public as to whether the NHS is balancing this critically important informational relationship or whether its approach is fit for purpose. The public would need to know what the purposes for the sharing of information are to assess whether it is indeed 'fit'.

This issue has been brought into sharp focus through the recent public debate about the NHS's attempt to roll out a programme of work ('care.data'[3]) which uses the public's data for purposes other than their direct healthcare ('direct care'). The programme uses only an ill-communicated[4] information leaflet telling patients they can 'opt out',[5] which brings the issue of consent and objections management to the forefront.

In direct contrast, the NHS Information Revolution publication[6] vowed to put patients at the heart of healthcare decisions, giving them 'choice' and 'control'. With hindsight, this was always going to be an empty promise, positioned before the revolution that promised patients the right to choose whether to control the sharing of their healthcare information or not. However to achieve this objective there is a need for the NHS to take several steps backwards before moving forwards. Unlike the system in the USA,[7] in England there is a web of seemingly unconnected law, regulations and policy pre-existing this state of 'patient empowerment'.

There is also a large distinction between sharing personal confidential data for direct care purposes and sharing personal confidential data for indirect care purposes. Direct care purposes are those of a clinician or care worker with a legitimate relationship to treat a patient. The sharing of personal confidential data for these purposes has a direct benefit for the individual. This is the type of sharing that the NHS has traditionally engaged in for the benefit of the individual in their care. Sharing for indirect care purposes is relatively new to the business of the NHS. These purposes are not for the primary treatment or care of an individual. They include the analysis of information for research,

2 Department of Health, 'Liberating the NHS: An Information Revolution' (2010), http://consultations.dh.gov.uk/information-revolution/informationrevolution.

3 www.hscic.gov.uk/gpes/caredata.

4 www.wired.co.uk/news/archive/2014-02/07/care-data-terrible-communication.

5 Stephanie Pritchett, 'Care.data – why should we care?' (2014) 14(4) *P. & D.P.* 14–16.

6 See note 2.

7 The US system was able to start from a 'blank page' when developing HIPPA as not much federal law preceded it.

commissioning or payment of service providers and audit of services. However, this big distinction has been blurred. This is partially due to the unclear areas of law outlined above. There could also be some purpose behind the blurring: whilst the uncertainty exists, those who currently rely on implied consent for direct care purposes might conveniently blur the boundaries to make their essentially indirect care purposes fit within the definition so that explicit consent is not sought for these purposes.

The *Caldicott Review*[8] highlighted the illegality of some practices, such as commissioning, which has led to various sticking plasters of legislation (namely s. 251 of the NHS Act 2006[9]) but no overarching solution. It also highlighted the need to share for direct care purposes to ensure that care is safe and effective. Nevertheless, in the midst of the confusion of yet another NHS reorganisation giving more power to the central NHS and less to the regions, the messages of the *Caldicott Review* which looked independently at the issues of information sharing without the clutter of other political agendas, have not been heeded. We purport that this has had two major impacts pushing in opposing directions, whereas the more difficult, yet more ethical, solution is staring us in the face. We argue that transparency and control for patients has still not been considered. As a result the first adverse impact has been on direct care, where some have begun to question the legality of the doctrine of implied consent. This is a common law concept that assumes that because someone presents for treatment they are consenting to their information being shared for these purposes. The pollsters show that people expect this to happen[10] and are concerned that it may have a negative, and sometimes fatal, effect if this does not happen. Despite this we see proposed changes to the European Data Protection Directive[11] making explicit consent the default for all handling of health data. The second adverse impact has brought about the current principal debate.

The Health and Social Care Act 2012 illustrated the will of Parliament to allow a government quango – the Health and Social Care Information Centre (HSCIC) – the right to direct other parts of the health service to send personal confidential data about individuals to them for purposes of analysis (indirect care) without the consent of those individuals. However, even before this was put in motion through the 'care.data' movement the then Secretary of State for

---

8 www.gov.uk/government/publications/the-information-governance- review.

9 For example see www.hscic.gov.uk/media/12029/s251-guidance-note/pdf/s251-guidance-note-may13.pdf.

10 Onmedica reported this to be 85 per cent. See www.onmedica.com/newsarticle.aspx?id=6e8f91d9-2945-45c7-aba1-1ccbeebae70c.

11 http://ec.europa.eu/justice/data-protection/.

Health publicly contradicted the law at the launch of the *Caldicott Report*, stating that the public would have the right to 'veto' the transfer of data from GPs to the HSCIC,[12] in contravention of the right to direct the HSCIC to collect personal data laid out in s. 254 of the Health and Social Care Act 2012.

While this suggestion is definitely contentious, perhaps more detrimental to the government was NHS England's attempts to honour this 'pledge' through a leaflet drop highlighting an individual's right to opt out of the 'care.data' scheme. The leaflet was compared to a 'pizza menu'[13] and led to a freeze of the rollout of the 'care.data' programme. Hence unsurprisingly we are currently in a position of stalemate, where fair processing and the 'right' to object are becoming too difficult for the government to control on their own. Patients are more aware than ever that they have the right to object to the sharing of some of their data but are still largely unaware of the data sharing that currently happens and that which doesn't happen which might lead to their harm. Likewise they are unaware of the benefits to society of sharing information, which could help to improve treatments or services.

In the spirit of pragmatism this book develops a way to address this lack of transparency and choice through the use of technology. It suggests that a portal could allow individuals to access their data, to add to it, to decide who else can see it and for what purposes and to understand when they do not have the choice because of a law which mandates either sharing or secrecy. This is becoming more important as the population is increasingly more geographically mobile. As society is travelling or working away more often than in the past, the idea of personal relationships with a local GP who solely holds and controls your paper health records to make decisions about your care is rapidly becoming outdated. Because it is this type of trust which gives rise to relationships of 'confidentiality', we must reconsider whether this ruling concept of 'confidentiality' in health is also becoming outdated or whether the nature of the relationship(s) can evolve with the times.

We must not forget that 'confidentiality' as a concept requires consent from the individual. This begs the question of whether we in fact need anyone to control our information on our behalf. Hence, we propose that using an internet-based portal could allow people to access and control their own data, or allow others to access it if the individual chooses that, wherever in the world they may need treatment. This book is therefore about empowering people to make informed choices about sharing their health data. But what if an individual does have a personal relationship with the GP, an unspectacular medical history

12 Jeremy Hunt, the then Secretary of State for Health, responding to the Caldicott Report, 26 April 2013 at www.youtube.com/watch?v=Udpaajqg3nE.

13 Margaret McCartney, 'Care.data Doesn't Care Enough about Consent' (2004) 348 *BMJ* g2831.

and has no desire to make choices about the sharing of their healthcare data? We argue that although it is a very reasonable choice to make, nevertheless it should be an 'informed choice'. What is particularly intriguing about this observation is the question that we pose – 'How do you know what you don't know?' It is this question that the model we propose addresses. Currently there is considerable uncertainty as to the legal and regulatory status of several essential aspects of sharing healthcare data across different jurisdictions. The application of established data protection concepts and rules for processing and sharing information in the context of the NHS can be problematic, with fundamental uncertainties as to what is regulated, who is responsible, which laws apply and the circumstances in which other authorities can obtain access to information. There is also a lack of clarity as to the subsistence and ownership of proprietary rights in data stored, processed and generated in this context.

It is not that information is not shared per se, but that it is controlled almost exclusively by the NHS on behalf of the patients. This inadvertently masks the individual's intended role and circumvents autonomy-based laws (and corresponding rights) designed for implementation by the individual. We assert that this paternalistic behaviour of the NHS consequently creates two unintended outcomes. Firstly, it places a limitation on the individual's power to be autonomous; secondly, and probably more importantly, it restricts the patient's ability to apply the law themselves.

This book suggests that we should re-examine this position. We argue that the *choice of* control over personal medical information should be moved to individuals which will render the concept of 'privacy', as it is currently viewed, as a largely negative concept, redundant. In parallel it should validate 'confidentiality' as a positive concept, activated legitimately by obtaining active consent from empowered individuals. This power shift would expose the overdue need for options allowing individuals to increase their individual levels of control over their medical information. We argue that the act of selecting the level of control that an individual would like over the sharing of their information will replace the 'privacy' concept.

The novelty in this book is in our proposition that the redundant concept of 'privacy' should move away from the current NHS's paternal 'proxy-individual' conception of privacy where the NHS makes information sharing decisions on behalf of the individual. It should move towards more optimal sociological conceptions of control, whereby individuals make sharing decisions themselves based on transparency around the risks and benefits to themselves and society about sharing that information and to achieve this we will develop a three-stage theoretical model for change to the roles of the NHS and of the individual. Not only is the aim of this text optimistically directed beyond the changing social norms and changing expectations of digital society, most importantly it contextualises broader political commitments – the government's Open Data agenda and the government's pledge to allow access to GP records are just two examples which signify the direction of travel.

This text on the management and protection of healthcare data covers the key legal and regulatory issues in sufficient detail to provide a comprehensive account for policy makers, regulators and lawyers who are called upon to advice on NHS data protection policy matters and for students and tutors of technology law. In summary the book will provide the following for readers:

a. an understanding of how health information is currently managed;
b. an understanding of the value and complementary nature of both individual privacy and 'collective transparency' in healthcare information;
c. the information to be empowered to make decisions around control of their healthcare information which could be put into practice given the government's pledge to allow access to GP records; and
d. the information to be empowered to share best practice from other countries' data protection/open data regimes.

Content and Structure of the Book

This book is split into three sections. Section one is the introduction and background.

Chapter 1 'Individual Privacy versus Collective Transparency' serves as both an introduction to the book and to the concept of information privacy and data sharing. It includes a short history of the emergence of information society. The chapter then highlights the purpose of this work which is to suggest an opportunity to eradicate negative and redundant connotations of 'privacy' and replace them with 'control' as a positive enabler. It also provides background discussion on the current government framework which contextualises this, including:

a. the Power of Information (the Information Strategy);
b. the government ICT Strategy;
c. the Caldicott Review Report;
d. the Statutory Code of Practice for Confidential Information (as per s. 263 of the Health and Social Care Act 2012) and Confidentiality Guide published under s. 265 of the Health and Social Care Act 2012);
e. NHS Constitution changes; and
f. Care Record Guarantee.

It places this government framework into informational privacy theory and differentiates the NHS from other organisations/sectors. To do this it outlines the core of data protection law and regulation (including the implications of the proposed Data Protection Directive) with the three additional controls which are always present in a healthcare setting:

a. additional laws/regulations which necessitate sharing of information in and beyond health;
b. laws which necessitate not sharing of information in and beyond health; and
c. common law, consent and professional judgement, which is born out of the relationship of confidence between a patient and their doctor for example.

The goal is to provide the context to establish the framework for addressing a variety of salient issues surrounding privacy and access to healthcare data.

Chapter 2 provides a critical analysis of how healthcare data is handled in Europe and the USA,[14] to look for best practice which could be applied within a framework such as that in the UK. We assert that there is one clear common denominator in healthcare across Europe – spiralling costs – something needs to change to make the current financial regime sustainable. We explore whether passing control of information over to the patient could contribute to this. Currently healthcare is barely managing to cover its costs. Not only are the methods for raising funds to cover its costs inadequate, but, of even greater concern, the costs themselves are set to soar[15] with an ever-increasing ageing population escalating the demand for care.

In Europe control of healthcare data is being positioned as *the* way to design healthcare by 2020 through the e-health Task Force.[16] The European Commission published two legislative proposals in January 2012: a Regulation setting out a general EU framework for data protection and a Directive. The Regulation continues many of the established principles of EU data protection law familiar to those in the health sector. Unfortunately the practicalities of some of the proposed changes leave a lot to be desired. The principle that individuals are the owners and controllers of their own health data, with the right to make decisions over access to the data and to be informed about how it

14 M. Pine et al. 'Harnessing the Power of Enhanced Data for Healthcare Quality Improvement: Lessons from a Minnesota Hospital Association Pilot Project' (2012) 57(6) *J. Healthcare Management*, 406–18, 419–20.

15 Economist Intelligence Unit, *Future of Healthcare in Europe* (Economist Intelligence Unit Limited 2011).

16 See http://ec.europa.eu/information_society/activities/health/docs/policy/taskforce/redesigning_health-eu-for2020-ehtf-report2012.pdf.

will be used, is outlined in EU law and European jurisprudence but is rarely fully implemented in health systems. Even in those countries which have invested in e-Health applications (such as Denmark, Sweden, Estonia, and Spain) we do not see an example of a population who can fully control their own health data. We examine why this is the case and to what extent alternatives have been tested.

This chapter then explores important aspects of healthcare data in the United States with its predominantly privately funded business model. It examines what (or who) drives the collection of these data and the accessibility of these data for new clinical insights. It analyses the role of the individual in controlling these data and reflects on how well these data are used and the key barriers to wider use. One clear barrier is that despite its size and the fragmented nature of its healthcare system, a unique patient identifier is not yet adopted.[17] This is a prerequisite for complete control by an increasingly geographically mobile population. We are therefore pleased to find that through the course of writing this book, a Private Members' Bill, The Health and Social Care (Safety and Quality) Bill,[18] to mandate the use of a unique identifier (the NHS Number) is being progressed and is well supported. The agenda behind this is to increase information sharing for direct care only and should not be confused with sharing information for purposes other than direct care.

We assert that there needs to be a leader nation which starts this process so that others can follow best practice (in both public and private sectors). That's not to say best practice does not exist within pockets worldwide. There are a number of advocates from America conducting studies, like Miller's,[19] to test levels of patient control but invariably they have shown progress is poor. However, it is the pockets of good practice – such as Kaiser Permanente's and Nautilus Health Care Management Group's[20]– portals that allow patients to view test results, as well as information on allergies, immunisations and past

---

17 http://online.wsj.com/article/SB100014240529702041242045771546618149 32978.html.

18 http://services.parliament.uk/bills/2014-15/healthandsocialcaresafety andquality.html.

19 Robert H. Miller, 'Satisfying Patient-Consumer Principles for Health Information Exchange: Evidence From California Case Studies' (2012) 31(3) *Health Affairs*, 537; www.eweek.com/c/a/Health-Care-IT/Web-Portals-Vital-to-Patient-Control-of-Health-Data-Study-257933/.

20 Miller's study examined five different health care organisations that collectively serve a full range of California patient populations: Kaiser Permanente, Nautilus Health Care Management Group, Santa Clara Valley Hospital and Health System, Inland Empire Health Plan and the Santa Cruz Health Information Exchange.

visits upon which we draw inspiration. We suggest the UK as a beacon early adopter for such technologies to empower patient control, building on the policy grounds which are rapidly emerging in the UK.

In Part II we extensively discuss the alleged root of the problem. Chapter 3 outlines the theoretical problem, concluding that three issues necessitate change – the mindset around informational privacy, the quality and 'ownership' of information and the use of innovation. Chapter 4 articulates the practical problem and highlights the historical role reversal, where law and technology are used as vehicles with the wrong drivers. We argue that firstly there must be a change of mindset around 'privacy', moving privacy from an individualistic concept to a societal concept. The balance required between 'individual privacy' and 'collective' transparency' reflects this. Secondly information within health records must be standardised and understandable and information must be controlled by the patient to the extent they choose to do this. Online records are required to facilitate this. Likewise, the third element requiring change is that innovation needs to be used by the patient as an impartial vehicle to deliver this control – allowing the individual to control their own information and to implement or invoke the autonomy-based laws, such as the Human Rights Act, as intended. At present technical controls within NHS information systems do reflect the principles of laws such as the Data Protection Act. However they are designed for control by patients but are controlled by clinicians.

The principle behind this is that when individuals have the choice of control they will be empowered to think of privacy as whatever they decide it means for them – be that an individualistic concept or a social concept – or anything in between. They can make their own informed decisions by controlling information through innovation appropriately. Information sharing is purported to be self-propelling as individuals will see the societal benefit of sharing. It is suggested that it is the current secrecy surrounding 'privacy' that makes people decide not to share.

In Chapter 4 we will discuss the irony inherent within the 'Information Revolution' publications.[21] They promise choice and control to patients but don't consider repositioning the control of information by individuals as an enabler. We suggest that the privacy framework per se is fit for purpose but that the way in which information is governed renders it unfit for purpose, therefore the roles of the individual and NHS need to be reconsidered. The NHS assumes a paternal 'proxy' individual role which means the role of the individual is masked so they cannot enforce autonomy-based laws. 'Confidentiality' is the ruling concept which governs the legal processing of

21 See note 2.

health data but it is not currently always underpinned by the consent of the patient so may often be illegitimate. Chapter 4 places this reconsideration of the roles of the individual and the NHS in information sharing into real life examples by outlining the technical information governance controls designed for individuals which are being exercised by the NHS through technology in information technology (IT) systems that contain patient information. It outlines what laws and policy direction underpin them.

In the final third part of the book we argue that the solution must be twofold. Firstly, the theoretical solution discussed in Chapter 5 provides a framework for options of varying levels of control over information for the patient to address the issues outlined in Chapter 3. In parallel, the practical technical solution (Chapter 6) applies technology as an impartial vehicle to deliver this, addressing the issues outlined in Chapter 4.

Chapter 5 analyses the theoretical framework for the solution we are proposing. We name this 'MI Information Revolution' which invalidates the self-imposed 'proxy-individual' role of the NHS and allows individuals to exercise autonomy-based law. The theoretical element binds the first two issues – mindset and information – by creating a framework of choices of varying levels of control of information which individuals may choose based on their individual definition of privacy. This will validate 'confidentiality' by patients consenting to the current 'proxy-individual' control or to accept varying levels of control.

In Chapter 6 the practical technical solution is proposed, through the use of internet based portals. To address the problem of 'privacy' being imposed on society as an individualistic concept, technology is suggested as an impartial vehicle, driven by individuals, to deliver choice. The practical implementation part of the solution is delivered through innovation – portals named the MIi Fit for individuals to control (and define) their own concept of 'privacy' and the WIi Fit for the NHS to transparently show how 'collective transparency' is complementary to individual privacy.

In concluding the book, it is suggested that combining theory and practice in this way means that the choice of 'control' of information could replace the 'privacy' myth. 'Control' of information is positioned as an alter ego of privacy, which in turn empowers the choice and control promised in 'the Information Revolution'.[22] We argue that control of information is a vital step towards empowering choice of safe and effective care and treatment so 'MI Information Revolution' should be considered as the 'Real Information Revolution' empowering the choice of a full (or partial) revolution from choice *of* control to choice *and* control.

---

22 Ibid.

BACKGROUND

Information Society and the Need for 'Collective Transparency' to Ensure the NHS Survives

The reader might be asking 'why now?' For a start, it is well known that now we live in an 'information society' and we all need healthcare. Likewise the NHS operates within the information society and must adapt to operate in a way which is financially sustainable. Following the behaviours of the pioneers in the information society is asserted as the way for the NHS to be financially sustainable. Sharing anonymous information (where it is very unlikely that an individual can be identified) to improve health services for others in society is termed 'collective transparency' throughout this book.

The information society, which many claim dates as far back as the 1970s,[23] has exploded recently. However it is difficult to see how it could progress further without first expanding on the existing strong foundations. Today, the creation, distribution, use, integration and manipulation of information is a significant economic, political, and cultural activity. 'Information society' has the aim of gaining competitive advantage internationally, through the use of IT in a creative and productive way. The knowledge economy is its economic partner, whereby wealth is created through the economic exploitation of information. People who can partake in this form of society are sometimes termed 'digital citizens'. We argue that patients are not always afforded the opportunity to become digital citizens.

Although the markers of this rapid change may be technological, economic, occupational, spatial, cultural, or some combination of these, there is no denying that economic efficiencies have played a huge part. Information society is seen as the successor to industrial society. In 2005, governments reaffirmed their dedication to the foundations of the Information Society in the Tunis Commitment and outlined the basis for implementation and follow up in the Tunis Agenda for the Information Society.[24] In particular, the Tunis Agenda addresses the issues of financing of information communication technologies for development and internet governance that could not be resolved in the first phase.

The issue of technologies and their role in contemporary society have been discussed in the scientific literature using a range of labels and concepts, including 'knowledge or information economy', 'post-industrial society', 'postmodern

---

23 James R. Beniger, *The Control Revolution: Technological and Economic Origins of the Information Society* (Harvard University Press 1986).

24 www.itu.int/wsis/docs2/tunis/off/6rev1.html.

society', 'network society', 'the information revolution', 'informational capitalism' and 'network capitalism'.[25]

Drucker has argued that there is a transition to be made from an economy based on material goods to one based on knowledge.[26] We are all in this transition at the moment and health has the opportunity to be a leader. Porat distinguishes a primary (information goods and services that are directly used in the production, distribution or processing of information) and a secondary sector (information services produced for internal consumption by government and non-information firms) of the information economy.[27] He uses the total value added by the primary and secondary information sector to the Gross National Product (GNP) as an indicator for the information economy. The OECD has employed Porat's definition for calculating the share of the information economy in the total economy (e.g., OECD 1981, 1986). Based on such indicators, the information society has been defined as a society where more than half of the GNP is produced and more than half of the employees are active in the information economy.[28]

Towards the end of the twentieth century, the concept of the network society gained importance in information society theory. For Castells, network logic is, besides information, pervasiveness, flexibility, and convergence, a central feature of the information technology paradigm.[29] One of the key features of informational society is the networking logic of its basic structure, which explains the use of the concept of 'network society'.[30] Castells' insight was that the network society is the result of '*informationalism*', a new technological paradigm. Jan Van Dijk[31] defines the network society as a 'social formation with an infrastructure of social and media networks enabling its prime mode of organization at all levels (individual, group/organizational and societal). Increasingly, these networks link all units or parts of this formation (individuals,

---

25 See for example J. Aronson, ' The Communication and Internet Revolution' in Baylis, J. and Smith, S. (eds), *The Globalisation of World Politics* (OUP 2001).

26 Peter Drucker, *The Age of Discontinuity* (Harper & Row 1969).

27 Marc U. Porat and Michael R. Rubin, *The Information Economy* (Office of Telecommunications Special Publication 77–12, 9 Vols, US Department of Commerce, Washington DC 1977).

28 Karl Deutsch, 'Soziale und politische Aspekte der Informationsgesellschaft' in Philipp Sonntag (ed.), *Die Zukunft der Informationsgesellschaft* (Haag & Herchen 1983) 68–88.

29 M. Castells, *The Rise of the Network Society. The Information Age: Economy, Society and Culture* (2nd edn, Vol. 1, Blackwell 2000) 69.

30 Ibid. 21.

31 Jan Van Dijk, *The Network Society: Social Aspects of New Media* (Sage Publications 2006) 20.

groups and organisations).'[32] For Van Dijk, networks have become the nervous system of society. Whereas Castells links the concept of the network society to capitalist transformation, Van Dijk sees it as the logical result of the increasing widening and thickening of networks in nature and society. Barney uses the term for characterising societies that exhibit two fundamental characteristics: 'The first is the presence in those societies of sophisticated – almost exclusively digital – technologies of networked communication and information management/distribution, technologies which form the basic infrastructure mediating an increasing array of social, political and economic practices. The second, arguably more intriguing, characteristic of network societies is the reproduction and institutionalisation throughout (and between) those societies of networks as the basic form of human organisation and relationship across a wide range of social, political and economic configurations and associations.'[33]

The factor that unites all of these theories of information society is access to information through technology to connect and empower people. This is a sweeping statement and in health the type of information is central to any discussions about 'information society'. Misunderstanding the finer details of the definitions of different types of information could contribute towards the uneasiness surrounding 'individual privacy' issues.

Definitions as Part of the Issue

It is important to clarify the type of information discussed in this book. It is about all information but it differentiates between information that identifies an individual, which we say should be 'controlled' by the individual and that which does not identify an individual and therefore can be freely used to help society without infringing on an individual's privacy. Although this seems a simple distinction, there are many myths propelled by the lack of understanding around this distinction.

'Confidential information' describes personal information about identified or identifiable individuals, which should be kept private or secret. For the purposes of this book 'personal' includes the Data Protection Act definition of personal data, but it is adapted to include dead as well as living people. 'Confidential' includes both information 'given in confidence' and 'that which is owed a duty of confidence' and is adapted to include 'sensitive' as defined in the Data Protection Act.

'Consent' is the approval or agreement for something to happen after consideration. For consent to be legally valid, the individual must be informed,

32 Ibid.

33 Darin Barney, *The Network Society* (Polity 2003) 25.

must have the capacity to make the decision in question and must give consent voluntarily. This means individuals should know and understand how their information is to be used and shared (there should be 'no surprises') and they should understand the implications of their decision, particularly where refusing to allow information to be shared is likely to affect the care they receive. This applies to both explicit and implied consent. Implied consent is what allows 'confidential information' to be shared by clinicians and others in the 'direct care' team who are involved in the treatment and care of an individual.

Personal information or data is information which relates to an individual who can be identified from those data, or from those data and other information which is in the possession of, or is likely to come into the possession of, the data controller (the NHS). It includes any expression of opinion about the individual and any indication of the intentions of the data controller or any other person in respect of the individual.[34] For the purposes of the Data Protection Act in a health context, sensitive personal data includes personal data consisting of information as to an individual's physical or mental health or condition.[35]

Anonymous information is information which has gone through the process of rendering data into a form which does not identify individuals and where there is little or no risk of identification (identification is not likely to take place). When one piece of data is linked with another the risk of combination and consequence of re-identification means it is not always straightforward to distinguish between anonymised data and personal data.[36] There is no 'bright light distinction' between

34 Data Protection Act 1998, s. 1.

35 Ibid. s. 2.

36 See e.g., *Common Services Agency v Scottish Information Commissioner* [2008] UKHL 47, [2008] 1 WLR 1550. It is worth noting that anonymous data do not lose their status because one organisation is able to make a link between these data and the individuals, as long as this organisation will not release information enabling such link to be made and have in place appropriate security measures. See R *(Department of Health) v ICO* [2011] EWHC 1430 (Admin), (2011) 155(17) SJLB 31: in this case, the Department of Health declined to provide, at the request of a pro-life's group, anonymised statistical information regarding the number of patients who had late terminations on medical grounds, as they feared that publication would allow the public identification of vulnerable women and medical practitioners. The court held that anonymised data that would not lead to the identification of a living person were not personal data, even though individuals could be identified from the statistics taken together with the other information in the Department's possession. In the Upper-tier Tribunal judgement *All Party Parliamentary Group on Extraordinary Rendition v ICO* (2011) (mentioned in Damien Wefare 'Clarifying the scope of personal data' in (2012) 12(7) *Privacy and Data*

anonymous and confidential data.[37] De-identified information on the other hand exists where information which identifies an individual has been removed, but there is still some risk of re-identification.

Sharing with Whom and For What Purpose

Another point of confusion is understanding what information is being shared with whom and for what reason. Every act of sharing needs to be legal. Explicit patient consent can make most sharing decisions legal so should be the 'trump card' but consent is often not obtained as a legal basis for sharing. The broad categories of sharing are outlined below but have been simplified for explanatory purposes:

The Law Commission in its Data Sharing Consultation Paper[38] outlines some key benefits of sharing information between public bodies, including:

a. informed policy making and improved provision of public services;
b. emergency planning and response;
c. research and the knowledge-based economy;
d. efficiency and cost effectiveness; and
e. transpar.ency.

Expectations of the public regarding the processing of their data are also increasing. The development of low cost information and communications technology makes it cheaper and easier to collect, share and combine information. As business is providing offers in line with peoples' tastes and needs, on the basis of personalised data obtained from internet users, public services are equally expected to be better tailored to people's needs. Data sharing may be instrumental in improving public services.

Protection), the Tribunal similarly held that fully anonymised data remained personal data in the hands of the data controller as long as he or she can continue to identify the individuals involved but cease to be personal data in the hands of the recipient where the public cannot identify any individual from it. See also Information Commissioner Office, 'Determining what is personal data' (2012) p 27, at https://ico.org.uk/media/for-organisations/documents/1554/determining-what-is-personal-data.pdf (last visited 28 March 2015); and Information Commissioner Office, *Proposed new EU General Data Protection Regulation: Article-by-article analysis paper* (12 February 2013) 7.

37 See e.g., R. Thomas and M. Walport, 'Data Sharing Review Report' (Ministry of Justice, UK, July 2008) 37; F. Caldicott, 'Information: To Share Or Not To Share? The Information Governance Review' (April 2013) 55.

38 Law Commission, 'Data Sharing Between Public Bodies' (Consultation Paper No 214, 16 September 2013) http://lawcommission.justice.gov.uk/docs/cp214_data-sharing.pdf.

Table 1.1. Direct Care and Indirect Care

Direct Care		
Sharing with...	**Can share confidential data?**	**Legal basis**
Within the care team in one setting (e.g., between departments in a hospital)	Yes	Implied consent
Within the care team outside the setting for continuing care (e.g., GP to care home)	Yes	Implied consent
Between public bodies (e.g., GP to the police for safeguarding)	Yes	Safeguarding – public interest test – common law Public Health (Control of Diseases) Act 1984 and amendments. See in particular the Heath Protection (Notification) Regulations 2010 (SI 2010/659)
With carers or family members	Yes	Explicit consent

Indirect Care				
Sharing for...	**Can share anonymised data?**	**Can share de-identified data?**	**Can share confidential information?**	**Legal basis**
Service planning	Yes – publish	Within a controlled environment if anonymised data is not fit for purpose	Only with a legal basis if de-identified or anonymised information is not fit for purpose	s. 251 NHS Act 2006 Section 60 of the Health and Social Care Act 2001 as re-enacted by s. 251 of the NHS Act 2006 allows the Secretary of State for Health to make regulations to set aside the common law duty of confidentiality for defined medical purposes The Regulations that enable this power are called the Health Service (Control of Patient Information) Regulations 2002. Any references to 'section 251 support or approval' actually refers to approval given under the authority of the Regulations

Indirect Care				
Sharing for…	**Can share anonymised data?**	**Can share de-identified data?**	**Can share confidential information?**	**Legal basis**
Commissioning (paying invoices for services)	Yes – publish	Within a controlled environment if anonymised data is not fit for purpose	Only with a legal basis if de-identified or anonymised information is not fit for purpose	s. 251 NHS Act 2006
Public Health (controlling infectious diseases etc.)	Yes – publish	Within a controlled environment if anonymised data is not fit for purpose	Only with a legal basis if de-identified or anonymised information is not fit for purpose	Public Health (Control of Disease) Act 1984 and Public Health (Infectious Diseases) Regulations 1988
Research (genetic illnesses, finding cures etc.)	Yes – publish	Within a controlled environment if anonymised data is not fit for purpose	Only with a legal basis if de-identified or anonymised information is not fit for purpose	s. 251 NHS Act 2006

Obstacles to Data Sharing

Obstacles to data sharing are said to be partly legal, partly non-legal. Among the legal factors, uncertainty is often identified as one of the main obstacles preventing public bodies from sharing data.[39] The legal and regulatory environment is commonly criticised as overly complex and a source of diverse interpretations, giving rise to uncertainties and, as a result, an overly cautious approach. Guidance is not always sufficient to dispel such uncertainty. Difficulties have also sometimes been attributed to insufficient powers to collect or share

39 See e.g., Scottish Government, 'A Scotland-wide Data Linkage Framework for Statistics and Research: Consultation Paper on the Aims and Guiding Principles' (March 2012) 14, at www.scotland.gov.uk/Resource/0039/00390444.pdf (last visited 28 March 2015).

data. Against this background, a new statutory fast-track procedure has been seen by those such as Thomas and Walport as one of the ways of removing legal obstacles.[40] Past proposals to introduce such procedures have, however, been controversial.

In the wake of the NHS centralising GP records onto databases such as 'care.data' and giving individuals the opportunity to 'opt out' of sharing their information for purposes other than their direct care, mistrust and rumours are at their highest. Two commonly cited aversions to sharing information are insurance companies obtaining information about individuals and using it to set their insurance premiums and that pharmaceutical companies will be sold their data. In the first case, arguably using anything but this risk-based approach would mean an individual was not disclosing relevant facts about their medical history and would therefore invalidate their insurance. In the second case the end result of a pharmaceutical company using data about them would be to develop medication and potential cures that would benefit their direct care. Propagation of the 'privacy myth' appears to be fuelling this mindset.

Parliamentary Opposition to Data Sharing versus an Obligation to Share Data: The Human Rights Act

Both the 2002 report *Privacy and data-sharing – The way forward for public services*[41] and the *Walport–Thomas Review*[42] proposed the enactment of a general power to enable information sharing gateways to be created by secondary legislation. An attempt to legislate such a power was made during the passage of what is now the *Coroners and Justice Act 2009*. Parliamentary opposition to the creation of such a wide power led to its withdrawal.[43]

Statutory gateways in general have raised concerns in terms of the adequacy of safeguards and parliamentary scrutiny. The Joint Committee on Human

---

40 See e.g., R. Thomas and M. Walport, note 37. They recommend that primary legislation should provide the Secretary of State, in precisely defined circumstances, with a power by order, subject to the affirmative resolution procedure in both Houses, to remove or modify any legal barrier to data sharing by repealing or amending other primary legislation; changing any other rule of law (e.g., the application of the common law of confidentiality to defined circumstances); or creating a new power to share information where that power is currently absent.

41 Cabinet Office, London, Performance and Innovation Unit, 'Privacy and Data-Sharing: The Way Forward for Public Services, (April 2002).

42 See note 40.

43 Joint Committee on Human Rights, 'Legislative Scrutiny: Coroners and Justice Bill' (Report of the Joint Committee on Human Rights, 2008–09), HL 57, HC 362.

Rights, in a report in the parliamentary session 2007–2008,[44] observed that in recent years there had been a marked increase in the number of provisions in Government Bills authorising wide powers to share personal information, including within the public sector. The Committee expressed its fundamental disagreement with the government's approach of including very broad enabling provisions in primary legislation and leaving data protection safeguards to secondary legislation. It highlighted that mere compliance with the Human Rights Act and Data Protection Act was not enough and that setting out the purposes of data sharing and the limitations of data sharing powers in primary legislation would give a clear message to public sector staff about data protection, given the *insufficient respect* in the public sector for the right to respect for personal data.[45]

This leaves an unresolved problem which fuels a myth around privacy which may leave the public feeling their information is 'unprotected'. Conversely, in some circumstances, the Human Rights Act 1998 can impose a duty on public bodies to share data. Section 6(1) of the Human Rights Act provides that it is unlawful for a public authority to act in a way that is incompatible with Convention rights. Both Article 2, the right to life and Article 3, freedom from torture and inhuman or degrading treatment, imply positive obligations on the state to undertake proper investigations and take preventive measures.

A low level of public trust in the way data sharing is undertaken by public services, along with negative media coverage, may constitute further hindrances. Anticipating this reluctance, public bodies may prefer not to share data when they suspect that individuals would not give their consent, although consent is not always necessary.[46]

Capability of Organisations to Securely Link Information

Qualitative problems of both legal and practical relevance, such as incomplete, out of date, inconsistent or other low quality data may be an obstacle to the transfer and linkage of data. For example, the fact that there may be several different 'unique identifiers'[47] in use can make it difficult to link sets of data

44 Joint Committee on Human Rights, 'Data Protection and Human Rights' (Report of the Joint Committee on Human Rights' 2007–08), HL 72, HC 132, 3.

45 Ibid.

46 Scottish Government (note 39) 14. Pointing to this deficit in trust in how governments use personal data, see e.g., World Economic Forum, 'Rethinking Personal Data: Strengthening Trust' (May 2012) at www3.weforum.org/docs/WEF_IT_RethinkingPersonalData_Report_2012.pdf (last visited 28 March 2015).

47 For example, a number or code relating to a unique individual.

from different systems.[48] Security issues, similarly addressed by the law, are also a key hindrance in data sharing and linkage. Safe processing requires a suitable technological infrastructure, including the IT hardware and software. It also demands organisational protective measures.[49]

The limited capacity of public sector organisations to analyse and make use of linked data is another commonly cited problem[50] which has been somewhat resolved in health by the 'safe haven' status afforded to the Health and Social Care Information Centre, as per the Health and Social Care Act 2012. This makes it a trusted environment for linkage of confidential data.

Cultural Issues

We finally also suggest that there are cultural issues which are reported to assume a prominent role as obstacles to data sharing. The *Thomas-Walport Review* reported only a few specific examples of situations where data sharing was being prevented by the legal framework.[51] By contrast, it reported several cultural and institutional barriers to data sharing such as an attitude of risk aversion, a lack of funds or proper IT, unsatisfactory legal advice and an unwillingness to put required safeguards in place or to seek the necessary consents to use data.

The *Caldicott 2 Review* published in April [52] also stressed the need for a cultural change in health and social care to shift from a 'risk-averse' culture to one of trust.[53] The review panel observed that mandatory training in information governance tended to focus more on processes rather than underlying principles and could be confined to a 'tick-box exercise'. When staff knowledge of data sharing rules was insufficient, staff lacked the ability or confidence to share information appropriately. This encouraged risk-averse attitudes to sharing.

---

48 Scottish Government (note 39) 11.

49 See e.g., Cabinet Office, 'Data Handling Procedures in Government: Final Report' (June 2008) at www.gov.uk/government/publications/data-handling-procedures-in-government (last visited 30 August 2013).

50 See note 39 at 12 and www.gov.scot/Resource/0039/00390444.pdf (last visited 28 March 2015).

51 R. Thomas and M. Walport, 'Data Sharing Review Report' (Ministry of Justice, UK, July 2008).

52 F. Caldicott, 'Information: To Share or Not To Share? The Information Governance Review' (April 2013) at www.gov.uk/government/uploads/system/uploads/attachment_data/file/192572/2900774_InfoGovernance_accv2.pdf (last visited 28 March 2015).

53 See note 51.

According to a round table discussion hosted by *The Guardian* newspaper in association with 'Objective' in February 2013,[54] the main challenge is to change cultures in the public sector. There is a lack of awareness by staff of the value of data sharing, partly because management is not actively involved in this area and does not provide enough incentives to share data properly. Insufficient value attached to information management in workplace education and training is also identified as one of the causes of this failure. This lack of awareness leads to a lack of engagement by members of the organisation; data sharing is not integrated into the routine work. Further, trust between partner bodies is often insufficient.

In line with the *Caldicott Report*, the Scottish government recently observed that an overly cautious approach prevailed in the public sector, fuelled by the fear of public disapproval of data processing. The Scottish government also suggested that 'a sense of "territoriality" stemming from the level of resources already invested in developing approaches to data linkage'[55] might explain a lack of willingness to share data.[56]

The Perceived Value of Privacy

Although society understands and appreciates the practical advantage of data sharing, there are contrary claims of principle which contest sharing. These are founded on a value judgement about the importance of privacy to individuals[57] which can be seen in an extensive amount of literature that has critically evaluated the 'value' of privacy. As a value, privacy is a broad concept, encompassing a number of issues including anonymity,[58] liberty,

54 J. Hirschleifer, 'Privacy: its Origin, Function and Future' (1980) 9 JLS 649, 649; D. Feldman, 'Secrecy, Dignity or Autonomy? Views of Privacy as a Civil Liberty' (1994) 47 *CLP* 41, 53; J. Rubenfeld, 'The Right to Privacy' (1989) 102 *Harv. L. Rev.* 737, 784–807; R. Thomas and M. Walport (see note 51). See also Dan Jellinek, 'Why sharing data can save services', *The Guardian* (London, 23 January 2013) at www.guardian.co.uk/public-leaders-network/2013/jan/23/public-sector-sharing-data (last visited 28 March 2015). "Objective Corporation" is a provider of content, collaboration and process management solutions for the public sector and regulated industries.

55 Scottish Government (note 39).

56 Ibid.

57 Para 2.20 Law Commission Data Sharing Consultation.

58 A. Westin, *Privacy and Freedom* (Atheneum 1970) 31.

intimacy,[59] dignity[60] and solitude.[61] In a seminal article Warren and Brandeis characterised privacy as 'right to be let alone'.[62] Prosser documented how privacy as a legal concept has come to constitute four distinct torts: (i) intrusion upon an individual's seclusion or solitude; (ii) public disclosure of private facts; (iii) negative publicity about an individual; (iv) appropriation of an individual's name or likeness.[63] The privacy interests underlying these torts included the protection of reputation and intangible property and protection against emotional distress. It is clear that any consideration of whether privacy is indeed a right of the individual will depend upon what definition of the individual we accept. Hence the state of privacy has been described as 'the condition of human life in which acquaintance with a person or with affairs of his life which are personal to him is limited'.[64] This includes intimacy and managing social relationships[65] and control of dissemination, use and retention of personal information.[66] However,

---

59 Ibid.

60 E. Bloustein, 'Privacy as an Aspect of Human Dignity: An Answer to Dean Prosser' (1964) 39 *NYU L. Rev.* 962; D. Feldman, 'Human Dignity as a Legal Value: Part 1' (1999) *PL* 682.

61 See note 58.

62 S. Warren and L. Brandeis, 'The Right to Privacy' (1890) 4 *Harv. L. Rev.* 193, 205–215.

63 W. Prosser, 'Privacy' (1960) 48 *Calif. L. Rev.* 383, 389. See *Prosser on Torts* (3rd edn, 1962 and his work on the *Second Restatement of Torts* (1965); E. Bloustein, 'Privacy as an Aspect of Human Dignity: An Answer to Dean Prosser' (1964) 339 *NYU L. Rev.* 962, 964.

64 H. Gross, 'The Concept of Privacy' (1967) 42*NYU L. Rev.* 34, 36; see generally, R.A. Posner, 'Privacy, Secrecy and Reputation' (1979) 28 *Buff. L. Rev.* 1; R. Gavison, 'Privacy and the Limits of Law' (1980) 89 *Yale L. J.* 421; A. Moore, 'Privacy: Its Meaning and Value' (2003) 40 Am Philos. Q. 215: W. Prosser, 'Privacy' (1960) 48 *Calif. L. Rev.* 383, 389. S.M. Journard, 'Some Psychological Aspects of Privacy' (1966) 31 *LCP* 307; O.M. Ruebhausen and O.G. Brim, 'Privacy and Behavioural Research' (1965) 65 *Colum. L. Rev.* 1184.

65 C. Fried, 'Privacy' (1968) 77 *Yale L. J.* 475, 477–484; see generally C. Fried, *An Anatomy of Values: Problems of Personal and Social Choice* (1971); R. Gerstein, 'Intimacy and Privacy', in F. Schoeman, *Philosophical Dimensions of Privacy: an Anthology* (CUP 1984); J. Rachels, 'Why Privacy is Important' (1975) 4 *Philosophy and Public Affairs* 323; J.H. Reiman, 'Privacy, Intimacy, and Personhood' (1976) 6 *Philosophy and Public Affairs* 26; R. Post, 'The Social Foundations of Privacy: Community and Self in the Common Law Tort' (1989) 77 *Calif. L. Rev.* 957, 974; D. Feldman, 'Secrecy, Dignity or Autonomy? Views of Privacy as a Civil Liberty' (1994) 47 *CLP* 41, 51–62; 'Surveillance: Citizens and the State', Second Report of the House of Lords Constitution Committee (2008–09), HL 18 para. 102.

66 D. Feldman, 'Secrecy, Dignity or Autonomy? Views of Privacy as a Civil Liberty' (1994) 47 *CLP* 41, 53; E.L. Beardsley, 'Privacy: Autonomy and Selective Disclosure' in

privacy is not simply an absence of information about us in the minds of others; rather it is the control we have over information about ourselves.[67] Concern for control over the retention of information has also driven proposals for a 'right to be forgotten'.[68] 'Privacy' therefore also provides for autonomy,[69] safeguarding social norms[70] and liberal democracy.[71] We argue that there is a basic similarity between each of the justifications for protecting privacy as a value, as a condition privacy provides the individual with a retreat from the conformist pressures of social norms.[72]

Pennock and Chapman (eds) *Privacy* (NOMOS XIII) in J.R. Pennock and J.W. Chapman (eds), *Nomos XIII* (NewYork: Atherton, 1971), 56–70; see generally, R.A. Posner, 'The Right of Privacy' (1978) 12 *Ga. L. Rev.* 393; G.J. Stigler, 'An Introduction to Privacy in Economics and Politics' (1980) 9 *JLS* 623; W. Parent, 'Privacy, Morality and the Law' (1983) 12 *Philosophy and Public Affairs* 269.

67 C. Fried, 'Privacy' (1968) 77 *Yale L. J.* 475, 482.

68 E. Reid, 'Data Protection: the Right to be Forgotten' (2012) 114 *Human Rights Updater* 14; J.L. Gray, 'A Right to be Forgotten: The Far-reaching Implications' (2011) 8(5) *Data Protection Law and Policy* 14; A. Roosendaal, 'Right to be Forgotten vs Need to be Remembered' (2012) 22(6) *Computers and Law* 10.

69 D. Feldman, 'Secrecy, Dignity or Autonomy? Views of Privacy as a Civil Liberty' (1994) 47 *CLP* 41, 53; see generally, J. Hirschleifer, 'Privacy: its Origin, Function and Future' (1980) 9 *JLS* 649; see also 'Surveillance: Citizens and the State', Second Report of the House of Lords Constitution Committee (2008–09) HL 18 paras 100 and 144; J. Rubenfeld, 'The Right to Privacy' (1989) 102 *Harvard Law Review* 737, 784–807; R. Thomas and M. Walport, *Data Sharing Review Report* (July 2008) para. 1.6.

70 C. Fried, 'Privacy' (1968) 77 *Yale Law Journal* 475, 487; R. Post, 'The Social Foundations of Privacy: Community and Self in the Common Law Tort' (1989) 77 *California Law Review* 957.

71 'Surveillance: Citizens and the State', Second Report of the House of Lords Constitution Committee (2008–09) HL 18 para. 14; F. Schoeman, *Privacy and Social Freedom* (CUP 1992); M.A. Weinstein, 'The Uses of Privacy in the Good Life' (1971) 13 *Nomos XIII* 88; J. Cohen, 'What is Privacy for?' (2012) 126 *Harv. L. Rev.* 1904, 1905–1912, 1913–1920. 'Big Data' refers to datasets so large or complex that it is beyond the ability of ordinary software to manage and analyse the data. Big Data techniques use trends and patterns in Big Datasets to draw inferences and make predictions. See McKinsey Global Institute, 'Big Data: The Next Frontier for Innovation, Competition and Productivity' (McKinsey and Company, May 2011) 1. Data mining consists of identifying unusual patterns in large datasets of personal information. One concern is that the results of data mining could be used to inform surveillance priorities without independent evidence to support the need for such surveillance.

72 J. Craig, 'Invasion of Privacy and Charter Values: The Common-Law Tort Awakens' (1997) 42 *McGill L. J.* 355, 360.

In light of these considerations, it is important that the types of information are not treated as the same when analysing the importance of data sharing versus the perceived value of privacy. Most of the value from data sharing via publication and analysis of information is from anonymous information. Conversely most of the value from sharing confidential information is from sharing between care providers for the direct care of an individual.

Current Political Framework

The confusion between types of data and the benefits of 'collective transparency' versus 'individual privacy' is confounded by a lack of communication with the public and a lack of public awareness campaigns. The suspicion which is bred from misinformation could manifest as a fear of invasion of privacy due to the lack of awareness and control of the individuals to which information arguably belongs. This book suggests an opportunity to eradicate negative and redundant connotations of 'privacy' and replace them with 'control' as a positive enabler.

It is surprising that this opportunity has not yet been taken, given that it underpins the current government framework. The current government framework which contextualises this includes The Information Strategy, The Government ICT Strategy, Open Government Initiatives, the *Caldicott Review Report* and the updated NHS Constitution.

All Information

The Power of Information (The Information Strategy) should logically be the backdrop for patient control. It sets out the choice and control agenda but does not mention the choice of control over information for patients. Information is only one of the components and there are strategies to cover the others. However, the *Government ICT Strategy*[73] revolves around making government ICT more open to the people and organisations that use the government's services, and open to any provider – regardless of size. Its other objectives seem to rule out patients and focus on competition for companies. The one objective which could be used for patients is enabling reuse of existing ICT systems and 'off the shelf' components, reducing duplication, over-capacity and saving money.

73 Cabinet Office 'One Year On: Implementing the Government ICT Strategy' (May 2012) www.gov.uk/government/publications/one-year-on-implementing-the-government-ict-strategy.

Enabling Patients to Access Electronic Health Records[74] is a government commitment starting with online access to GP records for individuals by 2015. Although this deadline has now moved back, it strikes us as an opportunity missed as it is about only viewing content, not controlling its use. If it was positioned as the start of a roll out plan, eventually leading to patient control of their information, it would be much more reassuring. For years before the Information Revolution the potential for patient control was recognised at points where progress seemed tantalisingly close. In 2002, the report on *Privacy and Data Sharing* concluded that: '*there is great potential to make better use of personal information to deliver benefits to individuals and to society, including through increased data-sharing*'.[75]

The Walport–Thomas Review[76] expressed a similar view but took the control away from the patient, recommending the setting up of a new statutory fast-track procedure to remove legal obstacles, where necessary, subject to parliamentary scrutiny. The Cabinet Office White Paper *Open Data* was also concerned with realising the potential of a transparency policy, including easing anonymised data sharing between public bodies for non-operational purposes, subject to compliance with robust safeguards.[77] We have expressed the view that as long as it is anonymised, we fully support this principle.

How to make the best use of public sector information to support economic growth was also the subject of the Shakespeare Review.[78] Highlighting the potential benefits of using these data, it warned against a risk averse approach likely to restrict the access to information, recommending instead increased

74 Enabling Patients to Access Electronic Health Records Guidance for Health Professionals – Version 1.0 (1 September 2010) www.rcp.org.uk/clinical-and-research/pratice-management-resources/~/media/files/informatics/health_informatics_enabling_patient_access.ashx.

75 Cabinet Office, London, Performance and Innovation Unit, 'Privacy and Data Sharing: The Way Forward for Public Services' (April 2002) 2.

76 Thomas and Walport (note 51).

77 *Open Data. White paper. Unleashing the Potential* (2012) Cm 8353. These data aim to facilitate analysis and improve the creation of evidence-based policy. They include e.g., data on offenders, benefit claimants and employees, shared between the Ministry of Justice, DWP and HMRC in order to analyse the employment and benefit outcomes for offenders.

78 *Shakespeare Review: An Independent Review of Public Sector Information* (Department for Business, Innovation & Skills, May 2013). See in particular Recommendation 5; at www.gov.uk/government/uploads/system/uploads/attachment_data/file/198752/13-744-shakespeare-review-of-public-sector-information.pdf (last visited 28 March 2015).

penalties in case of misuse of data.[79] Whilst this would satisfy the wishes of some patients, it neglects to ask the patients what their choice would be.

Anonymous Information

The Open Data[80] *White Paper* is much more encouraging. It acknowledges that 'citizens across the globe are proclaiming their right to data'. The *White Paper* sets out how government intends to use that energy to unlock the potential of open data for the first time that the technology exists to make the demand for greater openness irresistible. Using the tag line that 'transparency drives prosperity' they have a three stage plan with a 'prize' of 'effective, personalised, 21st-century democracy'. The first stage is access and looks for each government department to have an open data strategy. The second is that privacy should be put first, through technology. The third is for public services to share data more effectively using the latest technology. It is important to clarify that this is about publishing anonymised data about public services' performance, such as hospital waiting times.[81] This strategy aims to increase the transparency and accountability of government action, help individuals to make informed choices and to encourage business to create value from these data.[82] This policy is implemented by each government department through an open data strategy. It is supported by a series of statutes such as the Freedom of Information Act 2000, and the Re-use of Public Sector Information Regulations 2005,[83] and underpinned by the *Information Principles*,[84] which promote re-use and publication of public information. It is argued that many of the principles should extend to the patient's control of their own information.

---

79 According to the Shakespeare review, increased penalties in cases of the misuse of data are more innovation friendly because pre-emptive action for data protection purposes, including e.g., limiting the access to data through an accreditation process, could prevent the re-use of data and ultimately stifle innovation.

80 http://data.gov.uk/

81 In particular through the website www.data.gov.uk.

82 On the anticipated economic benefits, see *Shakespeare Review* (note 78).

83 SI 2005 No. 1515.

84 *Information Principles* (December 2011) at www.gov.uk/government/uploads/system/uploads/attachment_data/file/266284/Information_Principles_UK_Public_Sector_final.pdf (last visited 28 March 2015).

De-identified Information

In the area of research and statistics, the *Administrative Data Taskforce*[85] identified that the two main hindrances to access to and use of de-identified administrative data were data holders' concerns about disclosure of personal data and legal restrictions related to their use.[86] The report recommended the establishment of an Administrative Data Research Centre in each of the four countries of the UK in order to legally secure access to and linkage of data, supported by a generic statutory gateway. In the same area, the Scottish government is setting up a *Data Linkage Framework for Statistics and Research*[87] with a view to enhancing data linkage. A prior consultation revealed that uncertainty about the legalities and public acceptability of data sharing and linkage ranked first among the identified obstacles to data linkage.[88]

Confidential Information

In stark contrast to all of the above, the *Caldicott Report*[89] was actually developed using patients' and service users' views. The resulting 26 recommendations were accepted in full by the government in their response launched by the Secretary of State on 12 September 2013.[90] In contrast to the *Open Data White Paper* this is about confidential and de-identified data.

---

85 UK Administrative Data Research Network, 'Improving Access for Research and Policy' (Report from the Administrative Data Taskforce, December 2012) at www.esrc.ac.uk/_images/ADT-Improving-Access-for-Research-and-Policy_tcm8-24462.pdf (last visited 28 March 2015).

86 Ibid.

87 Scottish Government (note 39).

88 Scottish Government, 'Joined-up Data for Better Decisions: A Strategy for Improving Data Access and Analysis' (2012) 7, at www.scotland.gov.uk/Resource/0040/00408151.pdf (last visited 28 March 2015).

89 F. Caldicott, 'Information: To Share or Not To Share? The Information Governance Review' (April2013) 9 at www.gov.uk/government/uploads/system/uploads/attachment_data/file/192572/2900774_InfoGovernance_accv2.pdf (last visited 28 March 2015).

90 Department of Health, Information: To Share or Not To Share? Government Response to the Caldicott Review (September 2013), at www.gov.uk/government/uploads/system/uploads/attachment_data/file/251750/9731-2901141-TSO-Caldicott-Government_Response_ACCESSIBLE.PDF (last visited 28 March 2015).

The *Caldicott Report* called for a cultural change in the health and social sector in order to strike a new balance between sharing and protecting information, covering both anonymised and personal data. While the 1997 *Caldicott Review* emphasised preventing misuse of patient information outside of clinical control, the second review was primarily concerned with the lack of confidence of many clinicians about when it is safe to share confidential information. Despite a perceived consensus among professionals and the public that safe and appropriate sharing in the interests of the individual's direct care should be the rule, the review panel observed that a 'risk averse' culture generally prevailed: 'Over recent years, there has been a growing perception that information governance was being cited as an impediment to sharing information, even when sharing would have been in the patient's best interests.'[91] The *Review* put forward a number of recommendations to the government in order to improve data sharing. Importantly, these included recognising that the duty to share information can be as important as the duty to protect patient confidentiality.

Improvement of data sharing between health and care professionals and NHS organisations is also one of the objectives of the *digitalisation strategy*[92] pursued by the NHS. In line with the EU Digital Agenda for Europe 2010-2020, the NHS plans to become paperless by 2018, with hospitals being able to share digital data from April 2014.[93]

The Confidentiality Guide[94] published under s. 265 of the Health and Social Care Act 2012 was launched alongside the government's response to the *Caldicott Report* and presents as a type of implementation manual for the *Caldicott Review*. It provides a welcome layman's version of the implications of the law. The five rules are:

- Confidential information should be kept confidential.
- Confidential information should be shared for safe and effective care.

91 See note 89.

92 See for example www.jac.co.uk/files/Digitising-the-NHS-by-2018.PDF and http://jac.co.uk/wp-content/uploads/2013/03/Digitising_the_NHS_-_One_Year_On.pdf.

93 Department of Health, The Power of Information: Putting all of us in control of the health and social care information we need (May 2012); see also Secretary of State for Health Jeremy Hunt's announcements of 16 January 2013, at www.gov.uk/government/speeches/16-january-2013-jeremy-hunt-policy-exchange-from-notepad-to-ipad-technology-and-the-nhs (last visited 30 August 2013); European Commission, 'The Digital Agenda for Europe 2010–2020', at http://ec.europa.eu/information_society/digital-agenda/index_en.htm (last visited 28 March 2015).

94 www.hscic.gov.uk/confguideorg.

- Information used for the benefit of the community should be anonymised.
- The individual's right to object to confidential information about them being shared should be respected.
- Organisations should ensure that policies, procedures and systems are in place to ensure that the rules are followed.

Likewise, the *Code of Practice on Confidential Information*[95] published under s. 263 of the Health and Social Care Act 2012 is a legally binding code for the use of confidential information and focuses mainly on indirect care practices. Importantly it emphasises the need to respect objections by individuals and to share information.

The *NHS Constitution*[96] changes are equally significant. The introduction of the *right to have objections* to information sharing considered is exceptionally significant. A right to have any objections to use of an individual's personal information beyond their care considered is set out, including that if it cannot be followed then the reasons will be given. Amending 'you have the right of access to your own health records' to state 'you have the right of access to your own health records and to have any factual inaccuracies corrected' strengthens the concept of the patient's responsibility to provide feedback. However, less positively, it amends the proposed wording of the patient's right to be involved in discussions and decisions about their health and care to reflect the concern that it may not be practically feasible for patients to be fully involved in all discussions and decisions.

The additional rights are included to better advertise existing legal rights, rather than to create new ones. The Data Protection Act 1998 safeguards require those who hold personal data to inform individuals at their request about the specific processing of their identifiable information.

> Evidence suggests that people rarely know how their information is used and this can lead to issues where there is a mismatch between people's expectations and what the law allows NHS and social care organisations to do with data. It is also important that people understand how the law supports the use of information, what rights individuals have in relation to how their information is used and how to exercise those rights. Both patients and staff need to be aware of the duties of NHS staff to use and share that information safely across health and care services and protect confidentiality.[97]

95 http://systems.hscic.gov.uk/infogov/codes/cop.

96 www.gov.uk/government/publications/the-nhs-constitution-for-england.

97 www.gov.uk/government/uploads/system/uploads/attachment_data/file/170642/Consultation_on_strengthening_the_NHS_Constitution_Government_response.PDF.

The pledge that follows is to offer 'easily accessible, reliable and relevant information'[98] and it is difficult to evidence the additional words about:

a. providing information 'in a form you can understand';
b. supporting patients to use information; and
c. providing information on the *range* of services.[99]

The right to be involved in discussions and decisions and the inclusion of additional text about involvement of patients, their family and carers in decision making about health and care, including end of life care, is significant. However in the consultation document, the terms 'all' and 'fully' were included in the proposed wording of this right (i.e., 'you have the right to be fully involved in all discussions and decisions…'). However, during the consultation the Department of Health heard that this may not be practically feasible because of how these may occur (for example, a telephone conversation between practitioners). Accordingly, they have removed the words 'all' and 'fully' from this statement. This dilution could invoke suspicion without further communication but with this explanation it appears to be perfectly reasonable.

The pledge to provide the information you need to influence and scrutinise the planning and delivery of NHS services would be facilitated by 'collective transparency'. The insertion of words 'and support' after 'information' is intended to clarify that patients should not only be given information but should also be supported to understand it so that they can make meaningful decisions. At this point patients are not always even given the information, never mind supported.

The responsibility for patients to recognise that they can make a significant contribution to their own, and their family's, good health and well being and take some personal responsibility for it is emphasised and this book examines whether this is facilitated and how it could be further facilitated. Responsibilities about the use of and access to patient information include two new responsibilities:[100]

- 'to inform patients about the use of their confidential information and to record their objections, consent or dissent'; and
- 'to provide access to a patient's information to other relevant professionals, always doing so securely, and only where there is a legal and appropriate basis to do so'.[101]

98 Ibid.

99 Ibid.

100 Ibid.

101 Ibid.

These changes have been made to provide further clarity about staff responsibilities in relation to the use of patient information. The responsibility to record a patient's views on use of their confidential information goes further than the relevant patient right and pledge, which only refer to patient objections.

The Legal Framework

The intentions outlined in the political framework set out above must still operate within the legal framework. It is important to differentiate the NHS from other organisations/sectors in terms of legal bases for processing personal or confidential information. The two pieces of legislation which apply to all are the Data Protection Act 1998 (DPA) which deals with 'personal data' and the Human Rights Act 1998 dealing with private or confidential data. Unfortunately, many only see the DPA as the binding force and fail to acknowledge rights to a private and family life (Article 8) under the Human Rights Act. We must remember that the concepts of privacy and confidentiality interact in parallel in health therefore both need to be considered. The third element in health is the common law duty of confidentiality which is built up from case law.

Restrictions on the disclosure of information may also come from data sharing contracts,[102] contractual clauses and employment obligations.[103] There may be greater risks of professional consequences when sharing information incorrectly in a way that could breach confidentiality than risks of professional consequences for not sharing information.[104] This is not helpful when juxtaposed against the sometimes tragic consequences of not sharing information. However, such real life ethical considerations are aided by the new principle established by the *Information Governance Review* led by Dame Fiona Caldicott. The *Information Governance Review* argues that it is as important to share information for the benefit of the patient as it is to keep it confidential. This has been liberating for many doctors and care workers. However, it is still difficult to understand what takes precedence and which direction to take heed of at any given point. To examine how the laws should

102 A data sharing agreement is a set of common rules between organisations involved in a data sharing initiative. It usually specifies the basis for sharing, gives precise advice about which datasets may be shared, the rules for the retention and deletion of shared data items and sets out the data quality requirements and the technical and organisational security arrangements.

103 See e.g., General Medical Council, *Confidentiality* (GMC 2009) 30 onwards. Note that s. 38 of the Freedom of Information (Scotland) Act 2002 includes a deceased person's medical records within the definition of personal information.

104 C. Bessant, 'The Duty of Confidence' in C. Bessant (ed.) *Information Sharing Handbook* (Law Society, London 2009) 128.

interact this chapter will outline the core of data protection law and regulation (including the implications of the proposed Data Protection Directive) now and in the future.

The Data Protection Principles

The data protection principles place limitations on the sharing of personal data by data controllers. In health, the NHS as an organisation is a data controller. In a process of information sharing, at least two data controllers are involved. A data controller is the natural or legal person, such as a public authority, which alone or jointly with others determines the purposes and means of the processing of personal data.[105] Also, whenever legislation provides for the processing of data by a specific body, expressly or impliedly, the person required to process such data is the data controller.[106] Alongside data controllers, there may be numerous data processors, which process personal data on behalf of the controller but they do not have any statutory obligations under the Act.[107]

Prior notification

The obligations in relation to data sharing are actually set up for maximum transparency, including a duty of prior notification.[108] Data controllers must

105 Data Protection Act 1998, s. 1(1). In order for the controller to be regulated by the Data Protection Act 1998 when processing personal data, he or she must be established in the UK or using equipment in the UK for processing the data otherwise than for the purposes of transit (Data Protection Act 1998, s. 5(3)).

106 Data Protection Act 1998, s. 1(4).

107 Ibid., s. 1(1). On the difficulty to identify roles in increasingly complex relationships, see OECD, Working Party on Information Security and Privacy, 'The evolving privacy landscape; 30 years after the OECD privacy guidelines' (April 2011) 27.

108 Data Protection Act 1998, ss. 16–18. This obligation is subject to derogations, e.g., for maintenance of a public register and information that is not processed by means of equipment operating automatically. It is not always straightforward to establish whether the data subject has given consent. The condition will be met if the data subject has capacity to consent, is aware of the purpose(s) of the data processing and has given consideration to this question, on the basis of the specific circumstances existing at the time of the consent. Further, the data subject should feel that there is a genuine choice. The extent to which implied consent, widely relied on in some areas such as healthcare, is acceptable, is debatable. The question also arises whether an implied consent conforms to art. 2(h) of Directive 95/46 requiring that consent

give a notification to the Commissioner specifying the so called 'registerable particulars', including a description of the personal data, of any recipient to whom the data are to be disclosed, and of the purpose(s) for which the data are to be processed. The notification should also include a general description of the measures to be taken in order to comply with the security requirements. Such particulars should therefore include information on the public body to which information will be communicated, in a data sharing process. This should really lend itself to the fair processing notices for the public (an organisation's real stakeholders) as an adaptation of the notifications. However, it is disappointing to see that in 2014 Dame Fiona Caldicott's report on information is still calling for appropriate fair processing notices.[109]

The eight data protection principles set out in Schedule 1 Part 1 of the Data Protection Act 1998 and explained in Part 2 of Schedule 1 form the core of data protection regulation. Each controller must comply, subject to some maintenance of a public register and information which is not processed by means of equipment operating automatically. These principles essentially revolve around legitimacy[110] (determining when data sharing may occur); transparency[111] (imposing duties of

---

be 'specific'. Non-consensual sharing may be justified to protect the vital interests of the data subject, such as medical emergency (Data Protection Act 1998, Sch 2 para. 4. Information Commissioner's Office, *Data sharing code of practice* (May 2011) 16: e.g., disclosure of a person's medical history to an Accident and Emergency department treating the data subject for serious injuries). Sharing data may also be necessary for the purposes of legitimate interests pursued by the data controller or the recipients of the data, provided these interests are not overridden by the rights, freedoms and interests of the data subject. Article 8 of the European Convention on Human Rights is of major relevance in this exercise of weighing up the respective interests, rights and freedoms at stake. There is some doubt as to whether the 'legitimate interests condition' can be used by public bodies.

109 www.gov.uk/government/publications/iigop-annual-report-2014.

110 Principle 1 – Personal data shall be processed fairly and lawfully and, in particular, shall not be processed unless (a) at least one of the conditions in Schedule 2 is met, and (b) in the case of sensitive personal data, at least one of the conditions in Schedule 3 is also met.

111 The first principle requires not only that processing be lawful, but also that it be fair. What is or is not 'fair' processing is explained in Schedule 1 part 2 to the Data Protection Act 1998. Personal data are not to be regarded as being processed fairly where the data subject has been deceived or misled as to the purpose of processing. Further, the data subject must be provided with sufficient information, either prior

informing the data subjects); purpose limitations[112] (narrowing the use of the data on first and subsequent transfer); proportionality[113] (restricting the amount[114] of

---

to or at the time that the processing such as data sharing first takes place, or very soon afterwards. The information that should be provided to the data subject includes the identity of the data controller or any nominated representative; the purposes for which the data are intended to be processed; and any further information that is necessary in order for the processing to be considered fair having regard to the specific circumstances. Usually this requirement is complied with through the provision of 'fair processing notices' informing the data subject about any possible communication of the data to another body.

112 The purpose limitation rule derives from the second principle, which provides that at the point of the initial collection of personal data, the purposes must be specified and lawful, and that subsequent use must not be incompatible with those purposes. This principle partly overlaps with the transparency requirement flowing from the first principle.

113 Proportionality implies that the amount of data and the duration of its storage be commensurate with the purpose for which it is acquired and processed. It covers the third and the fifth principles of the Data Protection Act 1998.

114 The third principle, amounting to a 'minimality' requirement, reads as follows: 'personal data should be adequate, relevant and not excessive in relation to the purpose or purposes for which they are processed'. It is subject to a number of exceptions listed under Part 4 of the Data Protection Act 1998. The result is that in exempted areas, bulk transfers of data including irrelevant material could be lawful where separating particular fields or records from a dataset prior to a transfer would be impracticable or prohibitively expensive. Privacy Impact Assessments, to be carried out by a government department when introducing new policies or processes involving personal data, enable the departments to reach an informed decision about how much information needs to be shared. Moreover, according to the fifth principle, personal data should not be kept longer than is necessary in relation to the purpose for which it was collected. It means that the body which receives the information must make provision to ensure that the personal data it has received is kept no longer than is necessary for the purpose of the transfer. The retention period may be specified by statute; other retention periods will be determined by business need or risk analysis. Section 33 of the Data Protection Act 1998 provides an exemption to this principle, allowing data controllers to keep personal data indefinitely where necessary for historical, research or statistical purposes, provided that certain conditions are met. Further exemptions from this principle are allowed, when they are necessary to safeguard some overarching objective such as national security or economic interests.

information that may be shared and for how long); quality of data[115]; compliance with data subjects' rights[116]; and security.[117]

Exemptions

As if that wasn't confusing enough, it is important to recognise that the Data Protection Act 1998 provides exemptions from some or all of the data

115 The fourth principle requires that personal data is accurate, and, where necessary, kept up to date. In the context of data sharing, it means, as explained in part 2 of Schedule 1 that the receiving body must take reasonable steps to ensure the accuracy of the information they receive, having regard to the purpose for which the data was obtained and further processed. The sixth principle requires processing to be in accordance with the rights of data subjects conferred by the Act. These rights are set out in Part 2 of the Data Protection Act 1998. The data subject is entitled: (1) to be informed whether personal data are being processed and be given appropriate information about the processing (including a description of the personal data, the purpose of the processing, the possible recipients of the data and their source). The personal data of which the individual is the data subject must be communicated to him in an intelligible form.

116 These rights are subject to the right of others not to have their personal data (Data Protection ACT 1998, S7) and to restrictions in the context of 'unstructured' personal data held by public authorities (Data Protection Act 1998, S9A); to require the data controller to cease or not to process personal data, in particular where this would cause substantial and unwarranted damage or distress to him, subject to some exceptions (Data Protection Act 1998, s. 10(1)); to be compensated for failure by a data controller to comply with the Data Protection Act 1998 where the individual suffers damage or distress because of that failure (Data Protection Act 1998, s. 13); and to apply for the court to order the rectification, blocking, erasure or destruction of data (Data Protection Act 1998, s. 14.) In the context of public sector data sharing, both the sender and the recipient of the data have to comply with these rights.

117 Security requirements are dealt with by the seventh principle, which reads: Appropriate technical and organisational measures shall be taken against unauthorised or unlawful processing of personal data and against accidental loss or destruction of, or damage to, personal data (Data Protection Act 1998, Sch 1 part 1 para. 5). This principle requires for example that data controllers must take reasonable steps to ensure the reliability of any employee who has access to the personal data (Data Protection Act 1998, Sch 1 part 2 para. 10). Further, if a data controller resorts to a data processor, the processor must comply with appropriate security guarantees on the basis of a written contract (Data Protection Act 1998, Sch 1 part 2 para. 12. On the debated question of the respective roles of processors and controllers, *Encyclopaedia of Data Protection*, Sweet and Maxwell para. 1–206). High-profile data losses have resulted in greater emphasis on security and the imposition on all central government

protection principles in a number of situations. For example, where personal data are processed for:

a. the prevention or detection of crime;
b. the apprehension or prosecution of offenders; or
c. the assessment or collection of any tax or duty or of any imposition of a similar nature, the first principle (to the extent that it sets down transparency requirements) and the rights of information of data subjects contained in section 7 are disapplied.[118]

The exemption is not automatic and may only be applied to the extent to which the application of the exempted provisions would be 'likely to prejudice' any of these objectives. This is very subjective and the end result can leave the layman with no understanding of what is and what isn't allowed. This provision has been interpreted as requiring a more significant than merely fanciful chance of prejudice.[119] Subject information requirements may be waived in relation to health and social work data[120]; data processed by regulatory bodies for the purposes of protection of the public from misconduct of various sorts, subject to a 'likely to prejudice' test[121]; de-personalised data processed for research purposes, including statistical or historical purposes.[122] But where is the line drawn for health and social care data? How does a member of the public know?

---

departments of mandatory minimum security measures (Ministry of Justice, *Mandatory Minimum Measures for Protection of Personal Data*, annex E to the *Data Sharing Protocol*, at www.justice.gov.uk/downloads/information-access-rights/data-sharing/annex-e-mandatory-minimum-measures.pdf (last visited 28 March 2015)).

118 For example, provided that the processing of data occurs for one of these purposes and necessary for the exercise by a public body of any function conferred by an enactment or common law powers, the public body would not have to inform an individual that it is gathering personal information about him or her.

119 *R (Lord) v Secretary of State for the Home Department* [2003] EWHC 2073 (Admin), [2004] Prison Law Reports 65 at [99] and [100].

120 Data Protection Act 1998, s. 30. These exemptions are detailed in the Data Protection (Subject Access Modification) (Health) Order 2000, SI 2000 No. 413; the Data Protection (Subject Access Modification) (Education) Order 2000, SI 2000 No. 414; the Data Protection (Subject Access Modification) (Social Work) Order 2000, SI 2000 No. 415; and the Data Protection (Subject Access Modification) (Social Work) (Amendment) Order 2011 No. 1034.

121 Data Protection Act 1998, s. 31.

122 Ibid., s. 33. These data are also generally exempted from the second and fifth data protection principles.

Confidential and Private Information: Article 8 of the HRA

Even if you manage to unravel and understand the data protection rules, in parallel you must also grapple with the long-standing action for breach of confidence that protects private information from disclosure.[123] Disclosure may be prevented irrespective of the existence of a prior relationship between a confider and a confidant, provided the information is 'private'. The right to respect for private life, protected by Article 8 of the European Convention on Human Rights, is integral to the modern action for breach of confidence. Just when you thought you had a vague grasp of the data protection legislation, you might be frustrated to stumble across the notion that an action under the Human Rights Act can trump the Data Protection Act. The right to object to information about you being shared for purposes beyond your direct health and social care is a topical example of this.

The Law Commission's Data Sharing Consultation examines the issues which face public bodies sharing information and emphasises the Article 8 right:

> Protection of personal data is of fundamental importance to a person's enjoyment of his or her right to respect for private and family life as guaranteed by article 8 of the European Convention on Human Rights. Any encroachment on this right raises fears of the invasion of privacy. The potential threat to individual freedom posed by data sharing may be reinforced where the sharing occurs between large numbers of entities and translates into a centralisation of records.[124]

The contemporary action for breach of confidence reflects developments following the coming into force of the Human Rights Act 1998. Originally revolving around the breach of a trust underpinning a confidential relationship, it has come to centre on the private nature of the information itself. The House of Lords explained these developments in the *Campbell* case, which has been

---

123 The modern action for breach of confidence developed from the mid-nineteenth century: see *Prince Albert v Strange* (1849) 2 De G & Sm 652. This case was for example referred to as 'seminal' in *Campbell v MGN Limited* [2004] UKHL 22, [2004] 2 AC 457 at [43]. See also Breach of Confidence (1981) Law Com No 110 at 3.2; T. Aplin, L. Bently, P. Johnson and S. Malynicx (eds), *Gurry on Breach of Confidence* (2012) ch. 2, commenting that 'courts have been willing to protect confidentiality pragmatically by whatever mechanism is at hand'.

124 See e.g., *Database State. A Report Commissioned by the Joseph Rowntree Reform Trust Ltd* (Joseph Rowntree Reform Trust Ltd 2009) 4, at www.jrrt.org.uk/sites/jrrt.org.uk/files/documents/database-state.pdf (last visited 28 March 2015).

followed in many subsequent judgements.[125] These developments reflect the obligation of the courts, as public bodies, to act compatibly with human rights, including in the development of the common law, and to take into account the case law of the European Court of Human Rights.[126] But how would the man on the street even know about such case law to enable them to take it into account? To be fully informed and actively participate in controlling your health data must you be a lawyer? In the *Campbell* case, Lord Nicholls of Birkenhead hit the nail on the head when he described this as 'awkward' but in search of a more natural way to explain it he dehumanised the process, making the subject of the breach the information itself rather than the relationship between confidant and confider, stating that:

> The gist of the cause of action was that information of this character had been disclosed by one person to another in circumstances 'importing an obligation of confidence'.... Now the law imposes a 'duty of confidence' whenever a person receives information he knows or ought to know is fairly and reasonably to be regarded as confidential. Even this formulation is awkward.... The more natural description today is that such information is private. The essence of the tort is better encapsulated now as misuse of private information.[127]

However, the main elements of the action for misuse of private information are three-fold and only the first centres on the information itself, with the other two focusing on human relationships:

The information is not in the public domain

The private and confidential nature of the information is a prerequisite for any action for breach of confidence. Protected information must not be in the public domain.[128] Whether further disclosure has the potential

---

125 *Campbell v MGN Limited* [2004] UKHL 22, [2004] 2 AC 457. See e.g., *McKennitt v Ash* [2006] EWCA Civ 1714, [2008] QB 73 at [11]. However, this change is viewed by some as a distortion of the original cause of action: Lord Phillips of Worth Matravers in *Douglas v Hello* (No 3) [2005] EWCA Civ, [2006] QB 125 at [53].

126 Human Rights Act 1998, s. 6; R *(Alconbury Development Ltd) v Secretary of State for the Environment, Transport and the Regions and other cases* [2001] UKHL 23, [2003] 2 AC 295 at [26]; *Kay v Lambeth London Borough Council* [2006] UKHL 10, [2006] 2 AC 465 at [43] and [44].

127 *Campbell v MGN Limited* [2004] UKHL 22, [2004] 2 AC 457 at [13] and [14].

128 *Attorney-General v Guardian Newspapers Ltd (No 2)* (the 'Spycatcher' case) [1988] 2 WLR 805;'public property' or 'public knowledge' are sometimes alternatively referred to: see e.g., *Saltman Engineering Co Ltd v Campbell Engineering Co Ltd* (1948) 65 RPC 203,

to affect the interests of the person concerned may also be a relevant consideration.[129]

Information can retain its private character after the death of the individuals concerned. This was the approach taken in relation to medical data in the *Bluck* case by the Information Tribunal, in view in particular of the fundamental importance of such data in the case law of the European Court of Human Rights.[130] The High Court in *Lewis v. Secretary of State for Health* was similarly inclined to accept that 'an obligation of confidence imposed on the conscience of the confidant does survive, or at least is capable of surviving, the death of the confider'.[131] The European Court of Human Rights held that protection of medical confidentiality of a deceased person may constitute a legitimate interest overriding the right to freedom of expression, but recognised that this balance was highly time sensitive.[132] Similarly, the *Caldicott Review* of 2013[133] extended the definition of personal confidential data to include the deceased.

Information imparted in confidence

For a breach of confidence to occur, there must be a violation of a pre-existing duty to maintain the confidentiality of the information. This obligation arises in relation to private information. It may also arise out of a contract or implied contract or flow from a specific relationship between the parties, such as between a social worker and child. There is no closed list or hard and fast rule for ascertaining the nature of such a relationship. The test is whether 'the circumstances are such that any reasonable man standing in the shoes of the recipient of the information would have realised that … the information was being given to him in confidence'.[134] It is interesting to note that the action for breach of confidence does not require the claimant to show that damage

215; *Coco v A N Clark (Engineers) Ltd* [1969] FSR 415; see also T. Aplin, L. Bently, P. Johnson and S. Malynicx (eds), *Gurry on breach of confidence* (2012) para. 5.14, referring to the 'inaccessibility' of the information.

129 *Speed Seal Products Ltd v Paddington* [1985] 1 WLR 1327, 1332H.

130 *Bluck v Information Commissioner and Epsom and St Helier University NHS Trust* EA/2006/0090.

131 *Lewis v the Secretary of State for Health* [2008] EWHC 2196 (QB), [2008] LS Law Medical 559. See also *Toulson and Phipps on Confidentiality* (2nd ed. 2006) para. 11-053.

132 See *Plon v France* (2006) 42 EHRR 36 (App No 58148/00), relating to the publication of information about the health of the late President F. Mitterand.

133 www.gov.uk/government/uploads/system/uploads/attachment_data/file/192572/2900774_InfoGovernance_accv2.pdf.

134 *Coco v A N Clark (Engineers) Ltd* [1969] FSR 415, 421.

has resulted or will result from disclosure.[135] It is therefore another extremely broad and subjective concept which is likely to confuse the layman.

Respect for private life

Similarly, the concept of 'private life' is a broad one, not susceptible to exhaustive definition. The following information which has been considered to fall within the definition of 'private information' shows just how subjective this definition is: a person's health, including mental health, diet issues and drug dependency; personal feelings and opinions, more generally any personal information that an individual wishes.[136] The bottom line is that it is down to the individual to decide what is considered private to them. Of course, this only applies if they can transparently see what the candidate pieces of information are, along with the proposed usage.

Exceptions to the Duty of Confidence: Countervailing Public Interest

To illustrate this point further, we argue that confidentiality can be waived by consent, just as it is underpinned by consent. However, even though an obligation of confidence has arisen, a public body is allowed to pass on the information to another public body when the law requires this communication.[137] If we take a second to contemplate this juxtaposition of sentences, it seems somewhat contradictory.

At least – with a lot of work – the written laws can be researched and patients can understand why this is prioritised over their consent, meaning they are not in control of that piece of information. However, yet again, to add to this uncertainty, we enter the territory of a subjective assessment of the facts when discovering that disclosure will also be lawful when it meets a prominent public interest and does not go beyond what is necessary to reach this purpose. This public interest was understood initially as justifying a breach of confidence, in accordance with the so-called 'iniquity rule', when the secret hid a crime or a fraud. The exception to the rule of confidentiality was then extended to civil wrongs or misdeeds and finally came to cover any important public interest, for example endangering safety or even value for money.[138] The breadth makes 'confidentiality' as a concept almost meaningless.

135 *Duchess of Argyll v Duke of Argyll* [1967] Ch 302; *Coco v A N Clark (Engineers) Ltd* [1969] FSR 415; *Mc Kennitt v Ash* [2006] EWCA Civ 1714, [2008] QB 73.

136 *Prince Albert v Strange* (1849) 2 De G & SM 652; *Stephens v* Avery [1988] Ch 449.

137 The defence of the 'compulsion of law'.

138 *Gartside v Outram* (1857) 26 LJ Ch 113, 114; *Beloff v Pressdram Ltd* [1973] 1 All ER 241, 260; *Lion Laboratories Ltd v Evans* [1985] QB 526; *Initial Services Limited v Putterill*

However, there has been some clarity from Europe. Under the influence of the European Convention on Human Rights, this examination of the public interest defence has taken a more structured form of a balancing exercise in which the public and private interests in the preservation of confidentiality are weighed against other countervailing public interests requiring disclosure of information.[139] For a disclosure of confidential or private information to be lawful, the 'interference' with the right to respect for private life must be 'in accordance with the law', pursue a legitimate aim and be necessary for achieving that aim.[140]

Disclosure must be based on law, failing which there will be a breach of the right to respect for private life.[141] On face value this sounds simple enough if it were not accompanied by the proviso that the law must be formulated with sufficient precision to clarify the scope of discretion conferred on the competent authorities and the manner of its exercise. Case law tells us that instructions, administrative practices and guidance may be taken into account, in so far as they are clear and sufficiently publicised.[142] We are yet to find such artefacts.

Information sharing is likely to constitute an interference with private life in some contexts.[143] The disclosure of a person's medical record by a clinic to a Social Insurance Office for purposes of investigating fraud has been held to be interference.[144] Article 8(2) expressly provides for legitimate interference 'for the prevention of disorder or crime'[145] or 'in the interests of…. public safety' or 'the protection of rights and freedom of others'. Transparency and accountability in the use of public money are other legitimate aims.[146]

[1968] 1 QB 396; *Hubbard v Vosper* [1972] 2 QB 84; *London Regional Transport v The Mayor of London* [2001] EWCA Civ 1491, [2003] EMLR 4.

139 *Attorney-General v Guardian Newspapers Ltd* (No 2) [1990] 1 AC 109, 282.

140 European Convention on Human Rights, art. 8.

141 *Sciacca v Italy* (2006) 43 EHRR 20 (App No 50774/99).

142 *Silver v United Kingdom* (1983) 5 EHRR 347 (App Nos 5947/72 6205/73, 7052/75, 7061/75, 7107/75, 7113/75, 7136/75) at [88] to [89].

143 See *Marcel v Commissioner of Police of the Metropolis* [1991] 2 WLR 1118, 1130.

144 See e.g., *MS v Sweden* (1999) 28 EHRR 313 (App No 20837/92); joined cases C-465/00 and C-138/01 *Rechnungshof* [2003] ECR I-4989 at [74]; *Hilton v UK* App No 12015/86 (Commission decision).

145 Including the identification of offenders: *S and Marper v United Kingdom* (2009) 48 EHRR 50 (App Nos 30562/04 and 30566/044) (Grand Chamber decision); *R (Wood) v Commissioner of Police of Metropolis* [2009] EWCA Civ 414, [2010] 1 WLR 123 at [79].

146 See e.g., joined cases C-92/09 and C-93/09 *Volker* [2010] ECR I-11063 at [68].

The social impacts of privacy are only considered when information relates to a risk posed by an individual to other individuals. In such cases additional requirements include the assessment of evidence of the risk on the balance of probabilities, the need for taking into consideration the time elapsed since the events contained in the information, the interest of the recipient of the information and an assessment of the risks posed in case of non-disclosure.[147] In health it is arguable that the social impacts of privacy should almost always be considered but because you cannot see the impacts in a tangible way they are often neglected. For example, if a cancer patient refuses to share their information, the numbers of patients participating in research for the development and adoption of new drugs to cure cancer may not be high enough and this could pose a threat to the health of society. However this would never be considered in this context.

Additional Controls Specific to Health

The question of what privacy is and if it has been breached is complex enough in any setting but in a healthcare setting there are three additional controls that are always present.

1. Additional laws/regulations/obligations which *necessitate* sharing of information in and beyond health. These broadly include three categories:
   - Laws that mandate the sharing of confidential information, for example the Public Health (Control of Diseases) Act 1984 and amendments[148] which mandates the notification of infectious diseases to a 'proper officer' within a local authority.
   - Court orders ordering the disclosure of confidential information.
   - Informed consent of the individual. This is perhaps the least well used but most important.
2. Additional laws/regulations/obligations which *allow* sharing of information in and beyond health. Examples include:
   - The public interest test. These are generally cases relating to a single individual's information and the public interest will almost never provide

---

147 R *v Local Authority in the Midlands and another, ex parte LM* [2000] 1 FLR 612; *Woolgar v Chief Constable of Sussex Police* [2000] 1 WLR 25; R *(L) v Commissioner of the Police for the Metropolis* [2009] UKSC 3, [2010] 1 AC 410; *JR 57 Application for Judicial review (QB)* (NI) [2013] NIQB 33.

148 See in particular the Heath Protection (Notification) Regulations 2010 (SI 2010/659).

the basis for routine sharing arrangements. Confidential information can be disclosed to support the detection, investigation and punishment of serious crime and/or to prevent abuse or serious harm to others. Decisions to disclose confidential information when legal permission is available are complex. The holder of the information must believe that the public good that would be served by sharing the information outweighs both the obligation of confidentiality owed to the individual and the public good of protecting trust in a confidential service.

- The Crime and Disorder Act 1998 section 115, the Data Protection Act 1998 section 29, and the Police and Criminal Evidence Act 1984.
- Section 251 of the NHS Act 2006 (commonly referred to as 'section 251'). The Health Service Control of Patient Information Regulations 2002 are the regulations that allow the Secretary of State to exercise judgement as to whether the duty of confidentiality should be set aside.
- Safeguarding. There is legislation to protect children through sharing for safeguarding. The cases of *Baby P*[149] and *Victoria Climbie*[150] reinforce the need for this. For adults the *Winterbourne View*[151] episode, *Clwyd*[152] and *Francis*[153] reports suggest the same is required.

3. Laws that *necessitate that information is not shared* in and beyond health:

   - Information should always be shared in accordance with the law and organisations must abide by legal provisions which ban or limit the sharing of particular pieces of confidential information. One example is the law which makes the disclosure of information relating to assisted conception treatment (for example information about gamete donors and people receiving treatment) a criminal offence in most cases.[154] However, even these special cases are disputed. Parliamentary

149 www.haringeylscb.org/executive_summary_peter_final.pdf

150 www.gov.uk/government/uploads/system/uploads/attachment_data/file/273183/5730.pdf.

151 www.gov.uk/government/uploads/system/uploads/attachment_data/file/213215/final-report.pdf.

152 www.gov.uk/government/publications/nhs-hospitals-complaints-system-review.

153 www.gov.uk/government/news/francis-report-on-mid-staffs-government-accepts-recommendations.

154 Sections 33A and 41 of the Human Fertilisation and Embryology Act 1990.

opposition to a statutory duty to share information is evident. Both the 2002 report 'Privacy and Data-Sharing – The Way Forward for Public Services'[155] and the *Walport–Thomas Review*[156] proposed the enactment of a general power to enable information sharing gateways to be created by secondary legislation. An attempt to legislate such a power was made during the passage of what is now the Coroners and Justice Act 2009. Parliamentary opposition to the creation of such a wide power led to its withdrawal.[157] Therefore, there are checks and balances but they are based on what the government thinks is right, not on what the public wants.

Potential Changes to the Law

At this point the question we are compelled to answer is 'is it worth at this stage becoming adept in information law, when in parallel to the emerging political framework there are proposals to change the law?' We argue that although a change such as the proposed Data Sharing Directive is a potentially significant change, it signals positive moves for the public with an emphasis on explicit consent and privacy impact assessments. However, the Information Commissioner's Office (ICO) response[158] to the proposed Data Protection Directive reveals some of the practical implementation issues. They welcome the high standard of consent in Article 4(8),[159] but acknowledge that it is important that the strengthening of consent does not leave data controllers without a lawful basis for processing which is either necessary or unobjectionable. They purport that usually there need to be alternatives to consent. Wouldn't it be better if the public could voice that view, if indeed it is their view?

---

155 Cabinet Office, London, Performance and Innovation Unit, 'Privacy and Data-sharing: The Way Forward for Public Services' (April 2002). The report suggested introducing 'changes to legislative processes for establishing data-sharing gateways, to allow data-sharing gateways to be introduced through secondary legislation, subject to a codified list of tangible safeguards and adequate Parliamentary scrutiny'.

156 R. Thomas and M. Walport, 'Data Sharing Review Report' (Ministry of Justice, UK, July 2008).

157 Legislative Scrutiny: Coroners and Justice Bill (see note 43).

158 12.2.13

159 4(8) 'the data subject's consent' means any freely given specific, informed and explicit indication of his or her wishes by which the data subject, either by a statement or by a clear affirmative action, signifies agreement to personal data relating to them being processed.

Transparency and fairness – fair processing

It is this thought that brings us to re-examine Article 5, '*Principles relating to personal data processing*', which we believe requires some further consideration, around the distinction between transparency and fairness. The Data Protection Act tells us that 'Personal data must be

a. processed lawfully, fairly and in a transparent manner in relation to the data subject; and
b. collected for specified, explicit and legitimate purposes and not further processed in a way incompatible with those purposes.'

It is worth giving some thought to the distinction between the lawfulness and transparency provisions in (a) and the purpose limitation provisions in (b). In other European Union Member States, 'fairness' is primarily about transparency and not about fairness of use – which is generally treated as more of an 'incompatibility' issue. It is worth considering how 'fairness' could be used as a compliance tool – in the UK and elsewhere – once the new law is in place. Likewise, within Article 6 on 'lawfulness of processing', there is a danger that processing which is necessary for public authorities but not provided for by law will be prevented. The ICO asked for explicit recognition that processing may take place where it is clearly in the data subject's interests and does not override his or her fundamental rights and freedoms. Surely this would be better taken as an individual's decision?

Although there are informed consent provisions in 'Article 7 – Conditions for Consent', determining whether there is a 'significant imbalance' between an individual and a data controller is difficult to do in practice. The ICO accepts that genuine consent depends on freedom of choice, but that it is still possible to have genuine consent within a basically 'imbalanced' relationship – for example in respect of certain aspects of employer–employee data processing. This belief needs to be tested on the public at large. Perhaps the most important article for ensuring that individuals are in control of their information is Article 11 on 'Transparent information and communication'. The issue of whether privacy policies need to be merely accessible to data subjects or need to be actively communicated to them has always been a source of confusion. This is a real issue for data controllers and there is a need for clarification of the type of communication required. The wording of Article 11 as drafted does not provide clarity and perpetuates the uncertainty. It could be disproportionate to require data controllers to actively communicate their privacy policies in all circumstances, each and every time. The ICO believes that the transparency standard provided for should be linked to risk. The more unexpected, contentious or objectionable the processing, the more important it is that privacy policies are communicated actively to the data subject. However, it could be argued that if you are talking about something as subjective as the expectations of all of society you have to start by telling people what you expect them to know so you can know what they should expect.

Article 14 delves slightly deeper into this when broaching the subject of 'Information to the data subject':

1. Where personal data relating to a data subject are collected, the controller shall provide the data subject with at least the following information:
    a. the identity and the contact details of the controller and, if any, of the controller's representative and of the data protection officer;
    b. the purposes of the processing for which the personal data are intended, including the contract terms and general conditions where the processing is based on point (b) of Article 6(1) and the legitimate interests pursued by the controller where the processing is based on point (f) of Article 6(1);
    c. the period for which the personal data will be stored;
    d. the existence of the right to request from the controller access to and rectification or erasure of the personal data concerning the data subject or to object to the processing of such personal data;
    e. the right to lodge a complaint to the supervisory authority and the contact details of the supervisory authority;
    f. the recipients or categories of recipients of the personal data;
    g. where applicable, that the controller intends to transfer to a third country or international organisation and on the level of protection afforded by that third country or international organisation by reference to an adequacy decision by the Commission;
    h. any further information necessary to guarantee fair processing in respect of the data subject, having regard to the specific circumstances in which the personal data are collected.

The ICO has doubts as to how useful it is to provide a citizen with the contract terms set out in (b) and it does seem excessive for a data controller to have to provide these as a matter of course. Despite supporting greater transparency, they wonder how much, in reality, this will empower a citizen. The ICO would prefer the emphasis to be on clear, intelligible explanations of purpose, of data controller identity and the enhanced information about sources of data and disclosures, together with the purpose for which disclosures are made. They believe that this would provide a superior 'transparency' package for individuals that would also be less burdensome for data controllers. They would like to see some statutory recognition of the 'layered' privacy notices approach they have long supported, i.e., give people a basic notice but make a more detailed one available to those who want it. It would be very difficult to provide all the information set out above on a mobile device, for example. This is a particular issue given many individuals' apparent reluctance to read privacy notices and similar material. Another key point to consider on transparency is where data about an individual is collected from other people or organisations:

> Where the personal data are not collected from the data subject, the controller shall inform the data subject, from which source the personal data originate.[160]

Again, the ICO expresses concerns about practicalities around implementation. They 'generally like the idea of the data controller having to tell the data subject where the personal data came from – this is a valuable transparency measure – particularly in complex data sharing contexts where individuals may have little knowledge of – or control over – the sharing of their personal data'. However, they do not think it should have to be done in each and every case. The duty should be limited to those cases where a failure to provide this information would have particular consequences for the individual, or where the source would be wholly unexpected, for example. They would like to see an element of risk assessment introduced. Given the complexity of present-day information systems, as it stands this provision could result in a very large number of 'data obtained' notifications being sent to a very large number of individuals. In this book we question whether the onus needs to be on the NHS to send notifications out to individuals. It is surely impractical to send a notification every other day. Why not send one notification that all notifications can be found on a website or at local community centres or GP surgeries? Then the individual can take that risk decision themselves. This surely makes sense as they would suffer the consequences of any such risk-based decisions.

Data subject's right of access

The Article 24 right about Subject Access Requests (SAR) made to Joint Data Controllers is meant to make it easier for individuals to exercise subject access, and other rights, in respect of shared information. This would mean that an individual could make a single SAR in order to gain access to information about them that has been shared between other organisations without having to make a request to each organisation. The act of having to do this seems ludicrous; the current arrangement of having to pay, even more so. Why shouldn't access be instant?

160 https://ico.org.uk/for-organisations/guide-to-data-protection/key-definitions/.

Data quality

On first viewing the Article 17 right to be forgotten and to erasure does not seem hugely significant in the management of health data. However, it can be viewed as reflecting a subtle but significant change to the 'balance of power' between data subjects and controllers. Currently the default position is that controllers can process personal data about someone other than in certain limited circumstances. The situation under the Regulation is that the individual has the power to prevent the processing unless the controller can justify it. However, when this is extended to erasure it may be difficult or impossible to achieve and could lead individuals to believe falsely that they can achieve the absolute erasure of information about them. It can be impossible to remove information from the internet once it has been posted. This right, as billed, could mislead individuals as to the degree of protection the law can offer them in practice. Using data items for initiatives such as care. data can be likened to the switching on of a tap to top up a bucket of water. Once the data enters the existing pool of water surely it is almost impossible to separate it?

Right to object

This gives rise to the very topical and controversial right which Article 19 creates. This 'Right to Object' also features in the Confidentiality Guide and in the Secretary of State's speech mentioned above. But the ICO takes the view that the right to object would be more helpful if it were to be framed as a 'right to prevent processing'. The ICO feels the data controller should be able to refuse an objection where there are compelling and legitimate grounds for it to continue processing. This would deal with those situations where individuals expect the cessation of processing in unrealistic circumstances. The Confidentiality Guide and NHS Constitution both enshrine this as a right which must be respected. There is a difference however between a right to object and a right to stop processing. The right to object could actually be seen as patronising and paternalistic. It is essentially giving people freedom of speech – and then taking it away. Surely individuals should not need to object?

Impact assessments involving patients

Article 33 is even more promising in terms of 'data subject' involvement. It asserts that in data protection impact assessments 'the controller shall seek the views of data subjects or their representatives on the intended processing, without prejudice to the protection of commercial or public interests or the security of the processing operations'. The ICO welcomes the involvement of the public but suggest this is only really essential where a novel, large-scale and potentially privacy-invasive processing operation is envisaged but surely the public should have some way of knowing all activities proposed so they can make their own decisions about magnitude of scale. It should be made clearer that there is a requirement to take the public's views into account in this provision. The Secretary of State's 2014 commitment to put the Panel of the National Data Guardian on a statutory footing is a positive step in the right direction to encourage patient participation.

Summary

We argue that it is reassuring that the political and legal frameworks are moving in the right direction to empower patients and move away from a culture where the 'privacy myth' rules mindsets. We also see a movement towards a culture where the public can choose when they would like to contribute towards the 'collective transparency' the government aspires towards. However there is a strong sense that the NHS is still clinging on to the primary control of the information, without even a suggestion that the patient would have the primary control of their information. The fundamental starting point is therefore wrong and the rest of this book seeks to move the balance of control of information from the NHS to the individual for purposes other than their direct care. We further argue that this will satisfy each of the government's pledges outlined above and the proposed changes to EU data protection law. To take this theoretical concept through to the model's practical implementation, the book takes best practice from other countries and suggests theoretical models of 'privacy' and a technical portal to deliver it.

Chapter 2

Sharing Healthcare Data in Europe and the USA

Introduction

Healthcare in both the UK and Europe is barely managing to cover its operational costs. Not only are the methods for raising funds to cover costs inadequate,[1] but – and of even greater concern – costs are set to soar even higher,[2] with a burgeoning ageing population increasing the demand for care. While there is an ongoing debate about how to make changes to make healthcare remain financially sustainable, we argue that it is time to develop a new overarching strategy. Although there are clear attributes of different approaches to reform, that are more likely than others to slow cost growth, we only explore one such strategy which involves 'sharing of healthcare data' and sharing 'control' of healthcare data with the patients. The argument is simple, as information is 'power', by sharing healthcare data it is possible to deliver a modern, personalised and sustainable healthcare system. The purpose of this chapter is to consider what progress has been made to this extent and to compare and analyse how healthcare data is shared in Europe and the USA.[3] We specifically chose to compare USA and Europe because they face similar challenges, but more significantly, even with their very different health systems, both of them look to healthcare information technology as a critical means of addressing these challenges and are progressing in its adoption.[4]

---

1 Richard B. Saltman and Zachary Cahn, 'Restructuring Health Systems for an Era of Prolonged Austerity' (2013) *BMJ* 346.

2 Economist Intelligence Unit, Future of Healthcare in Europe (Economist Intelligence Unit Limited, 2011). According to the European Commission figures, the costs of health and social care will rise substantially to about 9 per cent of EU GDP in 2050.

3 We have separately discussed European and the US e-health, first for convenience of the reader, second perhaps more importantly to appreciate their very different health systems, as in comparing the USA and Europe we are comparing two extremes.

4 See National Information Board, 'Personalised Health and Care 2020 Using Data and Technology to Transform Outcomes for Patients and Citizens: A Framework for Action' (November 2014).

In Europe, control of healthcare data is being positioned as one key element in the redesign of healthcare by 2020.[5] A key component of 'control' of such data is the notion of 'privacy'. From a privacy point of view, 'health informational privacy is an individual's claim to control the circumstances in which personal health information is collected, used, stored, and transmitted'.[6] This brings to the forefront questions such as: Is the recipient of the information permitted to know the identity of the individuals which the information relates to? What is the minimum amount of information that will satisfy the purpose? And, ideally: Did the patient agree to the terms of the data collection? All questions that we argue become completely unnecessary if the patient is in 'control'.

We contend that the principle that individuals are the owners and controllers of their own health data, with the right to make decisions over access to the data and to be informed about how it will be used, is outlined in EU law and European jurisprudence. However, it is rarely fully implemented in health systems. In this chapter we try to understand why even in those countries that have invested in e-health applications (such as Denmark, Sweden and Spain), we do not find an example of a population that can fully control its own health data.

Finally, we discuss what (or who) drives the collection and the accessibility of these data in the pursuit of new clinical insights. It analyses the role of the individual in controlling these data and reflects on how well these data are used and the key barriers to broader applications. One clear barrier from the USA perspective is that, despite the size and the fragmented nature of the healthcare system in the USA, a unique patient identifier has not yet been adopted. This is a prerequisite for complete control by an increasingly geographically mobile population who may access care in different areas of the country. This observation is important, because it specifically points to a USA/Europe difference in approach.

We suggest that a leader nation must initiate this process so that others can follow best practice (in both public and private sectors, as care transverses geographical and financial boundaries). This is not to say best practice does not exist within pockets worldwide. There are a number of advocates from the USA conducting studies, including Miller,[7] to test levels of patient control, but invariably they have demonstrated that progress is poor. However, it is the

5 http://ec.europa.eu/information_society/activities/health/docs/policy/taskforce/redesigning_health-eu-for2020-ehtf-report2012.pdf

6 Lawrence Gostin, *Public Health Law: Power, Duty, Restrain* (2nd edn, University of California Press 2009) 316.

7 Robert H. Miller 'Satisfying Patient-Consumer Principles For Health Information Exchange: Evidence From California Case Studies' (2012) 31(3) *Health Affairs* 537, www.eweek.com/c/a/Health-Care-IT/Web-Portals-Vital-to-Patient-Control-of-Health-Data-Study-257933/.

pockets of good practice upon which we draw inspiration to suggest the UK as a potential beacon early adopter for such technologies to empower patient control, building on the policy grounds that are rapidly emerging in the USA, Europe and the UK.

E-Healthcare in Europe

The objective of this section is to discuss the concept of e-healthcare through a European lens and analyse the development of the European e-healthcare framework by focusing on the contemporary public discussion, policy and the legal landscape. We have also analysed the current perspectives for e-Health in light of opportunities and challenges identified in Europe.

The EU seeks to create a high-quality, patient-centred, equitable healthcare system for all patients.[8] However, the healthcare system we inherited was designed in the 1950s, and it has not evolved to respond to the modern environment. There are those who argue that it is no longer fit for purpose, even though the EU Member States have a range of different healthcare systems which can be divided into two basic types: 'Bismarck systems', which are insurance-based, and 'Beveridge systems' (centralised or decentralised), which are tax-funded.[9] Both systems share a common concern: the need to transform healthcare because of spiralling healthcare costs.[10] The urgency of this is increasingly

8 'eHealth can benefit citizens, patients, health and care professionals but also health organisations and public authorities. eHealth – when applied effectively – delivers more personalised "citizen-centric" healthcare, which is more targeted, effective and efficient and helps reduce errors, as well as the length of hospitalisation. It facilitates socio-economic inclusion and equality, quality of life and patient empowerment through greater transparency, access to services and information and the use of social media for health': see European Commission2012, 'European Union e-Health Action Plan 2012–2020: Innovative Healthcare for the 21st Century: EC 2012', COM(2012) 736. For a detailed explanation of the expansion of EU competence in the field of health law see Hervey, T. and McHale, J., *Health and the European Union* (CUP 2004); see also A. Beurden, 'The European perspective on e-health', in S. Callens (ed.), *E-health and the Law* (Kluwer 2003) 106–108.

9 W. Sauter, 'The Impact of EU Competition Law on National Healthcare Systems' (2013) E. L. Rev. 459. See E. Mossialos et al. (eds), *Health Systems Governance in Europe: the Role of European Law and Policy* (CUP 2010); see also M. McKee, E. Mossialos and R. Baeten (eds), *The Impact of EU Law on Healthcare Systems* (P.I.E.-Peter Lang 2002).

10 It is a constantly growing component of public finances, rising to 9 per cent of GDP and representing between 6 per cent and 15 per cent of government spending in most EU countries. See European Commission, 'e-Health Task Force

evident: these costs are driven by demographic changes, an ageing population, population movement,[11] a dramatic increase in chronic conditions linked to unhealthy lifestyles, expensive new technologies and products, the need for more specialised skills, and the demand for high-level care.[12]

The problem for Europe has been how to respond to these challenges; specifically, how to achieve an affordable and economically sustainable healthcare system, but at the same time one which is efficient and effective. Unsurprisingly e-Health, enabled by information and communication technologies, offers Europe solutions that can help avoid healthcare crisis.

In the past few years we have witnessed an increasingly sophisticated use of digital technology by healthcare providers in managing and sharing patient information to reduce cost, improve accuracy, and empower patients.[13] The European Commission has been investing in e-health research for more than 20 years[14] and

---

Report – Redesigning Health in Europe for 2020 (Publications Office of the European Union, 2012).

11 *Raymond Kohll v Union des caisses de maladie* (C-158/96) [1998] ECR I-1931, [1998] 2 CMLR 928; R (*on the application of Yvonne Watts*) *v Bedford Primary Care Trust and Secretary of State for Health* (C-372/04) [2006] ECR I-4325, [2006] 3 CMLR 5. See C. Newdick, 'Citizenship, Free Movement and Health Care: Cementing Individual Rights by Corroding Social Solidarity' (2006) 43 *CML. Rev.* 1645; J. van de Gronden, 'Cross-border Health Care in the EU and the Organization of National Health Care Systems of the Member States: the Dynamics resulting from the European Court of Justice's Decisions on Free Movement and Competition Law' (2009) 26 *Wisconsin Int. L. J.* 705.

12 European Commission, 'e-Health Task Force Report – Redesigning health in Europe for 2020' (Publications Office of the European Union, 2012).

13 M. Petkovic and L. Ibraimi, 'Privacy and Security in E-Health Applications' in Carsten Röcker and Martina Ziefle (eds), *E-Health, Assistive Technologies and Applications for Assisted Living: Challenges and Solutions* (IGI Global 2011) 23; see also Stroetmann, K.A., Jones, T., Dobrev, A. and Stroetmann, V.N. (2006) 'e-Health is worth it? The Economic Benefits of Implemented e-Health Solutions at Ten European Sites', E-Health IMPACT project study supported by the European Commission Information Society and Media Directorate-General (Luxembourg Office for Official Publications of the European Community), www.ehealth-impact.eu/download/documents/ehealthimpactsept2006.pdf.

14 E-Health initiatives can been seen across the world including creation of national/regional electronic health record (EHR) infrastructures such as RHIO's in the USA, the NHS Spine project in the UK and NICTIZ in The Netherlands. There are also commercial web-based personal health record (PHR) systems such as Microsoft HealthVault and Google Health. These applications process, store and exchange

has been responsible for developing targeted policy initiatives ('e-Health Action Plan'[15]) with the aim of fostering widespread adoption of e-health technologies across the EU.[16] Better use of information and more generally the implementation of electronic health records (EHRs) is at the heart of many of these initiatives.[17]

As a part of this process for policy development, in 2012, the EU created the e-Health Task Force (The Task Force) to assess the potential of ICT in healthcare innovation in the EU and to make recommendations on what might be done to ensure that Europe reaps the full benefits of e-health by 2020. The Task Force published a report entitled 'Redesigning Health in Europe

patient's medical information. See Petkovic and Ibraimi (note 13); Communication from the Commission for a Digital Agenda for Europe, COM (2010) 245 final/2, 29; Directive 2011/24/EU of the European Parliament and of the Council of 9 March 2011 on the application of patients' rights in cross-border healthcare (0J L 88, 4.4.2011, 45) and Commission Decision 2008/49/EC of 12 December 2007 concerning the implementation of the Internal Market Information System as regards the protection of personal data (0J L 13, 16.1.2008, 18); Karl A. Stroetmann, Jorg Artmann, Veli N. Stroetmann, 'European Countries on Their Journey Towards National e-Health Infrastructures: Final European Progress Report' (European Commission 2011); C. Pagliari, T. Shand and B. Fisher, 'Embedding Online Patient Record Access in UK Primary Care: A Survey of Stakeholder Experiences' (2012) 3(34) *J. R. Soc. Med.* Short Rep.

15 The Action Plan 2012–2020 being the most up to date. The Action Plan operates in the context of Article 14 of Directive 2011/24 on the application of patients' rights in cross-border healthcare. Its main objective is to support research and innovation. See also European Commission, 'e-Health – Making Healthcare Better for European Citizens: An Action Plan or European e-Health Area', SEC (2004) 539 COM (2004) 356 final, Brussels.

16 See European Commission (note 15); see also European Commission, 'ICT for Health and i2010, Transforming the European Healthcare Landscape' (Publications Office of the European Union, 2006); European Commission (2008) 'Legally e-Health: Putting e-Health in its European Legal Context, Study Report' (European Communities, Luxembourg March 2008).

17 'A longitudinal collection of patient-centric, healthcare information, available across providers, care settings, and time. It is a central component of an integrated health information system'; see US Institute of Standards & Technology, www.itl.nist.gov/div897/docs/EHR.html; see UK Department of Health. www.dh.gov.uk/Home/fs/en; see also C. Pagliari C. *Literature Review and Conceptual Map of the Area of e-Health* (NHS SDO 2005); see also A. Black, J. Car, C. Pagliari, C., 'The impact of eHealth on the Quality and Safety of Healthcare: A Systematic Overview' (2011) *PLoS Medicine* 8.

in 2020' which highlights the importance of health data, health literacy, and the exchange of strong practice protocol on e-health. The report also argues that the future of health research, diagnostics and healthcare delivery will depend upon how effectively we manage healthcare data. The first section of the report describes five levers for change that could create the momentum for a fundamental reorganisation of healthcare to make use of already existing information technologies. The Task Force has identified:[18]

- 'My data, my decisions': Individuals are the owners and controllers of their own health data, with the right to make decisions over access to the data and to be informed about how it will be used.[19]
- 'Liberate the data': Governments should ensure that health data is accurate, reliable, and up to date; that it is gathered in a standard way; and that it is anonymised before it is made available to anyone who can add value to it in the best interest of the patient.
- 'Connect up everything': The digital environment is evolving rapidly, with an increasing trend toward interaction and sharing. Healthcare needs, therefore, to reap the benefits of the digital age in order to provide more integrated and personalised care to patients rather than 'only' interventions.
- 'Revolutionise health': By this we mean creating the necessary conditions for patients to be able to make more informed choices about where and how they want to be treated. This will have a real impact on resource allocation in health, as funding follows the patients and not the other way round.
- 'Include everyone': The needs of the vulnerable communities that are outside the reach of e-health tools need to be accommodated; otherwise, the chances are that e-health could ultimately exacerbate existing inequalities rather than reduce them.[20]

---

18 European Commission, 'e-Health Task Force Report – Redesigning Health in Europe for 2020' (Publications Office of the European Union, 2012) 9–14.

19 According to the task force this represents a shift in power relationships within healthcare; away from the authority of the medical professional and towards a more collaborative partnership with patients who would be expected to take greater responsibility and participation in managing their own well-being. The task force also highlighted how it would be possible to share ownership between the patient and the health system depending on the use; for example it suggested that in possible way patients could be the owners of personal health information but allowing the health system to use depersonalised or 'pseudonymised' data for epidemiological purpose with or without requiring additional consent: see European Commission (note 18) 9.

20 European Commission (note 18).

On the basis of these five levers, the second section of the report provided five recommendations for action in order to achieve the vision of e-Health by 2020. These are developed with policymakers at the European and national levels in mind as the primary audience. The first recommendation called upon policy makers to act quickly to create a legal framework and space to manage the explosion of health data. As part of this effort, safeguards need to be put into place that will allow patients to use e-health services with confidence that their data is handled appropriately.[21] The second recommendation is for European and national policy makers to create a 'beacon group' of Member States and regions committed to 'open data' and 'e-health'. There is no unique e-health model that can be imposed across Europe, but the experience of others can be shared, and lessons can be learned. The third recommendation calls upon policy makers at all levels to support health literacy among patients. Health-literate patients have better awareness of and knowledge about medicine use, and they take greater responsibility for their own health. The fourth recommendation calls for an effort to overcome the 'silo mentality' and lack of cooperation in primary, secondary, and tertiary health institutions. Unfortunately, this silo mentality mirrors the manner in which health professionals guard their own competence and areas of expertise. Finally the last recommendation calls for the promotion of user-driven innovation in health as opposed to technology-driven innovation.[22] Importantly for our purposes, the next phase would see an investment in tools patients can use to support their well-being and manage their lives, which would close the gap between innovation and the market, and between the market and patients.[23]

Also significant for our analysis is the fact that originally the EU had far more ambitious objectives which sought to integrate all patient information from primary to tertiary settings, and to include emergency and in-patient care,[24] which at an early stage was further expanded by the EU Commission by setting 2015 as the target year for EHR interoperability, to ensure that key

21 J. Cruickshank, C. Packman and J. Paxman, 'Personal Health Records: Putting Patients in Control' (2020health.org, September, 2012) 24.

22 See note 18.

23 The most recent major publication from the EU has been the 'e-Health Action Plan 2012–2020: Innovative Healthcare for the 21st Century' in which the Commission reaffirms the vision and impact of eHealth systems and identifies some of the barriers to adoption and strategies for removal of these barriers.

24 European Union, Directive 2011/24/EU of the European Parliament and of the Council of 9 March 2011 on the Application of Patients' Rights in Cross-border Healthcare, OJEU, L 88/45.

EHR[25] datasets could span European borders in conformity with medical rules and other relevant legal frameworks. However, neither of the objectives was fulfilled because of a number of challenges, one of which was, and still remains, technological in nature. This is to specify, develop, test, and deploy standardised tools, common architectures, and vocabularies within secure, real-time, and scalable networks, and to achieve all of this within the fast-changing world of information and communication technologies. It is important to note that, despite the significant and continuing effort, cultural differences still remain a formidable barrier.

In fact, to a degree, it is felt that this initial setback is a positive turning point, as the EU Commission acknowledged that a 'Single eHealth Area' across Europe and a pan-EU electronic health record (EHR) system would be unrealistic, impractical and would not be technically feasible, cost effective or even medically justified.[26] Crucially, such severe criticism resulted in freeing strategic space for working towards a realistic and achievable alternative, which was in the form of developing the European Patient Smart Open Services (epSOS).[27] This interoperable, inter-regional, but most importantly, realistic, project aimed at the more modest goal of connecting 12 nations to a secure database and sharing only basic patient summaries and prescription records. It also aimed to fulfil a longstanding political objective to sell European e-Health to the public and enable emergency treatment for Europeans travelling outside their home countries. epSOS underscored a strategic shift in EU thinking about using information technology in healthcare. The central premise was to develop 'a practical e-Health framework and ICT infrastructure'[28], with a

25 European Commission's Seventh Framework Programme (FP7) has funded a number of projects on interconnecting EHR with innovative delivery solutions and making better use of data for early detection and prevention. See www.ecoquip.eu/cms/resources/uploads/File/EcoQUIP%20Workshop%20Provocation%20Paper.pdf.

26 See 'European Countries on their Journey towards National e-Health Infrastructures' www.ehealth-strategies.eu/report/eHealth_Strategies_Final_Report_Web.pdf.

27 It is important to note that the epSOS Services are offered on a pilot basis. As a pilot, the primary objective of the initiative is to gather information and evidence in order to facilitate subsequent full deployment. The epSOS project came to an end in June 2014.

28 The overarching goal of epSOS is to develop a practical e-Health framework and Information and Communication Technology (ICT) infrastructure that will enable secure access to patient health information, particularly with respect to a basic patient summary and e-Prescription, between European healthcare systems. The project is co-financed by the European Commission within the Competitiveness and Innovation Programme.

two-phased[29] approach (much like the USA's approach, detailed later in this chapter).

Unfortunately, there has been very little dialogue internationally about what works and what doesn't work[30] despite the fact that many countries have had spectacular failures alongside some amazing successes. The European experience suggests that the critical challenge of any e-Health strategy is primarily delivery and implementation. We also argue that an essential element of e-Health is making patient data available to concerned parties. The rationale is simple and well established: data sharing[31] can lower costs and improve quality. For example, data sharing in the airline industry, banks and in the retail sector has improved productivity, reduced costs, and improved customer satisfaction. Banks have also reaped substantial benefits by making data available to customers online. There is no reason to assume that it would not produce the same positive response in the healthcare system. However, it is important to note that how this will work can be expected to vary greatly between countries.

International experience has shown that e-Health deployments are complex undertakings and need specific focus. Governments across the world are in various stages of planning initiatives designed to leverage advances in healthcare information technology. Among the European countries, Spain is already a leader in e-Health with many of its regions having invested early and productively in healthcare IT adoption and health information exchange. For example, the southern province of Andalusia has implemented an EHR system called Diraya, covering eight million inhabitants. Indeed, epSOS itself was highlighted in the January 2011 empirical report as a way to build bottom-up and outwards from local or regional EHR initiatives such as the Spanish Diraya effort.[32] It integrates patients' health information and intervention details in primary care, emergency services, mental health services and ambulatory specialised care in the region. While Spain's decentralised system has driven

29 Phase I included the Patient Summary (access to key medical data for patient treatment) and cross-border use of e-prescriptions. Phase II involved integration of pan-EU 112 emergency services, integration of the European Health Insurance Card (EHIC) and patient access to data.

30 H. McConnell, 'International Efforts in Implementing National Health Information Infrastructure and Electronic Health Records' (2004) 40(1) *World Hospitals and Health Services* 33–37, 39–40, 50–52.

31 For example between a company and its customer.

32 Spain is working towards developing a national set of standards for interoperability within and between systems: www.ihe-online.com/feature-articles/electronic-health-records-the-european-and-american-experience/trackback/1/index.html.

leading practice at the regional level in connected health, at the national level it is also seen as a barrier to development. There is now a general agreement in Spain that priority should be to have an electronic medical record for each citizen, accessible from anywhere in the country.

Denmark is generally recognised as being a 'shining light' in terms of e-Health in Europe. What can we learn from Denmark? A distinctive feature of Denmark's e-Health is its strong governance, which has ensured that end users are comfortable with sharing data and clinical work processes – a key factor in creating further impetus for information sharing across the system. In 2003, Denmark launched a universal EHR system and a national PHR Service with full clinical functionality and a strong emphasis on cross-national governance of healthcare IT. The government-run PHR portal is Sundhed.dk with differentiated access for health staff and the public.[33] Denmark's EHR centres on the 'e-Journal' which began in 2009 and is now available to all hospitals and all GPs across the country. The e-Journal makes extracts of registered patient data available via the MedCom secure network, and it ensures that hospital doctors and GPs have access to patient data no matter where the patient has been hospitalised previously. MedCom is considered one of the most interesting examples for the bottom-up development of a national health communications network.[34] This framework has been developed based on clear protocols, which are well embedded, along with a comprehensive and secure infrastructure that has allowed for the effective and secure sharing of data across Denmark's five regions.[35]

---

33 The portal provides general information on health and treatment options and access to individuals' own medical records and history: 'the citizen can … view treatments and diagnoses from his own hospital patient record, book appointments with his GP, renew prescription drugs, monitor own drug compliance, survey shortest waiting lists for operations and quality ratings of hospitals, register as organ donor, and get access to local disease management systems in out-patient clinics': note 21.

34 David Blumenthal and Marilyn Tavenner, 'The "Meaningful Use" Regulation for Electronic Health Records' (2010) 363 *N. Eng. J. Med.* 501, 501.

35 Denmark has continued to make substantial progress in developing innovative Healthcare IT solutions. Recently the Odense University Hospital started working with MedCom International to facilitate high-quality care in patients' homes. Patients with lung disease are equipped with a 'briefcase' that allows live images and sound as well as data measurement to be monitored at home and quickly transferred to the hospital either via the internet or a satellite connection. At the hospital, the doctor can evaluate and guide the patient as if the patient was present at the hospital. The data transmitted from the patient's home enable the hospital to perform systematic monitoring and control the quality of the treatment. See 'Connected Health: The Drive to Integrated

As we have already argued, online access to records has the potential to be one way of enabling individuals to become more empowered in relation to their health and healthcare. It is certainly clear that there is a gap between what patients say they want and need; and that such a gap must be bridged before e-Health generally and EHRs particularly are widely adopted. In addition, while we acknowledge that Healthcare IT can be disruptive in nature, it is not entirely new and many other industry domains have been using similar systems for many years. Indeed, e-Health technologies have been evolving steadily; however, their adoption has been slow due to various factors that have acted as barriers. These barriers will need to be removed and will themselves become key enablers once this has happened. It has also been noted that the impediments to adoption are not limited to the 'technical' challenges. Considerable legal challenges[36] also exist regarding the use of e-health tools and applications at the European and national/regional levels[37] – in particular, the lack of regulations related to privacy, confidentiality, liability, and data protection[38]. Some countries are already well advanced in the implementation of electronic medical records and national network infrastructures, predominantly the Scandinavian countries of Denmark, Finland, Norway, and Sweden.[39] Although we think that these systems are yet to achieve the full benefit and it is difficult to place them definitively on a continuum of progress or to draw definitive normative judgements of success, we certainly can identify patterns of progress emerging within and across these

---

Healthcare Delivery', Accenture Institute for Health and Public Service Value, 2012 www.accenture.com/connectedhealthstudy.

36 Karl A. Stroetmann, Jörg Artmann, Jos Dumortier and Griet Verhenneman, 'United in Diversity: Legal Challenges on the Road Towards Interoperable e-Health Solutions in Europe' (2012) 8(2) *Eur. J. Biomed. Informatics* 3–10.

37 C. George, Internet Pharmacies: Global Threat Requires Global Approach to Regulation' (2009) 9(3) *Telehealth Law* 37–52.

38 See C.P. Friedman, I. Lakovidis, L. Debenedetti, and N.M. Lorenzi, 'Across the Atlantic Cooperation to Address International Challenges in e-Health and Health IT: Managing Toward a Common Goal' (2009) 78 *Int. J. Med. Informatics* 778–784; see also K.A. Stroetmann, J. Artmann and V. Stroetmann, 'Developing National e-Health Infrastructures – Results and Lessons from Europe' (AMIA Annual Symposium Proceedings, 2011) 1347–1354.

39 Rachelle Kaye, Ehud Kokia, Varda Shalev, Dalia Idar and David Chinitz, 'Barriers and Success Factors in Health Information Technology: A practitioner's perspective' (2010) 3(2) *J Management & Marketing in Healthcare* 165, 163–175; the Estonian Government has recently (July 2014) decided to set up the e-Health Task Force to operate within the Government Office, with the goal being to develop a strategic development plan for Estonian e-Health until 2020, www.ehealthnews.eu/development/3989-estonian-government-launches-ehealth-task-force.

countries. We argue that the UK could use examples of good practices from these countries to its own effect.

Healthcare Data in Europe

The EU e-Health Task force report on 'Redesigning health in Europe for 2020', as mentioned above, argues that individuals should be the 'owners' and 'controllers' of their own health data, along with the right to make decisions over access to the data and to be informed about how that data will be used.[40] We believe that this radical shift moves the focus about the ownership and control of data from healthcare organisations to each individual, who would be the subject (and not the object) of data management. Incidentally this level and extent of reform is also connected with a crucial recommendation of the report which is about 'building a new legal basis for health data in Europe'.[41] The e-Health Task force report[42] also suggests that the governments across Europe should ensure that health data is made freely available to anyone who can add value to it. It is expected that this 'open data' approach would encourage many entrepreneurs to innovate rather than creating a monopoly or market domination as a service provider. But why do we need to act now? The argument is that gaps within the system are becoming increasingly apparent. Even though the data liberation theme has been at the very heart of the European e-Health Summit ('My data, my decision', and 'Liberate the data') it still needs careful considerations along with proactive policy making when moving from theory to practice.[43]

One of the most fiercely debated issues is how patients' data should be handled. But perhaps a far more intriguing and relevant question is how patients want their data to be handled. Should they be able to 'opt in' to a system of shared data or should they have to 'opt out'? And who will be the 'owners' and custodians of the data – the patients themselves or the caregivers and facilities that created the data? Issues of data ownership also raise questions about the legitimacy of secondary uses of data, such as in research and audit.

We argue that healthcare data in the UK represents a comprehensive resource funded by the taxpayers, inherently valuable and which could

40 European Commission, 'e-Health Task Force Report – Redesigning health in Europe for 2020' (Publications Office of the European Union, 2012).

41 See note 40.

42 Ibid.

43 Anne Moen et al., 'eHealth in Europe – Status and Challenges' (2012) 8(1) *Eur. J. Biomedical Informatics Informatics* 2–7.

stimulate innovation and economic growth and therefore should be used in an anonymised form in further research for public benefit.[44] However, the cost and practical obstacles[45] raise serious questions about the feasibility of the process.[46]

As we know, sharing patient information across even the NHS is not a straightforward task. In this section we look at the legal framework for the UK's care.data programme of work which is part of the NHS's plan to bring together data from GP practices, hospitals and other healthcare providers. The point of this discussion is to hightlight that the problems identified in this section and also in the chapter itself are not necessarily difficult to address; they have simply been overlooked. Historically, the sharing of health related data raised concerns about patient privacy as was experienced in the Icelandic medical database fiasco.[47] Whether this is a real obstacle may depend on a number of factors such as social aspects, which includes whether people trust their government and its privacy laws; technical aspects, whether, for example, the electronic patient record (EPR) is implemented as a new system under central control, or by providing messaging facilities between local systems. Emerging evidence indicates that while the UK appears to favour the former approach, countries like Sweden, the Netherlands, Germany, and France are moving towards the latter.

It is our view that an essential part of ensuring that people are comfortable with systems such as care.data would be to give them more control. Although we accept the importance of allowing individuals to 'opt out' of the scheme, we agree that everyone who opts out weakens the ability of the NHS to manage care effectively. Hence, in this section we also look at the experience of other European countries to understand what would be the ideal approach that would work in UK, which on the one hand ensures individuals have greater control

44 Elizabeth M. Hill, Emma L. Turner, Richard M. Martin and Jenny L. Donovan, '"Let's get the best quality research we can": public awareness and acceptance of consent to use existing data in health research: a systematic review and qualitative study' (2013) 13 BMC Medical Research Methodology 72.

45 Ibid.; see S. Noble, J. Donovan, E. Turner et al, Feasibility and Cost of Obtaining Informed Consent for Essential Review of Medical Records in Large-Scale Health Services Research' (2009) 14 *J Health Serv Res Policy* 77–81; see also P. Singleton and M. Wadsworth, 'Consent for the Use of Personal Medical Data in Research' (2006) 333 *BMJ* 255–258.

46 See Nadia Sirc, 'Data Protection and the NHS: Putting Patients First?' (2005) 2(50) *D.P.L & P* 6–7; the article discusses issues of personal privacy raised by the implementation of the National Programme for IT (NPfIT) by the NHS.

47 In the 1990s, there was a huge public outcry about Iceland's national genealogy database – a plan eventually quashed by the Supreme Court for violating the constitution.

over the underlying data, allowing them to see the information, correct it and use it themselves if they wish. On the other hand it provides enough incentives to them to allow their data to be used to create knowledge that will benefit all.

As valuable as the impact of sharing of healthcare data could be, it is worth remembering that 'trust' is the key word in healthcare.[48] The protection of an individual's privacy and personal health information requires attention when developing e-health systems, particularly since they have a significant impact on e-Health uptake.[49] Although better collection and analysis of anonymised data may save lives, cut costs, and expand access to care,[50] it is not without the risk that an individual patient could be re-identified. This has led stakeholders to rethink the traditional position regarding medical information – while not necessarily taking into consideration the full realm of current uses and the evolving nature of health information (in terms of what data usage is possible and the controls that might be created through the use of technology).[51]

As is the tendency with any still developing area, increasing involvement of information technologies in healthcare is raising challenges for privacy and data protection in ways we have never confronted before, primarily because e-health systems were designed without consideration for the privacy protection of the numerous participants in such environments. The rules pertaining to who has access to and control over data, at what point in time, and for what purpose, and regulations that determine when this data can be released, altered, and deleted, must be firmly established.

Even though privacy had been a minor issue in the past, it is now centre stage in the design and development of medical systems.[52] For example, one of the centrepieces of an e-health strategy is 'patient care records systems',[53] which

---

48 G. Laurie and E. Postan, 'Rhetoric or Reality: What is the Legal Status of the Consent Form in Health-related Research' (2013) 21 *Med. L. Rev. 371–414*, 372; see also P. Hustinx, 'Ensuring Trust in e-Health through Strong Health Data Protection' (European Policy Summit 'Planning Europe's Healthcare Revolution' Friends of Europe, Brussels, 2 December 2009).

49 See 'Broken Records: the Worrying Lack of Security Around Your Medical History, and How It Could Be Changing for the Worse', Big Brother Watch UK, March 2010, available at www.bigbrotherwatch.org.uk/brokenrecords.pdf.

50 F. Pasquale, 'Grand Bargains for Big Data: The Emerging Law of Health Information' (2013) 72 *Md. L. Rev.* 683, 682–772.

51 P. Singleton et al., 'Public and Professional Attitudes to Privacy of Healthcare Data: A Survey of the Literature' (General Medical Council 2007).

52 Ibid.

53 Personal health records offer a way to manage health data while lessening healthcare costs, improving patient data quality, and fostering healthcare efficiency.

enable healthcare workers to gain access to a patient's medical data regardless of their location. These systems have been cited for raising considerable problems in maintaining confidentially, whilst still providing wider access and availability.[54] This is a good example of where the benefits of sharing for direct care – to save lives – are lost because of the mass hysteria around 'privacy for the sake of privacy'. Meanwhile, patient surveys in the UK such as the Ipsos MORI poll have found that patients expect their information to be shared between the care professionals who treat them and are surprised and disappointed to find that this is not always the case.[55] Similar studies from Germany and Austria indicate high patient interest in these technologies.[56] Although medical records research is common, there have been substantial developments in how this information is used in health research[57] that challenge the rules around consent.[58] Responses to a Department of Health consultation on patient perceptions of secondary uses of data demonstrate some evidence of this sense:

> "It's my data – information should not be used for secondary uses without my consent, even if it is anonymised";[59] the information "belongs" to the patient who has allowed medical staff to have it as part of their care. Once given to medical staff for

---

See Inmaculada Carrión Señor, José Luis Fernández Alemán and Ambrosio Toval, 'Personal Health Records: New Means to Safely Handle Health Data?' (2012) 45(11) Computer 27–33.

54 See Ruth Halperin and James Backhouse, 'A Roadmap for Research on Identity in the Information Society' (2008) 1(1) *Identity in the Information Society* 71–87.

55 Ipsos MORI, Public attitudes to the use and sharing of their data Research for the Royal Statistical Society, July 2014.

56 A. Hoerbst, C. Kohl, P. Knaup and E. Ammenwerth, 'Attitudes and Behaviors Related to the Introduction of Electronic Health Records among Austrian and German Citizens' (2010) 79(2) *Int. J. Med. Informatics* 81–89.

57 See Graeme Laurie and Nayha Sethi, 'Towards Principles-Based Approaches to Governance of Health-Related Research Using Personal Data' (2013) *EJRR* 43–57; see also The Academy of Medical Sciences, 'A New Pathway for the Regulation and Governance of Health Research' (2011); Sabrina Fortin and Bartha Knoppers, 'Secondary Uses of Personal Data for Population Research' (2009) 5 *Genomics, Society and Policy* 80.

58 D.J. Willison et al., 'Alternatives to Project-specific Consent for Access to Personal Information for Health Research: What Is the Opinion of the Canadian Public?' (2007) 14 *J. Am. Med. Informatics Assoc.* 706, 706–712.

59 Department of Health, 'Summary of Responses to the Consultation on the Additional Uses of Patient Data' (2010), www.dh.gov.uk/en/Consultations/Responsestoconsultations/DH_109310,27.

> this purpose, it should not pass out of the patient's ownership for whatever reason, however good, allowing others to use patient's information without their permission is unethical and does not have any part in a "patient led" NHS.[60]

There is a perceived lack of understanding by the public at large of how medical records are 'produced', used and shared within the healthcare system as a whole, because healthcare policy in relation to privacy of healthcare data has been based on historic ethical and legal considerations, in conjunction with technical and financial practicalities, rather than on the basis of what individuals might want or expect.[61]

In the UK the Health and Social Care Act 2012 provided for the creation of a corporate body, the Health and Social Care Information Centre (HSCIC), or the 'Information Centre', which was empowered to collect and collate hospital and personal physician (GP) data of all UK citizens.[62] However, the will of parliament was seemingly challenged when the Secretary of State for Health promised citizens a 'veto' right to object, which has caused much controversy leading to a pause on the care.data programme, which is the HSCIC's centrepiece project to extract the greatest value from data for indirect care purposes.[63] Grace and Taylor[64] also point out that the Health and Social Care Act 2012 allows these data to be used for purposes that extend beyond patient care (e.g., for research) without any consultation, i.e., without the patients' knowledge[65] 'since the direct recipient of the information from the patient, the patient's physician, is obliged to forward such information to the "Information Centre", which itself is not

---

60 Ibid.

61 P. Singleton et al., 'Public and Professional Attitudes to Privacy of Healthcare Data: A Survey of the Literature' (General Medical Council 2007); see also U. Macleod, and G.C.M. Watt, 'The impact of consent on observational research: a comparison of outcomes from consenters and non-consenters to an observational study'(2008) 8(15) *BMC Medical Research Methodology* 1–6.

62 Sigrid Sterckx, 'The UK National Health Service's "Innovation Agenda": Lessons on Commercialisation and Trust' (2014) 22(2) *Med. L. Rev.* 221, 223.

63 Health and Social Care Act 2012 under the care.data scheme would allow the Health and Social Care Information Centre (HSCIC) power to compel the gathering of certain patient data gathered from GP surgeries in England under the 2012 Health and Social Care Act. This data is to be added to the patient data already gathered by hospitals unless individuals opt out.

64 J. Grace and M.J. Taylor, 'Disclosure of Confidential Patient Information and the Duty to Consult: the Role of the Health and Social Care Information Centre' (2013) 21(3) *Med. L. Rev. 415–447.*

65 See note 62.

obliged to inform the patient of the use of such data once "anonymised"'.[66] This has far-reaching consequences: the Information Centre will have the power, under section 259 (of the Health and Social Care Act 2012), to require the disclosure of confidential patient information (and other information) from health and social care bodies[67] to the 'Information Centre', in response to a requirement that it be provided. Such disclosure will not constitute a breach of the common law duty of confidence and will satisfy the requirement that there is a lawful basis for the processing of sensitive personal data under Schedule 3 to the Data Protection Act 1998.[68] Consequently, the right of a patient to object to the processing of his or her personal data on the basis that it would be likely to cause significant harm or distress to the individual, or to another individual, and that that harm or distress is or would be unwarranted,[69] is removed as a result of the Health and Social Care Act 2012: the responsibility to consult the patient and provide him or her with the opportunity to object is lifted from the 'Information Centre' as well as health professionals if disclosure of the information is required by the 'Information Centre'.[70]

In the UK, consent is not required to allow data to be shared – for example, between a GP and a hospital to which a patient has been referred, as part of what is called primary care delivery. Most of the time, consent for the sharing of the data in this environment is considered to be implied. There are times when patients are asked for consent at the point of care, such as before an operation. In some circumstances, this is because the data can be used for what is known as a secondary/indirect purpose. When it comes to the use of data for secondary purposes outside of the immediate care setting – for example, commissioning, research, clinical audit outside of the immediate care setting, for example – the law stipulates explicit consent.[71]

However, under certain circumstances consent requirements are sometimes overridden through legal solutions under section 251,[72] which allows personal data to be used without direct patient consent, or where the data are managed by a secure organisation – for instance, the Health and Social Care Information Centre.

66 According to the 'consent or anonymise' interpretation of the legal framework in the UK, in particular of the Data Protection Act 1998, if data contains any information which might identify a data subject – that is, if it is not anonymised – it is thought that explicit consent must be sought from that individual.

67 See note 64.

68 See note 64.

69 Section 10 of the Data Protection Act 1998.

70 See note 64.

71 The Academy of Medical Sciences, 'A New Pathway for the Regulation and Governance of Health Research' (London: Academy of Medical Sciences 2011).

72 NHS Act 2006.

Without clear communication of this to the public it could represent an erosion of patient autonomy[73] and would contradict one of the key phrases in Equity and Excellence: Liberating the NHS,[74] the 2010 report on NHS reforms planned by the coalition government, 'no decision about me, without me'.[75] This report, promised that patients would have increasing control over their care records starting with access to the records held by their GP and, over time, extending to health records held by all providers, with patients determining who else can access their records. However, as Grace and Taylor's analysis convincingly shows that the Health and Social Care Act 2012 has the opposite effect, patients now have less control over who can access and use their healthcare data.[76]

Establishing public concerns about the privacy of health data poses problems. However, from the few surveys that have been performed, it appears that only a small proportion of the public has a strong opinion.[77] As we have mentioned before, patient surveys such as Ipsos MORI's have found that patients expect their information to be shared between care professionals,[78] and that they have an understanding of the complex issues that need to be weighed up when arriving at an opinion.[79] Currently in the UK, 'informed' consent must be sought from individuals for any use of their identifiable data beyond their direct care, including when conducting a secondary review of a medical record.[80] Campbell et al. found that only about 28–35 per cent of patients would not have any problem if their health information – such as age, gender, ethnicity, reason for treatment, medical history, personal habits impacting health, type of treatment obtained, and side effects of treatment – was being used by physicians for other purposes.[81]

---

73 See note 62.

74 www.gov.uk/government/uploads/system/uploads/attachment_data/file/213823/dh_117794.pdf> see section 2.11, 14.

75 Ibid.

76 See note 62.

77 P. Singleton et al. (see note 61).

78 Ipsos MORI, 'Public Attitudes to the Use and Sharing of Their Data', Research for the Royal Statistical Society, July 2014.

79 P. Singleton et al. (see note 61).

80 N. Nicholas and S. Nicholas, 'Understanding Confidentiality and the Law on Access to Medical Records' (2010) 20 *Obstet. Gynaecol. Reprod. Med.* 161–163.

81 B. Campbell et al. 'Extracting Information from Hospital Records: What Patients Think about Consent' (2007) 16(6) *Quality and Safety in Healthcare* 404–408; see Maclean, A., 'Giving the Reasonable Patient a Voice: Information Disclosure and the Relevance of Empirical Evidence' (2005) 7 *Med. L. Int.* 1 at 12; however Heywood et al.'s empirical research project found that 'the patients found difficulty in relating to the true purpose of consent. However, they welcomed preoperative information

Interestingly, 'only 10 per cent of the patients expected to be asked for permission if their doctors used their health information for a wide variety of purposes, including combining data with other patients' data to provide better information to future patients, sharing treatment outcomes with other physicians, teaching medical professionals and writing research articles about diseases and treatments'.[82]

It is undeniable that inappropriate use of healthcare data can cause significant distress or harm to patients.[83] There is no absolute 'right to consent' or 'right to withhold consent' in the same way that there are moral and legal rights to privacy or confidentiality. Confidentiality between physicians and patients serves three core policy objectives: (1) to maximise unfettered patient communication with medical professionals, so that public disclosure will not deter people from seeking medical help and securing adequate diagnosis and treatment; (2) to encourage medical professionals to be candid in recording confidential information in patient medical records; and (3) to protect patients' reasonable privacy expectations against disclosure of sensitive personal information.[84] Jenkins et al.[85] forcefully argued in a recent study on medical confidentiality that a section of the public is very uncertain about confidentiality and what it may mean. This work corroborates a large literature which highlights the perceived gap in public understanding regarding privacy and confidentiality, and how privacy and confidentiality are legislated for by governments, healthcare organisations, and professionals.

---

and thought that being kept informed was beneficial for a number of reasons' see R. Heywood, A. Macaskill and K. Williams, 'Patient Perceptions of the Consent Process: Qualitative Inquiry and Legal Reflection' (2008) *J. Professional Negligence* 106; see also 'Share with Care: People's views on Consent and Confidentiality of Patient Information' (NHSIA 2002).

82 A. Appari and M. Johnson, 'Information Security and Privacy in Healthcare: Current State of Research' (2010) 6(4) *Int. J. Internet and Enterprise Management* 285, 279–314. However, an empirical research by Katherine C. Chretien et al., reported based on their national study of online postings by medical students in the United States that out of the 60 per cent of US medical schools that responded to the survey (78/130), of these schools, 60 per cent (47/78) reported incidents of students posting unprofessional online content. Violations of patient confidentiality were reported by 13 per cent (6/46). See K.C. Chretien, 'Online Posting of Unprofessional Content by Medical Students' (2009) 302(12) *JAMA* 1309–1315.

83 Marc Stauch, Nikolaus Forgó and Tina Krügel, 'Using EHRs to Design Drug Repositioning Trials: A Devolved Approach to Data Protection (2014) 28(2) *Int. Rev. L.* 237–248.

84 Jennifer Clark, 'HIPAA as an Evidentiary Rule? An Analysis of Miguel M. and Its Impact' (2013) 26 *J.L. & Health* 1, 9.

85 G. Jenkins, J.F. Merz, and P. Sankar, 'A Qualitative Study of Women's Views on Medical Confidentiality' (2005) 31 (9) *J. Med. Ethics.* 499–504

In *I v Finland*,[86] the European Court of Human Rights regarded confidentiality of health data as being central to realising legitimate policy goals – namely, in maintaining the patient's sense of privacy and his or her confidence in the medical professional and the healthcare system in general. One may argue that health data transmitted over national and international networks pose new challenges to confidentiality.[87] In at least some contexts, there is a very real tension between privacy and the need for sharing and dissemination of healthcare information and also the understanding of the public varies based upon the actual legislative instruments that are in place.[88] This may indicate a set of presumptions and expectations on the part of the public that are unrealistic and unachievable.[89]

As a final aside, it is worthwhile re-emphasising that at the European level, the EHR Report[90] states unequivocally that 'any processing of personal data in EHR systems has to fully comply with the rules for the protection of personal data; further, Directive 95/46, article 8.3 (and article 81 of the proposed regulation) allows processing in the presence of two cumulative conditions, namely:

> (a) The processing is "required" for the purposes of preventive medicine, medical diagnosis, the provision of care or treatment or the management of healthcare services (recall that the data minimisation principle still applies, i.e., that the processing must be necessary); and
>
> (b) The processing is conducted by a health professional subject to national law or rules established by national competent bodies imposing the obligation of professional secrecy or by another person also subject to an equivalent obligation of secrecy.[91]

Although consent permits the use of data which may otherwise be impermissible, problems arise from the propositional nature of consent and the circumstances in which it is often sought. The European Commission's proposed

86 ECHR 17 July 2008, appl. no 20511/03 para. 38.

87 R.J. Rodrigues, 'Opportunities and Challenges in the Deployment of Global e-Health' (2003) 5(3/4/5) *Int. J. Healthcare Technology and Management* 348, 335–357.

88 See note 85.

89 See note 77.

90 Article 29 Data Protection Working Party, 'Working Document on the Processing of Personal Data Relating to Health in Electronic Health Records' (Working Paper No. 131, 2007) available at http://ec.europa.eu/justice/policies/privacy/docs/wpdocs/2007/wp131_en.pdf.

91 Eugenio Mantovani and Paul Quinn, 'e-Health and Data Protection – The Letter and the Spirit of Consent Legal Requirements' (2013) *Int. Rev. L. Computers & Tech.* 222–236.

data protection reform[92] provides some relevant clarifications on the current data protection legal framework on the processing of medical data, including the role attributed to consent.[93] According to the EU Article 29 Working Party, in respect of EHR, 'free consent' can only be voluntarily given by an individual without coercion of any kind – be it social, financial, or psychological. However, where a health professional has been forced to process personal data in an EHR system due to unavoidable consequences of a medical condition, it would be misleading if he or she further sought to legitimise this processing through consent. Reliance on consent should be confined to cases where the individual data subject has a genuine 'free choice' and is subsequently able to withdraw the consent without detriment.[94] Even when consent is possible, in instances where the patient has a free choice, several additional requirements often apply.[95]

By now it should be apparent that there are differences in approach to privacy of healthcare data depending which country you live in. What if an individual has a second home in Europe and spends half of his/ or her time in the UK and half in Europe? Or what if an individual lives in one country and works in another? What differences can be expected?[96] Are there specific

---

92 On 25January 2012, the European Commission released a proposal for a General Data Protection Regulation.

93 Article 7.4 of the proposed regulation explicitly states that 'consent shall not provide a legal basis for the processing, where there is a significant imbalance between the position of the data subject and the controller'."Articles 14 and 15 propose that in order to allow individuals to be able to truly give informed consent, it should be possible to know what data and processing is actually required, thus, the proposed regulation increases the amount of information that must be provided to individuals with regards to both rights to information and access: see Mantovani and Quinn, note 91.

94 See note 91.

95 First, consent must be explicit, which means that only consent obtained in an opt in, rather than an opt out (meaning silence or inactivity) manner, is considered lawful. Second, consent must be obtained in writing. In Belgium, for example, explicit consent must be in writing. However, there are countries where written consent is not mandatory. Third, data should be processed only for those purposes specified. Care must be taken to ensure that individuals have given consent to the processing of data, and this calls for methods to ensure that patients remain aware that their data may be transmitted elsewhere when treatment via electronic means becomes routine. See note 91.

96 Directive 2011/24/EU on the application of patients' rights in cross-border healthcare was published in April 2011. The Directive applies to individual patients who decide to seek healthcare in a Member State other than the Member State of affiliation. Article 5(d) of the Directive states the following: 'The Member State of affiliation shall ensure that patients who seek to receive or do receive cross-border healthcare have remote access to or have at least a copy of their medical records, in conformity with,

national rules on consent from the patient to set up EHRs? Can patients update their record, modify, and erase EHR content? Are patients entitled to access their EHRs? Are there specific national rules on consent from the patient to share data? Does the law say who will be entitled to use and access these data?

A particularly interesting observation emerges when one compares the EU countries we studied which have invested in e-health applications (such as Denmark, Sweden, Estonia and Spain), governments that are striving to create coherent and consistent policies and have national legislations in place regarding electronic handling of patient data in healthcare. In most of these countries, data are owned by the healthcare provider, and the responsibility for data accuracy also lies with the healthcare provider; however there are differences as to whether the healthcare provider is a local or regional organisation.

In Europe, Scandinavian health systems are at the forefront of e-Health and offer useful and instructive case studies. Denmark's EHR system, since 2003, has allowed patients to access and partially edit their individual health records. The system allows users to send information on their previous treatments and diagnoses, book appointments with GPs, renew prescriptions, view waiting times and quality ratings for local providers, and connect to other patients and carers through chat facilities. The Danish National Health Portal was introduced in 2005 and gives patients electronic access to their EHRs and facilitates electronic communication between patients and their regional health service.[97] Patients' electronic records are kept separate for hospitals and physicians, and hospitals do not have access to GPs' systems. However, GPs have access to hospital EHR data. Although GPs own their patients' records, when a patient changes GP, the EHR is transferred electronically to the new GP.[98] Legislation allows physicians access to the medication profiles of patients, but all other health professionals must obtain patients' consent before viewing health information. Every Danish citizen has a unique national personal identification number that is used when healthcare is obtained.[99] In our view the use of a universal ID number has been a major enabler of change. Under the Danish system it is possible for a patient

---

and subject to, national measures implementing Union provisions on the protection of personal data, in particular Directives 95/46/EC and 2002/58/EC.'

97 Bradford H. Gray, Thomas Bowden, Ib Johansen and Sabine Koch, 'Electronic Health Records: An International Perspective on "Meaningful Use"' (2011) 1565 (28) *Issues in International Health Policy* (Commonwealth Fund publication).

98 M. Hartlev, *Study of Legal Framework of Interoperable e-Health in Europe – Nation Profile Denmark* (Copenhagen, Denmark: European Commission Directorate General Information Society, 2008).

99 See note 97.

who does not want his/her information available on the e-Health portal, to ask for the information to be kept private.[100]

The Swedish legislative framework is rather general when it comes to regulating healthcare data to be included in EHRs and was developed in support of its National e-Health Strategy.[101] The Patient Data Act, passed in 2008, allows healthcare providers, with patients' consent, to digitally access a patient's entire care history from different levels within the health and medical care services and provides a nationwide share of locally stored information. It strengthens an individual's participation by enabling it to determine who is to be given access to their overall medical record and showing what personnel had access to medical records. Further, the patient can block certain data from being shared. This raises the interesting and difficult question of how to reconcile the needs of a complete health information system with the patients' rights (especially the right of non-participation)?[102] To us, the question seems to highlight the striking similarity between the UK and Sweden. Furthermore, the Patient Data Act introduces more rights to an individual through the development of 'care choice models'.[103] The 'care choice models' have created more need for common access to information about patients and users as well as for comparable information on the results and quality of health and social care provision, providing a basis for choice. However, the Patient Data Act allows processing of personal data for the purpose of the patient's journal even when the patient does not agree. As a consequence, in case of an exception on that specific rule or in case the processing is not allowed on the basis of the Patient Data Act, the patient has to expressly agree to the data processing in order for it to be legitimate. The Act restricts access to the personal data; access is only allowed in cases explicitly enumerated. The bottom line seems to be that for Sweden, the vision is to have

---

100 It is only about 1 per cent of all patients in Denmark who say they do not want to give their general practitioners access to their medical data, and of this 1 per cent the majority are teenagers, see Claus F. Nielsen et al., *Strategic Intelligence Monitor on Personal Health Systems: Country Study: Denmark,* Scientific and Policy Report by the Joint Research Centre of the European Commission (Luxembourg: Publications Office of the European Union, 2013); Marianne Kristensen, *Addressing the Challenges of an Ageing Population through e-Health* (Danish Health and Medicines Authority, 2012).

101 In the beginning of 2014 a new authority was established – the Swedish eHealth Agency (Ehälsomyndigheten).

102 Patients here in the UK can also use 'choose and book' and electronic transfer of prescriptions.

103 Such models allow patients and users of the health and social care services to choose from different providers, while the providers themselves have free right of establishment in order to increase the range of options open to patients.

an infrastructure that makes necessary information available at the point of need, independent of where the information was produced. This will include both healthcare and social care.

The concept of exclusive 'ownership' often overly complicates things. In Spain, national legislation gives ownership to healthcare centres where care is provided. In Estonia, ownership by the healthcare provider ends once data is passed to the EHR, when it falls under the ownership of the Estonian National Health Information System (ENHIS). Furthermore, Estonian citizens have access to their personal data held within an EHR. In many instances, legislation stipulates that this can be obtained at least in paper format. Limitations to access relate to any harm that might be caused to a patient as a result. In most of these EU countries (such as Denmark, Sweden, Estonia and Spain), citizens are unable to modify their own data on the EHR.[104] In Estonia, citizens can add personal data to ENHIS (e.g., contact information, declarations of will, and provisions of access rights). Although Estonian citizens can close the element of their record that includes their data if they want to, they cannot delete it from the records of healthcare providers. In Finland and Sweden, patients have the right to request restrictions; for example, in Finland, patients can request restrictions regarding who sees their data.

Some jurisdictions take the view that explicit, opt-in consent is a prerequisite to the provision of healthcare, while other jurisdictions argue that in a doctor-patient relationship, consent should not be used as a basis for the processing of personal data in the healthcare delivery context. Implied consent is always present in direct care settings, but there may not be express consent. In Spain, there is essentially an 'opt-out' model, where patients have the right to refuse consent, which allows their data to be omitted from the registry whereas in Estonia, patient consent is not needed for creating EHRs or for processing EHRs for the purpose of providing healthcare. However, Estonian law has established an 'opt-out' system for the sharing of EHRs in the ENHIS – the patient can prohibit sharing EHRs in the ENHIS with healthcare providers.

Our research further found that healthcare authorities in these countries are adopting a number of other measures to help prevent medical data breaches. These include audits to monitor how data is used, stored and transferred, allowing patients to determine which data can be freely shared and to consider which health professionals need access to patients' personal information

---

104 Exceptions to this approach do exist however. For example in Aragon, Spain, citizens will have the right to ask for deletions and will be able to hide information in their EHR in the future.

as well as educating healthcare providers on security issues. For example, in Madrid, Spain, the HORUS system[105] has mechanisms to safeguard against the improper use of patients' health data which ensures that the clinicians who are consulting with a particular patient have free access to that person's data on the system (although patients are themselves able to request the partial deletion or hiding of particular aspects). Those accessing patient data outside of this arrangement would require consent to justify their access to and use of it on the system, and can only override system safeguards in certain emergency situations. The use of HORUS is continuously tracked, so system auditors can monitor who has accessed particular records, and assess any inappropriate usage.

We acknowledge that although healthcare information systems provide crucial advantages for the improvement of health systems, such technological intervention is also confronted with existing privacy regulations.[106] The European Commission must create a legal framework and space to manage the massive amounts of health related data. However, when considering European legislation in relation to the privacy and security issues posed by EHRs, it is important to recognise that in the field of healthcare, the EU has no formal legal powers to enact EU-level legislation. The EU does have competence in several other policy domains that influence health policy, including privacy and data protection, and European governments will need to find a way to improve collection and transparency of health data in order to prioritise investment decisions.[107]

The Data Protection Directive makes a fundamental distinction between regular and 'special data', the latter being subject to more stringent rules.[108] According to the Directive, any data related to health is 'special'.[109] Although there is no definition of health data included in the Directive, 'health informational

105 Accenture Implements Madrid Healthcare Information Exchange With 15 Million Medical Records, www.accenture.com/SiteCollectionDocuments/PDF/Accenture-Region-of-Madrid.pdf.

106 C.T Di Iorio and F. Carinci, 'Privacy and Health Care Information Systems: Where is the Balance?', in George, C., Whitehouse, D. and Duquenoy, P. (eds), *E-Health: Legal, Ethical and Governance Challenges* (Springer-Verlag 2012) 77.

107 Economist Intelligence Unit, *Future of Healthcare in Europe* (Economist Intelligence Unit Limited, 2011).

108 T. Hooghiemstra, 'Introduction to the Special Privacy Issue' (2002) 9 *EJHL* 181; S. Brillon, 'The European Data Protection Legislation and the Medical Records' in S. Callens (ed.), *E-Health and the Law* (Kluwer 2003).

109 Vassilis Hatzopoulos, "Is It Healthy to Have an EU Health Law?' (2005) 30(5) *E. L. Rev.* 705, 697–711.

privacy' is defined as an individual's claim to control the circumstances in which personal health information is collected, used, stored, and transmitted.[110] Under Article 8 of DPA, specific provisions are made under categories which are deemed to be particularly sensitive. Specifically, 'Member States shall prohibit the processing of personal data revealing racial or ethnic origin, political opinions, religious or philosophical beliefs, trade-union membership, and the processing of data concerning health or sex life'.[111] Whilst Article 8 prohibits processing of sensitive health data as a general principle, it is not absolute. Limited exceptions to this principle are laid down in the same article, particularly if processing is required for specified medical and healthcare purposes and follows certain guidelines, including:

- That the explicit informed consent of the data subject is obtained, contrary to the required unambiguous consent referred to in electronic healthcare records: 7(a) of the Directive.
- To protect the vital interest of the data subject or of another person when the data subject is physically or legally incapable of giving consent.
- For the purposes of preventive medicine, medical diagnosis, the provision of care or treatment, or the management of healthcare services, if the data are processed by a health professional subject to the obligation of professional secrecy or by another person also subject to an equivalent obligation of secrecy.

These specific rules for the area of health reflect the fact that there can be situations where sensitive health data need to be processed in order to allow public health authorities to take the appropriate measures to protect patients and citizens.[112] In the *Renewing Health* report, the particular sensitivity of personal health data was addressed as follows: 'unauthorised disclosure of personal health information such as a medical condition or diagnosis could negatively impact on an individual's personal and professional life. Maintaining health data in an electronic format increases the risk that patients' information could be accidentally disclosed to or accessed by unauthorised users'.[113]

---

110 L.O. Gostin, *Public Health Law: Power, Duty, Restraint* (2nd edn, University of California Press 2009). 316.

111 Art. 8 1(1).

112 http://eur-lex.europa.eu/LexUriServ/LexUriServ.do?uri=CELEX:31995L0046:en:HTML.

113 Regions of Europe Working Together for Health (2011): D7.1 Report on security and privacy issues, at a regional, national and European level.

Thus far, we have sought to show what rights patients have regarding healthcare data that refer to them, with particular emphasis on 'consent'. We have analysed the current governance framework in the UK and in the EU which conceptually and practically, in our view, over-protects 'individual privacy'. It is also evident that while many governments and health organisations are quite rightly prioritising information governance initiatives to improve data privacy and security, there is a feeling that some of these issues may actually be exaggerated – either by powerful privacy advocates or by those who wish to retain the status quo.

In this context there is still one final element to this discussion: health care data interoperability, which has been cited as a key force that can help lower costs and encourage more sharing of information among patients and providers. We believe that the EU Commission through the proposed Data Protection regulation has made an important contribution to the broader discussion on the establishment of interoperability between data systems, particularly health data systems, as before, 'a general right to system interoperability does not exist under EU law'.[114] It is undeniable that EHR systems create a significant new risk scenario in the processing of personal data concerning health when implementing interoperable e-health record systems. Such systems call for innovative safeguards and counterbalances that uphold the legal standard of confidentiality established within a traditional paper record environment. Even then, these systems may be insufficient in safeguarding the privacy interests of a patient once electronic health records are placed online.[115]

114 P. De Hert, and V. Papakonstantinou, 'The Proposed Data Protection Regulation Replacing Directive 95/46/EC: A Sound System for the Protection of Individuals' (2012) 28(2) *C.L.S. Rev*, 130–142.

115 Article 4(f) of Directive 2011/24/EU states that 'in order to ensure continuity of care, patients who have received treatment are entitled to a written or electronic medical record of such treatment, and access to at least a copy of this record in conformity with and subject to national measures implementing Union provisions on the protection of personal data, in particular Directives 95/46/EC and 2002/58/EC'. This means that patients seeking treatment in a different Member State of the EU should be allowed to have access to a copy of their medical records in their home state. See Commission Recommendation of 2 July 2008 on cross-border interoperability of electronic health record systems, document number C (2008) (3282); (2008/594/EC), at 9 www.epractice.eu/files/media/media2134.pdf.

In the UK, in what could be perceived as a step in the right direction, the Health and Social Care (Safety and Quality) Act 2015[116] may be hugely significant in terms of interoperability. The Act now requires clinicians to share patients' information with other care and health professionals, for direct care purposes to ensure continuity as long as it is in the patient's best interests. It is mandating the use of a single identifier to make interoperability more efficient. However, the Act also contains protective provisions where the identifier would not be used under certain circumstances, including when the individual objects or would be likely to object and when the information concerns the provision of services by an anonymous access provider.[117] The Caldicott review of information governance[118] highlighted that a culture of anxiety prevents information from being shared between organisations, with care providers having a risk averse attitude to sharing. The review also suggested that the duty to share information in certain circumstances can be as important as the duty to protect patient confidentiality.

We argue that at the European level, the problem is that for data portability to be possible, there must be common structures, starting from standards for data items in personal health records and, importantly, interoperability between national systems; however, a right to system interoperability is nowhere to be found in EU law. Directive 2011/24/EU does not create any common e-health infrastructure, either. However, Article 14 of the Patients' Rights Directive purports 'to support and facilitate co-operation and the exchange of information among Member States working within a voluntary network connecting the various national authorities responsible for e-Health'.[119] Additionally, the Commission 'shall adopt the necessary measures for the establishment, management and transparent functioning of e-health'. The proposal for a right to data portability and the provisions of the Patients'

116 http://services.parliament.uk/bills/2014-15/healthandsocialcaresafetyandquality.html.

117 Health and Social Care (Safety and Quality) Bill, Second Reading, 7 November 2014 www.publications.parliament.uk/pa/cm201415/cmhansrd/cm141107/debtext/141107-0001.htm#14110771000001.

118 Department of Health, 'Information: To share or not to share? The Information Governance Review' (April 2013).

119 P. Quinn, and P. De Hert, "The European Patients' Rights Directive: A Clarification and Codification of Individual Rights Relating to Cross Border Healthcare and Novel Initiatives aimed at Improving Pan-European Healthcare Co-operation' (2012) 12(1) *Med. L. Int.* 28–69.

Rights Directive seem to be a step in the right direction; however, it remains to be seen whether and how these new developments will be able to balance the practical requirements of the processing of personal health records for direct care and the protection of individuals and society against paternalistic management of healthcare information.

E-Healthcare in the USA

The US healthcare system, unlike the healthcare systems of many European countries,[120] is composed of private, independent individual and group providers, hospitals, ambulatory care centres, and long-term care centres that compete with one another. The US health system has both considerable strengths and notable weaknesses. The system is non-centralised, with multi-payers.[121] However, in the last four decades, US healthcare has undergone revolutionary changes and has evolved from a patient–physician dyadic relationship[122] into a complex network linking patients to multiple stakeholders[123] driven by advances in technology and legislations such as the Health Maintenance Organizations Act of 1973, the landmark Health Insurance Portability and Accountability Act (HIPAA) of 1996, and national initiatives such as the 'State Alliance for e-Health', started in 2007 by the National Governors Association's Centre for Best Practices.[124]

We have seen that since 2009, Congress has allocated a substantial amount of economic resources for development of healthcare IT[125] to ensure the implementation of the Health Information Technology for Economic and Clinical Health Act (HITECH) of 2009.[126] Similarly to Europe and particularly

120 Most of European healthcare system has its origins in the 'mutual aid societies' created in the early nineteenth century.

121 J.G. Anderson, 'Social, Ethical and Legal Barriers to E-health' (2007) 76 *Int. J. Med. Informatics* 481, 480–483.

122 See Jennifer Clark, 'HIPAA as an Evidentiary Rule? An Analysis of Miguel M. and Its Impact' (2013) 26 *J. L. & Health* 1, 9.

123 A. Appari and M. Johnson, 'Information Security and Privacy in Healthcare: Current State of Research' (2010) 6(4) *Int. J. Internet and Enterprise Management* 297, 279–314.

124 Ibid.

125 See Mark Faccenda and Lara Parkin, 'Meaningful Use – What Does It Mean To You?' (2011) 23(10) *Health Law* 10.

126 See Note 27.

to the UK, the US government also has pushed for wide-scale adoption of universal electronic health records (EHR). However, in stark contrast to the UK, particularly England, the US has adopted a 'bottom-up' implementation approach, where 'meaningful use'[127] goals to improve patient care[128] relating to EHRs have been centrally decided by a government agency,[129] but where hospitals have considerable choice in how these goals are achieved.[130]

The onus in the USA seems to be on regulating healthcare providers, and HIPAA mandates a unique identifier for health providers and healthcare plans – the National Provider Identifier. If only the priority was on producing an identifier for individuals in the same way (such as the NHS number), interoperability could extend from cross-organisational interoperability to interoperability at an individual health record level, which would enable individuals to control their record. However, it does match the responsibility attributed to organisations regarding the repercussions for breaches, attracting criminal penalties of up to five years in prison.

Likewise at an organisational level, the American Recovery and Reinvestment Act (ARRA) 2009 encourages Health Information Exchanges (HIE). The National Health Information Exchange is a confederation of stakeholders at the forefront of health information exchange, including federal agencies, state, regional and local health information organisations, integrated delivery networks, and private organisations. HIE's governance includes standards, services and policies that foster secure health information exchange over the internet. They have also introduced Data Use and Reciprocal Support Agreements for all states, which reflect consensus amongst the entities on issues such as

- privacy and security obligations
- multi-party agreements

127 The standards were stated in terms of objectives (e.g., maintaining an active medication list for patients) and measures for qualifying for incentive payments (e.g., recording at least one entry as structured data for at least 80 per cent of patients).

128 See note 125.

129 The Office of the National Coordinator at the Department of Health and Human Services published regulations in July 2010 that set forth standards to define the 'meaningful use' of EHRs. See D. Blumenthal and M. Tavenner, 'The 'Meaningful Use' Regulation for Electronic Health Records' (2010) 363(6) *N. Engl. J. Med.* 501–4.

130 Kathrin M. Cresswell et al., 'Comparative Case Study Investigating Sociotechnical Processes of Change in the Context of a National Electronic Health Record Implementation' (2012) 18(4) *Health Informatics J.* 251–270. As discussed already England has embarked on a 'top-down' implementation of EHRs characterised by large-scale government-led procurement.

- participants actively engaged in Health Information Exchange
- requests for information based on permitted purpose
- duty to respond
- future use of data received from another participant
- respective duties of submitting and receiving participants
- autonomy principles for access
- use of authorisations to support requests for data
- participant breach notification
- mandatory non-binding dispute resolution
- allocation of liability risk.

The American Recovery and Reinvestment Act (ARRA) 2009 also stipulates that all healthcare organisations must implement the use of electronic health records by 2015,[131] which is in line with the aspirations of England.

The USA has, from the outset, been pragmatic and flexible in its EHR planning. It has fashioned regulatory requirements from the inside out, developing the backbone of a national healthcare ICT and phasing it into local/regional systems as these systems continue to evolve. Evidence of such a hands-off approach is not hard to find. Unlike Europe, with its technology-led rather than user-driven philosophy, US regulators have paid scant attention to differences in Electronic Medical Record (EMRs) – best described as a partially-completed EHR – as opposed to the real thing. For example, the US Centres for Medicare and Medicaid Services note simply 'very often an Electronic Medical Record or EMR is just another way to describe an Electronic Health Record or EHR, and both providers and vendors sometimes use the terms interchangeably'.[132] In contrast, according to the EU Commission, such 'definitions have often been controversial or vague, and therefore acronyms were used wrongly'. Though it accepts the need to use 'EHR' and 'EHR system' interchangeably, it proceeds to painstakingly try to delineate boundaries between Automated Medical Records (AMR), Computerised Medical Records (CMR), Electronic Medical Records (EMR), Electronic Patient Records (EPR) and Electronic Health Records (EHR).[133] There is great potential for patient control and democratic contributions of individuals through the Patient Health Record (PHR).

131 www.ironmountain.com/Knowledge-Center/Reference-Library/View-by-Document-Type/General-Articles/E/Electronic-Health-Records-Security-and-Privacy-Concerns.aspx#sthash.LC0GzGZQ.dpuf.

132 www.cms.gov/Regulations-and-Guidance/Legislation/EHR.

133 www.ehr-impact.eu/downloads/documents/EHRI_D1_2_Conceptual_framework_v1_0.pdf.

Healthcare Data in the USA

The US healthcare system has a critical view about patient ownership of health records[134] as it seems counterintuitive that the protections which patients currently enjoy under the Health Insurance Portability and Accountability Act (HIPAA) Privacy Rule are surprisingly similar to those they would have if they owned their data.[135] However, it is undeniable that the USA has a confusing[136] and sometimes conflicting patchwork of federal and state laws and agencies that deal with the 'right to privacy'[137] and the right to avoid 'disclosure of personal matters',[138] which include information related to healthcare (health records).[139] The 'right to privacy' was established by the US Supreme Court in *Griswold v Connecticut*[140] and in *Lawrence v Texas*.[141] 'A person's medical profile is an area of privacy infinitely more intimate, more personal in quality and nature than many areas already judicially recognized and protected.'[142] In *Whalen v Roe*, 'the U.S. Supreme Court recognised

134 Although five states – Alaska, Colorado, Florida, Georgia and Louisiana – have done so with respect to genetic information, and a number of other states are considering whether to recognise patient ownership of health records, letting patients own their health records may not be an effective way to improve confidentiality. N. Ram, 'Assigning Rights and Protecting Interests: Constructing Ethical and Efficient Rights in Human Tissue Research' (2009) 23(1) *Harv. J. L. & Tech.* 141.

135 Barbara J. Evans, 'Would Patient Ownership of Health Data Improve Confidentiality?' (2012) 14(9) *Am. Med. Assoc. J. Ethics* 724–732.

136 See Bruce L. Watson, 'Disclosure of Computerized Health Care Information: Provider Privacy Rights under Supply Side Competition' (1981) 7 *AJLM* 265, 269; see *Johnson v Phelan,* 69 F.3d 144, 154 (7th Cir. 1995). Judge Posner stated that 'the term "right of privacy" bears meanings in law that are remote from its primary ordinary-language meaning ... One thing it means in law is the right to reproductive autonomy; another is a congeries of tort rights ...; still another is the right to maintain the confidentiality of certain documents and conversations. Another and overlapping meaning is the set of interests protected by the Fourth Amendment, which prohibits unreasonable searches and seizures.'

137 See note 121.

138 Jos Dumortier and Griet Verhenneman, 'Legal Regulation of Electronic Health Records: A Comparative Analysis of Europe and the US' in Carlisle George, Diane Whitehouse and Penny Duquenoy (eds), *e-Health: Legal, Ethical and Governance Challenges* (Springer 2013) 33.

139 *Whalen* v *Roe*, 429 US 589,599 of 1977 and *US* v *Westinghouse Electrical Corporation* 638 F.2d 570, 577 (3rd Cir. 1980).

140 381 US 479,484.

141 497 US 261.

142 *Board of Med. Quality Assurance v Gherardini,* 93 Cal. App. 3d 669, 678 (Cal. App. 1979).

a limited Constitutional right to individual privacy with respect to information held in governmental databases. The question of constitutional protection of health information privacy remains largely unresolved because attempts to apply Whalen to informational privacy more generally have been inconsistent.'[143] For a long time, healthcare privacy was almost entirely regulated by common law[144] and by various state laws and regulations[145] that, before the enactment of HIPAA, were characterised as follows: 'instead of providing for broad privacy protection, the state provisions were relatively reactive and limited to unique factual circumstances',[146] which proved slow, inconsistent, and inadequate.[147]

On the other hand, a large body of research (see for instance Keshavjee et al.[148]) on practices in the US conversion to an electronic health record (EHR) system has shown that many patients wish to have influence over the use of their personal health information.[149] In a 2006 survey, 62 per cent of the interviewees said 'the use of electronic medical records makes it more difficult to ensure patients' privacy'.[150] It was also reported elsewhere that about

---

143 *Whalen* v *Roe*, 429 U.S. 589, 603-04 (1997). See Melissa Goldstein, Lee Repasch and Sara Rosenbaum, 'Emerging Privacy Issues in Health Information Technology' in David Blumenthal et al. (eds) *Health Information Technology in the United States: Where We Stand* (Robert Wood Johnson Foundation 2008) 96, available at www.rwjf.org/files/research/3297.31831.hitreport.pdf.

144 Ilene N. Moore et al., 'Confidentiality and Privacy in Health Care from the Patient's Perspective: Does HIPAA Help?' (2007)17 *Health Matrix* 215, 219–27; see e.g., *Doe* v *Cmty. Health Plan–Kaiser Corp.*, 268 A.D.2d 183, 186–87 (N.Y. App. Div. 2000).

145 Amalia R. Miller and Catherine Tucker, 'Privacy Protection and Technology Diffusion: The Case of Electronic Medical Records' (2009) 55(7) *Management. Sci.* 1077, 1083.

146 Janine Hiller, Matthew S. McMullen, Wade M. Chumney and David L. Baumer, 'Privacy and Security in the Implementation of Health Information Technology (Electronic Health Records): US and EU Compared' (2011) 17(1) *Boston U. J. Sci. & Tech. L.* 1.

147 See note 144.

148 Keshavjee K., Bosomworth J., Copen J., Lai J., Kucukyazici B., Liani R., Holbrook A.M., 'Best practices in EMR implementation: a systematic review. *Proceedings of the 11th International Symposium on Health Information Management Research*, 2006, 1–15.

149 Ibid. However, concern over electronic medical records is not a new phenomenon in USA. The 1993 Harris-Westin found that 70 per cent of respondents were worried about the extensive use of computers in a national healthcare system to manage and monitor healthcare operations.

150 Karen Donelan and Paola D. Miralles, 'Consumers, EHRS and PHRs: Measures and Measurement' in David Blumenthal et al. (eds), *Health Information Technology in The*

75 percent of patients in the USA are concerned about health websites sharing information without their permission,[151] a perception fuelled by the fact that medical data disclosures are the second highest reported breach.[152] The survey highlighted that individuals have expressed concerns about increased sharing of information without their knowledge.[153] However, very limited research has examined patients' perceptions of sharing anonymised health records,[154] with the exception of studies that examine patients' perceptions about consent for data use.[155] The academic literature lacks systematic investigation procedures to identify and classify various sources of threats to health information privacy and security.[156] Following Rindfleisch,[157] Appari and Johnson have broadly categorised threats to health information privacy into two areas:[158]

- organisational threats that arise from inappropriate access to patient data by either internal agents abusing their privileges or external agents exploiting a vulnerability of the information systems;
- systemic threats that arise from an agent in the information flow chain exploiting the disclosed data beyond its intended use.

United States: Where We Stand (Robert Wood Johnson Foundation 2008) 66, available at www.rwjf.org/files/research/3297.31831.hitreport.pdf.

151 See A. Raman, 'Enforcing Privacy through Security in Remote Patient Monitoring Ecosystems' (6th International Special Topic Conference on Information Technology Applications in Biomedicine, Tokyo, Japan, 2007) 298–301. An interpretive study based on interviews of 15 privacy officers of major US healthcare organisations found that privacy breaches in the USA show human error as the cause of a significant number of violations of HIPAA Privacy Rule. See Divakaran Liginlal, Inkook Sim, Lara Khansa and Paul Fearn, 'HIPAA Privacy Rule Compliance: An Interpretive Study Using Norman's Action Theory' (2012) 31 *Computers & Security* 206–220.

152 A. Appari and M. Johnson, 'Information Security and Privacy in Healthcare: Current State of Research' (2010) 6(4) *Int. J. Internet and Enterprise Management* 279–314.

153 See note 150.

154 See note 152.

155 G. Bansal, F.M. Zaheid and D. Gefen, 'The Impact of Personal Dispositions on Privacy and Trust in Disclosing Health Information Online', Americas Conference on Information Systems, Keystone, CO, USA. http://aisel.aisnet.org/amcis2007/57; see also B. Campbell, et al.. 'Extracting Information from Hospital Records: What Patients Think about Consent' (2007) 16(6) *Quality and Safety in Healthcare* 404–408.

156 See note 152.

157 T.C. Rindfleisch, 'Privacy, Information Technology, and Health Care' (1997) 40(8) *Commun. ACM* 93–100.

158 See note 152.

For many decades, healthcare privacy protection in the USA was driven exclusively by professional ethics, primarily for healthcare providers, and a patchwork of state privacy laws.[159] There was no consistent federal baseline standard.[160] For a considerable period of time, there has been ongoing debate about the extent of control patients should have over their electronic health records. Patient Privacy Rights, an advocacy organisation dedicated to ensuring that Americans control access to their health records, argues that a lack of safeguards poses risks to a person's wellbeing, livelihood and financial stability,[161] and because of this, 'patients should have total control over their personal health records to ensure that information that a patient wishes to be kept private is kept that way'.[162] On the other hand, the Centre for Democracy and Technology's Health Privacy Project argues, 'patients intuitively want control of their data, but requiring consent for every exchange of health information is sometimes not the best approach for ensuring privacy'.[163]

The ultimate question this gives rise to is: Who owns health data, and who has the right to access the data and for what purposes?[164] The law provides incomplete, unclear, and somewhat inconsistent answers. But does this matter? Does it matter more that the laws are different in different countries but people are more geographically mobile? People may work in a country where their data are owned by them and live in a country where their data are owned by the state. It is needless to say that this question has much wider implications for the use of data for both direct and indirect care purposes. Even for the USA, economically benefiting from healthcare data by sharing is an unfamiliar and

---

159 *Sorrell v IMS Health, Inc.*, No. 10-779, the Supreme Court upheld a decision by the US Court of Appeals for the Second Circuit striking down a Vermont law that restricts the use of prescriber histories for purposes of marketing or promoting prescription drugs to physicians. The case involves data mining for pharmaceutical companies, the decision is very important for the ability of all marketers to collect and use information about consumers in order to target their messages to the right audience.

160 K. Nahra, 'Analysing the US HIPAA Legacy and Future Changes on the Horizon' (2013) 10(2) *DPL & P* 1–6

161 Diana Manos, 'Privacy Experts Debate Patient Consent' (2009) *Healthcare IT News* (21 September 2009), available at www.healthcareitnews.com/news/privacy-experts-debatepatient-consent.

162 Ibid.

163 Ibid.

164 Charles Safran et al., 'Toward a National Framework for the Secondary Use of Health Data: An American Medical Informatics Association White Paper' (2007) 14(1) *J. Am. Med. Informatics Assoc.* 3.

potentially troubling idea, therefore it is worth pausing to briefly characterise the conventional wisdom (if there is any) on this issue.

With regard to patient data, the law does not clearly delineate property interests.[165] Particularly relevant for our purposes is the work by intellectual property scholar Pamela Samuelson. She argues that 'the traditional view in American law has been that information as such cannot be owned by any person, unless specially protected by intellectual property laws'.[166] In most states, patient medical records are regarded as physical property owned by physicians and hospitals, and patients and insurers are allowed to access these records.[167] This does not mean, however, that healthcare providers can own a

---

165 Barbara J. Evans, 'Congress' New Infrastructural Model of Medical Privacy' (2009) 84 *Notre Dame L. Rev.* 585, 596–597 (discussing the current status of ownership of health data and human tissue specimens); David L. Silverman, 'Data Security Breaches: The State of Notification Laws' (2007) 19 *Intell. Prop. & Tech.. L.J.*, at 5, 8 (discussing the 'precarious' nature of ownership of database content under current law). But see Susan E. Gindin, 'Lost and Found in Cyberspace: Informational Privacy in the Age of the Internet' (1997) 34 *San Diego L. Rev.* 1153, 1195 (noting several cases where courts have recognised patients' ownership of medical records).

166 Pamela Samuelson, 'Privacy as Intellectual Property' (2000) 52 *Stan. L. Rev.* 1130–1131, 1125, 1170–1171 (stressing 'the lack of clarity in this country about the nature of the interest that individuals have in information about themselves: Is it a commodity interest, a consumer protection interest, a personal dignity interest, a civil interest, all of the above, or no interest at all?').

167 Although some commentators argue in favour of patient ownership of data to enhance patient privacy. See Deborah C. Peel, 'Written Testimony Before the HIT Policy Committee, Electronic Privacy Info. Center' (18 September 2009), http://epic.org/privacy/medical/Peel_PPR%20Written%20testimony%20HIT%20Policy%20Committee.pdf (indicating that 'twenty focus groups held across the country in order to understand consumers' awareness, beliefs, and fears concerning [health information technology]' discovered that '[a] majority want to "own" their health data'); Principles: More Patient Privacy Principles, Patient Privacy Rights, http://patientprivacyrights.org/principles (last visited 21 December 2011) (listing a set of eleven 'Patient Privacy Principles [that] should be included in all Health [information technology] legislation' and listing as the first such principle, 'recognize that patients own their health data'). Patient data ownership advocates often ground their position in the claim that privacy is a state in which patients exercise full control over their own health information. See Richard H. Thaler, Show Us the Data. (It's Ours, After All.), *New York Times* (23 April 2011) at BU4 (discussing 'a host of privacy issues' raised by collection and dissemination of personal data and calling for persons whose data is stored to have access to it); Leslie A. Saxon, 'Owning Your Health Information: An Inalienable Right',

patient's medical information per se. One important caveat is that the law does not grant providers exclusive ownership of the data in these records, and these data can be transferred relatively easily.[168] According to the American Medical Informatics Association's (AMIA) white paper, published by its expert panel,[169] 'the focus needs to be on data access and control, not data ownership'.[170] In our view, overcoming fractured ownership is critical to constructing a functioning e-Health system but we wouldn't use ownership per se as a lever, we would use the concept of control which has slightly different, more liberal, implications than legal ownership per se (it is a discussion that goes well beyond the, already broad, scope of this chapter).

In response to increasing threats to health information and privacy, the USA at the federal level enacted HIPAA,[171] which regulates and establishes the security and privacy requirements of patient data.[172] This law includes two sections on avoiding the improper use of personal information: the Privacy Rule, also referred to as the Standards for Privacy of Individually Identifiable Health Information, and the Security Rule,[173] which defines how and when a patient must consent before a physician may disclose the patient's medical records to anyone else.[174] The Preamble to the Privacy Rule adopted to enforce

---

The Huffington Post (7 October 2009), www.huffingtonpost.com/leslie-a-saxon-md/owning-your-healthinform_b_312852.html (discussing data ownership as a way to enhance patients' access to data). Another desired aspect of privacy is for patients to be able to control others' access to and use of the patients' data.

168 Marc A. Rodwin, 'Patient Data: Property, Privacy & the Public Interest' (2010) 36 *American Journal of Law & Medicine*, 587, 588, 586-618.

169 See note 164.

170 See note 164 at 6.

171 HIPAA itself was not initially conceived of as a privacy statute. As its name (the Health Insurance Portability and Accountability Act) implies, HIPAA was intended to promote health insurance portability for workers when they change or lose employment. See, e.g., Kendra Gray, 'The Privacy Rule: Are We Being Deceived?' (2008) 11 *Depaul J. Health Care L.* 89, 90–94.

172 J. Rodrigues, I. de la Torre, G. Fernández and M. López-Coronado, 'Analysis of the Security and Privacy Requirements of Cloud-Based Electronic Health Records Systems' (2013) 15(8) *J J. Med. Internet Res.* e186.

173 HIPAA and its Security Rule and Privacy Rule are explicitly intended to establish federal minimum standards, but many states opt to enact legislation that imposes stricter privacy and security requirements on organisations with operations in the state in question or that serve patients or other customers who are state residents.

174 Kari Bomash, 'Privacy and Public Health in the Information Age: Electronic Health Records and the Minnesota Health Records Act' (2009) 10(1) MINN. J.L.

HIPAA states: 'the existence of a generalized right to privacy as a matter of constitutional law suggests that there are enduring values in American law related to privacy. For example, the need for security of "persons" is consistent with obtaining patient consent before performing invasive medical procedures. Moreover, the need for security in "papers and effects" underscores the importance of protecting information about the person contained in personal diaries, medical records or elsewhere'.[175]

Importantly, it attempts to balance individual privacy and interests promoted by information sharing, including law enforcement and research.[176] In broad terms, the Privacy Rule defines what 'health information' governs its subset of 'protected health information' which is (1) individually identifiable, and (2) either transmitted electronically, maintained in electronic media; or transmitted or maintained in any other form or medium.[177] Pollio developed five guiding principles of the Rule which help to contextualise it within any geographical setting: '(1) consumer control – consumers should not have to trade their health privacy in order to obtain healthcare; (2) boundaries – disclosure of health information should be for healthcare reasons only; (3) security – consumers should have faith that their health information will be protected; (4) accountability – punishment for misuse of information; and (5) public responsibility – privacy should be balanced with the need to support medical research and law enforcement.'[178]

As we have discussed in Chapter 1, privacy is a complex and multifaceted concept which scholars have struggled to break down into its elements.[179] The Privacy Rule, however, combined with the subsequent regulations intended

---

SCI. & TECH. 119, 117–141. Alicia Ouellette and Jacob Reider, 'Practical, State, and Federal Limits on the Scope of Compelled Disclosure of Health Records' (2007) 7 *Am. J. Bioethics* 46, 46–47.

175 Melissa Goldstein, Lee Repasch and Sara Rosenbaum, 'Emerging Privacy Issues in Health Information Technology' in David Blumenthal et al. (eds), *Health Information Technology in the United States: Where We Stand* (Robert Wood Johnson Foundation 2008).

176 Erin B. Bernstein, Health Privacy in Public Spaces (2015) 66(5) *Alabama L. Rev.* 989.

177 Kevin B. Davis, 'Privacy Rights in Personal Information: HIPPA and the Privacy Gap Between Fundamental Privacy Rights and Medical Information' (2001) 19 *J. Marshall J. Computer & Info. L.* 545, 535–556.

178 Marie C. Pollio, 'The Inadequacy of HIPAA's Privacy Rule: The Plain Language Notice of Privacy Practices and Patient Understanding' (2004) 60 *NYU Ann. Surv. Am. L.* 579.

179 Ilene N. Moore et al., 'Confidentiality and Privacy in Health Care from the Patient's Perspective: Does HIPAA Help?' (2007) 17 *Health Matrix* 221.

to improve it, focuses almost entirely on ensuring consumer confidence by restricting access to information instead of granting access to information. The expectation that consumers desire confidentiality with respect to their personal healthcare information begins with the traditional doctor–patient relationship. 'The ethos of confidentiality derives from privacy interests of the patient. Privacy, generally described as the right to be let alone, is linked to autonomy, i.e., the ability to control one's destiny and limit others' physical access to one's person or to information about oneself.'[180]

Fundamentally, the privacy of medical information centres on the ability to control circulation.[181] According to HIPAA, patients have certain rights regarding their electronic medical records. The patient has a right to receive notice of the privacy policies of covered entities, including how they use and disclose PHI and the respective rights and duties of the patient and the entity. The mandate states that patients may:

- Request a copy of or gain access to their medical records.
- Request a rectification of any typographical errors or incorrect information.
- Receive notification about the usage of the medical records as well as who has access.
- Select the communication method with the healthcare provider.
- Receive notification if an unauthorised user gains access to any medical information.
- File a complaint with the Office for Civil Rights if there are any suspected violations from a healthcare provider.[182]

Something prevalent in the American model of private healthcare and which will undoubtedly increase as European states evolve is the value of data in the wrong hands. Protecting the confidentiality of health information also protects against the perceived and real potential for economic harm resulting from discrimination in health insurance and employment. The HIPAA Privacy Rule establishes that Protected Health Information (PHI) must be made available in order to provide the patient medical treatment, either through a court order or

180 See note 179.

181 *Board of Med. Quality Assurance v Gherardini*, 93 Cal. App. 3d 669, 678 (Cal. App. 1979) as citied in Kevin B. Davis (see note 177).

182 www.ironmountain.com/Knowledge-Center/Reference-Library/View-by-Document-Type/General-Articles/E/Electronic-Health-Records-Security-and-Privacy-Concerns.aspx#sthash.LC0GzGZQ.dpuf.

the authorisation of the patient. 'The goal for HIPAA was therefore to assure individual healthcare consumers that their autonomy would remain intact despite the newly rampant dissemination of healthcare information. HIPAA executed that goal based on the theory that consumers would be satisfied with these confidentiality-oriented protections.'[183]

The introduction of HIPAA regulations was positive as it forced the reluctant healthcare industry to adopt uniform formats for health data exchanges and uniform code sets to identify internal and external health services activities, and HIPAA compliance became a requirement of all applications.[184] However, even these rules reflect both inconsistent internal approaches, and therefore often provide little assistance with or overall confidence in more difficult situations.[185] Patient authorisation is not required to share health information for the purpose of direct care, particularly when it is being used for treatment, payment or healthcare operations, and the entity has taken steps to secure the information in a reasonable way, which depends on the method used to communicate that information. Communication methods include oral, written, telephone or fax communication.[186] For example, guidance provided by the Centres for Medicare and Medicaid Services states that patients are not required 'to sign consent forms before doctors, hospitals or ambulances can share information for treatment purposes'.[187] Furthermore, patients' prior authorisation is not required when information is shared for purposes of public health, payment, treatment, healthcare operations, research and support of a healthcare exchange. In our view it is the latter assumption that makes it shift to a regime of non-consensual access – that is, access without authorisation or informed consent – in indirect care situations.

HIPAA is well intended, but a patient's ability to restrict electronic health record access remains significantly limited. It also failed to make patients' own health information readily accessible. Not only must patients pay to access their own information, the process for obtaining that information is nearly as difficult as it was prior to the implementation of the HIPAA regulations.[188]

---

183 Jana Sutton, 'Of Information, Trust, and Ice Cream: A Recipe for a Different Perspective on the Privacy of Health Information' (2013) 55 *Ariz. L. Rev.* 1178.

184 R.J. Rodrigues, 'Opportunities and Challenges in the Deployment of Global e-Health' (2003) 5(3/4/5) *Int. J. Healthcare Technology and Management* 336, 335–357.

185 See note 160.

186 See HIPAA – Frequently Asked Questions, US Department of Health & Human Services, www.hhs.gov/hipaafaq/providers/smaller/482.html.

187 *Understanding Health Information Privacy* US Department of Health & Human Services, www.hhs.gov/ocr/privacy/hipaa/understanding.

188 See note 183.

The HIPAA framework defines two categories of potential disclosures: required and permissive. There are only two types of disclosures within the required category: 'a covered entity's provision of a patient's own PHI to the patient or to the patient's representative, and requests by the HHS Secretary for PHI for audit or other enforcement purposes'.[189] Any other disclosures 'are considered permissive or "allowed" but not "automatic" – even disclosures that may be required by other federal or state laws'.[190] Permissive disclosures are further categorised as '(1) those that require patient authorization, and (2) those that can be made without patient authorization'.[191] However, 'if a covered entity desires to disclose PHI, it generally can find a way to do so. HIPAA essentially permits covered entities to substitute their own institutional practices and policies for variable state disclosure laws'.[192] In essence, the healthcare provider has more control than the patient over what information will be disclosed.

Under existing HIPAA regulations, a covered entity or business may not disclose PHI when the organisation receives remuneration for the exchange, unless the patient has authorised such a transaction.[193] This applies to direct and indirect remuneration. In contrast, under HITECH, additional conditions apply regarding a patient's authorisation to sell information used for marketing or fundraising. However, exceptions stipulate that patient authorisation is not needed if the marketing related remuneration is for

- the transfer of data for public health research and treatment;
- the sale, transfer, merger, or consolidation of all or part of the covered entity;
- due diligence associated with a business entity transfer; or
- payments for services under a business associate agreement.[194]

We have found an interesting example of sharing PHI in the form of the Alaska Community Health Aides and Practitioners (CHA/P) and the Electronic Health Record (EHR) system. In May 2009, the Alaskan legislature unanimously passed Senate Bill 133 (SB 133) to create a statewide Health Information Exchange[195] (HIE) system that is interoperable and compliant with state and

189 See note 175.

190 Ibid.

191 Ibid.

192 Ibid.

193 Health Information Technology for Economic and Clinical Health (HITECH) Act, sec. 13405(d), Pub. L. No. 111-5, 123 Stat 115 (2009).

194 Ibid., (2)(A)-(G) (2009).

195 In March 2010, DHSS entered into a cooperative agreement with ONC to create an HIE in Alaska.

federal specifications and protocols for exchanging health records and data.[196] Broad adoption of interoperable HIE/EHR systems is widely regarded to be an essential element of health reform in Alaska, specifically designed to provide a patient-centric approach to sharing and receiving medical records, which allows individuals to have access to their records in order to better understand and control their own health and healthcare. Alaska health information exchange allows individuals to opt out of participating in the system. In our view, the Alaskan model has its inherent merits. As an example of good practice it demonstrates a community agreeing together to the offer of free healthcare in exchange for a community health record which is shared to improve medical insights. Incidentally, there is no shortage of innovative ideas and alternative models. According to Hall, which model ultimately prevails, and in what form, will be a product depending upon three factors: '(1) how well a given model actually works, (2) the basic legal framing of competing rights in medical information, and (3) the information's economic value.'[197]

The Department of Health and Human Services released its omnibus HIPAA/HITECH regulation, implementing changes to the HIPAA Privacy, Security and Enforcement Rules, as well as the interim final regulation on breach notification and certain changes to the Privacy Rule as required by the Genetic Information Non-discrimination Act (GINA Act).[198] These changes result from the 2009 passage of the HITECH Act. The schizophrenic nature of the HITECH law has been well documented. Simply put, Congress desired to incentivise – meaning *pay* – healthcare providers to implement electronic health records systems. Congress decided that it would impose new privacy compliance obligations on those entities that chose to use electronic health records, and it would then create a new set of privacy obligations for everyone else, unconnected in any way to the use of these electronic health records. This statute reflected an ongoing mix of priorities. Congress attempted to remedy for one of the key gaps of the original legislation and rules by applying the enforcement reach of HIPAA not only to covered entities, but to their 'business associates' as well in the final regulation, HHS also extended this to downstream contractors of the business associates. It increased the available penalties for HIPAA violations, cut down on permitted marketing, and modified and expanded certain individual rights.

---

196 The Alaska eHealth Network (AeHN) was incorporated in July 2008 as a 501(c)(3) Alaska non-profit corporation organised and managed by Alaskans. As a network of public and private organisations and businesses involved in healthcare, AeHN has been actively working on adoption of EHRs.

197 Mark A. Hall, 'Property, Privacy, and the Pursuit of Interconnected Electronic Medical Records' (2010) 95 *Iowa L. Rev.* 642.

198 See note 160.

Despite its recent expansion, the HIPAA is still not a general medical privacy law. While its scope has broadened, its protections still depend on where healthcare information starts, with a healthcare provider or health plan. That leaves enormous gaps in protection, particularly given recent technological and philosophical developments that are encouraging consumer involvement in healthcare and providing the technology to make this goal a reality. Although this legislation does not turn business associates into covered entities, it does impose – for the first time – direct accountability on these business associates, with potential civil and criminal liability for a failure to meet these requirements. But aside from some modest clarifications (such as ensuring that health information exchanges are treated as business associates), the HITECH law did not fundamentally broaden the overall HIPAA scheme, nor did it address in any way the tensions between HIPAA and the thousands of applicable state laws.

Conclusion

It is obvious from the discussion in this chapter that the central problem in the debate is how to address the conflict between patients' desire to control their data and the public's need to use those data for various worthy purposes. As we have already argued, it is undisputable that the patient/consumer protection is – and should be – at the core of e-healthcare. We observe that global integration of patient healthcare information is creating a record that functions as a patient analogue in the medical decision-making space, affecting the patient treatment as well as how others relate to the patient along the continuum of care.[199] This viewpoint is consistent with the trend of legislation and professional guidance on the management of personal health data: that we should respect and handle information about the patient as we would expect to handle the patient himself or herself.

Needless to say, the question of who owns the rights to a patient's healthcare data, and who should control that information, has been difficult to answer. Here the essential differences between US and EU law are crucial to our understanding particularly for the purpose of developing the theoretical framework, for the solution we have proposed, which we argue stems from the differing foundations of individual privacy. In the EU, the basic privacy right already existed under a human right to privacy, even before the adoption of the directives, whereas the USA established the right of an individual to health information privacy through a specific statute. We have examined two sets of explanations that we labelled 'legal' and 'behavioural'. The EU framework begins with detailed considerations about whether the information may be collected

199 Kluge E.H.W. Patients, Patient Records, and Ethical Principles' in Greenes, R.A. et al. (eds), (*Medinfo* 8, Pt 2 1995) 1596–1600.

and how to protect patients in the original collection process and the EU policy contemplates that protections should be implemented to prevent coercion of a patient into participation. Whereas, HIPAA works on the assumption that health information will be collected from the individual; its focus is on the subsequent protection, use, and sharing of that information; hence, it can be argued that patients in the USA have no real choice as to whether to participate in the system. There is no evidence that the European system is more efficient.

Arguably, the US policy stipulates that such information must be provided to individuals as part of the privacy notices of a covered entity. The EU Data Protection Directive contains information that must be made available 'whenever any individually identifiable information is used'. The transparency of health systems, notices, and ease of information sharing can also be found in the Working Party EHR Report. The Cross-border Recommendation encompasses the use of alternate means of notification, incorporation of easy-to-use technology to facilitate access and consideration of notice that is appropriate for persons with special needs.[200]

A particularly interesting observation emerges when one compares sharing and collection of information in the USA and Europe. The most striking difference is the EU's emphasis on actual patient understanding of information collection and sharing, depending on individual circumstances, which sets it apart from less specific US requirements. They have substantial differences in their frameworks on issues related to a patient's choice and consent to share personally identifiable health information with third parties. Evidently, they also have diametrically opposed starting points in terms of what health information may be collected. HIPAA contains many exceptions to when a patient's consent is needed to share information, although HIPAA provides a patient the right of access to his or her health records.[201] However, even though the patient may request changes to the record, the entity is not required to implement those changes. Hence, in practice it seems HIPAA offers limited instances for patient choice; it is argued that HIPAA should 'empower patients to assert control' over their health information.[202] In contrast, the DPA does allow individuals to correct their data, albeit through 'Subject Access Requests'. Neither are ideal positions, particularly as their medical safety often depends on the availability of accurate data.[203]

---

200 J. Hiller, M. McMullen, W. Chumney and D. Baumer, 'Privacy and Security in the Implementation of Health Information Technology (Electronic Records): US and EU Compared' (2011) 17(1) *Boston U. J. Sci. Technol. L.* 1.

201 Ibid.

202 Ibid.

203 Ibid.

The EU's emphasis on patient control of health information underpins its approach to access and accuracy. Therefore, the policy emphasises security aspects such as ensuring that the person requesting the information is properly identified as the patient. In fundamental ways, EU law has made more significant progress towards the dual goals of effective implementation of EHRs and the protection of individual privacy through enabling patient control. Even though the US legislative framework attempts to regulate organisations by focusing on information sharing, in the absence of a stronger governmental protection mechanism, it does not really empower individuals in the same way that some countries in Europe do at present. The USA has yet to establish whether the HITECH framework will sufficiently enhance the authority of the FTC and bolster its participation in healthcare privacy.[204]

Europe seeks to create a pan-European interoperable electronic health record (EHR). However, the introduction of a pan-European federal EHR raises important questions about whether and how people should be informed of those uses; when consent may be required and when research may be exempted from requiring consent; how one's willingness to participate in research might be recorded in the EHR; and the governance over use of information from the EHR for research purposes. There is evidence to suggest that public attitudes to protection and use of personal health information across Europe and even in the USA vary considerably depending on the sensitivity of the information, the mechanism of recording this information, the healthcare setting, and how the information may be used.

In summary, we argue that when considering patient control of information and transparency with regard to how that data is being used, the USA has an admirable approach of not being concerned with who 'owns' it. The idea of patient ownership of healthcare data is injudicious both legally and conceptually. In the USA, the focus is on access to the data and transparency, ensuring that the patient can know what the data is being used for. There is a lot to learn from the USA in terms of how the laws and regulations have been developed. They had the benefit of being able to develop a completely new federal legislative framework based on the needs and rights presented at the time, as they did not have a legacy framework or a 'patchwork' of sometimes conflicting legislative directions, which is present both in the EU and in the UK. Although this cannot be directly imposed in the UK, it could be used to influence new policy decisions and legislation. Overall, the US approach, focusing on benefits realisation, strongly supports our notion of 'collective transparency' required to release benefits to society at large. In contrast, in Europe the focus is on who has the right to decide how to use information. It is about obtaining

204 Ibid.

patient consent. The focus here lends support to the other notion, which we purport must balance 'collective transparency' – that of 'individual privacy'. We create this balance in the following chapters by highlighting, in contrast to both approaches, how the UK has specific issues to address in Chapter 3, as a starting point. Taking influence from both the USA and the EU model in the suggested solutions, we constantly use the two approaches as a check and balance to try to achieve the optimal balance point between both approaches.

Part II

THE PROBLEM

Chapter 3
The Theoretical Problem
The Three Issues Necessitating Change: Mindset, Information, Innovation

Introduction

This section focuses on the fundamental problems which we assert propel the 'privacy myth'. Chapter 3 sets the scene by analysing the theoretical problem. We argue that there are three issues which necessitate change – the *mindset* around informational privacy, the quality and ownership of *information* and the use of *innovation*. In the next chapter (Chapter 4) we explore some of the implications of the practical problem. It highlights the historical role reversal where the NHS is in control of information via technology, which masks the individual's rights and inadvertently circumvents the law.

In this chapter we develop a fuller account of the theoretical underpinning of the problem. We assert that the solutions to the problem are threefold. We argue that there must be a change of mindset around 'privacy', moving privacy from an individualistic concept to a concern for society. The balance required between 'individual privacy' and 'collective transparency' reflects this. We suggest that we should take influence from the European focus on individual rights and the US focus on collective transparency outlined in Chapter 2 and balance the two. Information within health records must be standardised and understandable and information must be controlled by the patient to the extent that they choose to do this. Online records are required to facilitate this so that consent issues are handled proactively rather than being relegated to reactive 'objection' decisions. Likewise, innovation should be used by the patient as an impartial vehicle to deliver this control – allowing the individual to control their own information and to use the autonomous laws as intended. At present technical controls within NHS information systems are designed for control by patients but are largely controlled by clinicians.

We have developed a model which demonstrates the reflective changes in roles required for both the NHS and the individual (Figure 3. 1 below). It is essentially a role reversal.

The principle behind this is that when individuals have the choice of control they will be empowered to think about 'privacy' in a way that allows consideration of its impact on society and on their own clinical safety. Individuals can make

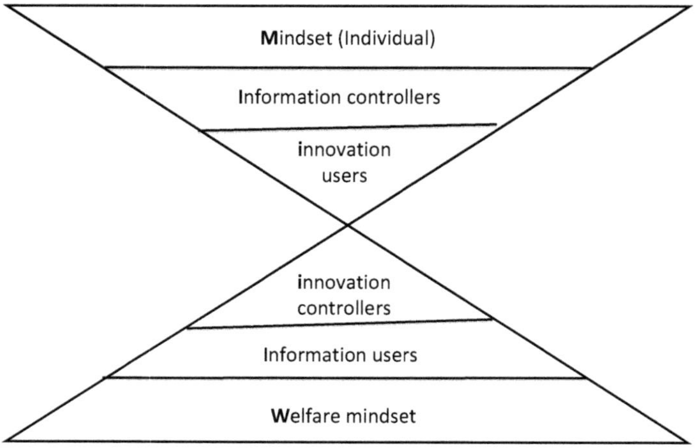

Figure 3.1 The reflective – and currently reversed – roles of the NHS and individuals in the management of information

their own informed decisions on what privacy means for them and enact these decisions directly by controlling information through innovation appropriately. It is purported to be self-propelling as individuals will see for themselves the direct societal benefit of sharing. It is suggested that it is the current secrecy surrounding 'privacy' that makes people decide not to share information. They are currently not privy to the information which would allow them to understand the negative impacts of not sharing information, both to their own clinical safety (e.g., not being able to correct incorrectly recorded allergy information or incorrect dosages of medication; or a care home not having a discharge plan from a hospital, therefore not knowing that an individual needs more regular food intake, resulting in a diabetic coma) and that of others, such as a person trialling a new HIV drug not allowing their outcome information to be part of a trial resulting in the potentially life-saving drug not being commissioned and saving lives – there could even be more direct benefits to the individual's family missed in the case of information not being included in research of rare genetic diseases, for example.

In Chapter 1 we touched upon the confusion around the handling of different types of information and the examples above illustrate how many different uses of information there are. This is further complicated by the roles of the NHS and of individuals in information management. To put it simply, if the individual manages their own information – of any description – the concept of privacy is redundant because (within legal limits) the individual can decide what is 'private'. There are some legal limitations which means that the NHS must handle some of the information as data controllers and the NHS must or may legally disclose or not disclose certain pieces of confidential information about an individual, however and the individual should see when this is the case. Generally when disclosure is for direct care, the information can be disclosed. Of course in general circumstances the boundaries are not definitive between what information the NHS should control and what information the individual should control and where this is the case, the most transparency is required.

Four key current issues are highlighted throughout to illuminate these issues. Firstly, the blurring of boundaries between direct care (provided by a clinician or care worker) where implied consent is accepted as a legal basis for sharing information within the care team and indirect care (research, commissioning and audit etc.) where another legal basis is required (the most desirable is asserted as patient consent). A particular issue drawn out from the comparison between the UK practices is insurance companies requiring access to patients' personal information for the payment of bills. This is acceptable practice where the system depends on insurance companies to balance the risk of healthcare not being available free of charge. However, there is much debate in the UK about information being disseminated to the insurers in the UK when it should not, including a House of Commons Health Select Committee hearing highlighting this very topic.[1]

Secondly, the current controversy around fair processing and the care. data patient information leaflet, opt out and objections and associated rights in the HRA and DPA. This is heightened by the Secretary of State's public commitments regarding the patient's right to 'veto' their information going from their GP surgery to Health and Social Care Information Centre for secondary uses. Thirdly, the problems surrounding legal definitions of anonymised, pseudonymised and identifiable data are illuminated.

And finally, new legal direction for organisations is pushing in the wrong direction, adding extra safeguards to the sharing of confidential information on

1 Health Select Committee footage can only be found in YouTube links, so that authors have chosen to cite this here as the only available source: www.youtube.com/watch?v=wCigjQsZYmA See also newspaper headlines signalling public outrage. 'The society which used data on every NHS patient – and used it to guide insurance companies on premiums.' *Mail Online UK* (Web) (27 February 2014), Amie Keeley. www.dailymail.co.uk/news/article-2566397/The-insurance-firms-buy-data-NHS-patient.html?ITO=1490&ns_mchannel=rss&ns_campaign=1490; see also 'Patient data should never have gone to insurers', *Daily Telegraph* (25 February 2014) 2, Laura Donnelly. A spokesman for the Health and Social Care Information Centre (HSCIC), which is now in charge of NHS data, said its predecessor body was wrong to sell the information to the insurance industry.

organisations, through Acts such as the Health and Social Care Act 2012 and the Care Act 2014. Juxtaposed alongside this is the proposed new legal direction for individuals through the Data Protection Directive which should give individuals more control on individual privacy and explicit consent.

The Theoretical Problem

With these issues in mind we outline the theoretical problem as three issues necessitating change – the mindset around 'informational privacy', the quality and ownership of information and the use of innovation. There are two perspectives to consider for each of the three issues – 'individual privacy' versus 'collective transparency'. Chapter 4, as we have mentioned before, articulates the practical problem and highlights the historical role reversal, where technology is used as a driver in itself to reflect the law instead of vehicles for the delivery of rights and choices. In contrast, we argue that the current privacy framework per se is suitable for the purposes of the Information Revolution, but we posit that the current roles of the national organisations create the problem.

Privacy is a surprisingly difficult concept to define, as there are many different definitions within the literature generated by different academic disciplines that examine privacy.[2] Researchers[3] recognise that the definition of privacy is multi-dimensional,[4] potentially extending over information, activities, decisions, thoughts, bodies, and communication, and is shaped by complex social, economic and political processes.[5] A full theory of privacy would need to take into account all of these dimensions, even if, eventually, it asserted theoretically grounded exclusions. However, the goals of this book are more limited; a detailed exploration of privacy theory is beyond the scope of this book, which aims not for a full theory of privacy, but only the right to privacy as it applies to information about people.

---

2 See Basu, S., 'Privacy Protection: A Tale of Two Cultures' (2012) 6(1) *Masaryk University Journal of Law and Technology* 1–34.

3 See Alan F. Westin, *Privacy and Freedom* (New York: Atheneum 1970); David Lyon, *Surveillance Society: Monitoring Everyday Life* (Open University Press 2001); James R. Beniger, *The Control Revolution: Technological and Economic Origins of the Information Society* (Harvard University Press 1986); Judith Wagner DeCew, *In Pursuit of Privacy: Law, Ethics and the Rise of Technology* (Cornell University Press 1997).

4 See note 2.

5 Alan F. Westin, 'Social and Political Dimensions of Privacy' (2003) 59 *Journal of Social Issues* 431.

It is pivotal to highlight the irony in the fact that finding a starting point for the definition of privacy is part of solving the problem of the 'privacy myth'. What the courts previously labelled 'confidentiality' has now moved to the more stringent constraints of 'privacy',[6] despite being distinct concepts. This is enumerated in the cases post the enactment of the Human Rights Act 1998. These definitional changes in health often appear to be driven somewhat by major breaches that hit the media spotlight, such as the Her Majesty's Revenue and Customs (HMRC) breach in 2007.[7] The pendulum seems to swing from a focus on confidentiality to one on privacy based on the latest incidents and media coverage. This is why we welcome the recent clarity from Dame Fiona Caldicott's Information Governance Review which created a new principle: that it can be as important to share information when it is for the benefit of the patient, as it is to keep it confidential. This allows for the human element of judgement required in each case.

We argue that there is a need for each member of the public to individually define privacy for themselves, so that it does not accompany the negative connotations attached to privacy's relationship with deception, secrecy and anonymity[8] which fuels the self-propagating 'privacy myth'. In turn, this can fuel 'privacy myopia', where individuals believe that legislative protection exists to protect organisations' rights to collect and disclose information, escalating the fear of what 'illegitimate activities'[9] others may undertake if unmonitored.[10] Conversely, many emphasise 'privacy' as positive, protecting a behaviour 'valued by society',[11] which facilitates individuals' positive 'freedoms'.[12] We assert that the differentiating factor between the perceptions of privacy as positive and as

6 See T. Aplin, 'The Development of the Action for Breach of Confidence in a Post-HRA Era' (2007) *IPQ 19*. Courts no longer analyse the action for breach of confidence in the terms of the three-limbed test of *Coco v Clark (Coco v A N Clark (Engineers) Ltd* [1969] RPC 41). Rather, the key question is whether the information is 'private' and, if it is, an obligation of confidence arises. Courts will then engage in a balancing exercise between Arts 8 and 10 of the ECHR.

7 www.computerweekly.com/feature/HMRC-data-breach-highlights-need-for-data-compliance.

8 See S. Margulis, 'Privacy as a Social Issue and Behavioral Concept' (2003) 59(2) *J. Social Issues* 243.

9 Such as misuse of a public office as noted by A. Westin, *Privacy and Freedom* (New York: Atheneum 1970).

10 A. Froomkin, 'The Death of Privacy?' (2000) 52 *SLR* 1461,1462.

11 C. Warren and B. Laslett, 'Privacy and Secrecy: A Conceptual Comparison' (1977) 33 *J. Social Issues* 43.

12 See S. Fredman, Human Rights Transformed (Oxford: OUP 2008).

negative lies in whether or not the correct amount of control and visibility rests with the individuals to whom the data refers.[13]

As definitions depend on this balance of power, synergies between Altman's[14] and Westin's[15] theories of informational privacy, which focus on the process of regulating levels of social interaction and on types and functions of privacy, provide a working definition. Both theories build on 'restricted access' approaches, dealing with how individuals and groups control access to personal information as a continuing dynamic of changing conditions.

Informational Privacy in the NHS: Mindset

The Ideal Theoretical Stages of Informational Privacy

This book focuses on 'informational privacy.' Wacks argued that the protection afforded by the law of privacy should be limited to information,[16] which, in his words, 'relates to the individual and which it would be reasonable to expect him to regard as intimate or sensitive and therefore to want to withhold or at least to restrict its collection, use, or circulation'.[17] This places the onus firmly on the individual to make a subjective 'reasonable' judgement about information. Wacks'[18] detailed account of privacy policy suggests that privacy is an enduring value and a legal, essential human right. This respect for 'privacy' as core to the very existence of an individual is one which Bloustein defends as a requirement for human dignity.[19]

Throughout history, 'informational privacy' has remained predominantly positioned from this individualistic[20] starting point which we term in our proposed model of privacy (outlined below in Figure 3.2), as 'stage one' or 'individualistic concept of privacy'. However, as we have seen in Chapter 2 best practice is rapidly moving towards the use of cyberspace for information storage and management. In cyberspace the unlimited interaction with society

13 Positive definitions of privacy depend on control.

14 I. Altman, *The Environment and Social Behaviour: Privacy, Personal Space, Territory, Crowding* (Brooks/Cole 1975).

15 A. Westin, *Privacy and Freedom* (New York: Atheneum 1970).

16 R. Wacks, *Personal Information - Privacy and the Law* (Clarendon Press1993).

17 Ibid. at 26.

18 Ibid.

19 See E. Bloustein, 'Privacy as an Aspect of Human Dignity: An Answer to Dean Prosser' (1964) 39 *NYU L. Rev.* 962.

20 S. Warren and L. Brandeis, 'The Right to Privacy' (1890) 4 *Harv. L. Rev.* 193, 195.

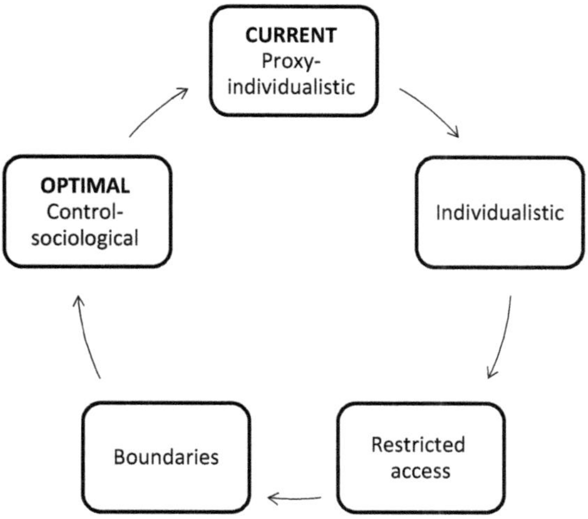

Figure 3.2 MI information revolution allowing individuals the choice to conceptualise privacy as one of four options

necessitates a move from an individualistic starting point towards models based upon 'restricted access'[21] and 'boundaries'[22], which we term as the second and third stages, respectively. Today, the concept of 'informational privacy' should aim to turn a full revolution towards a 'sociological' starting point – which we term as the final fourth stage. The specific stage in this revolution that individuals may choose to define as 'privacy' is termed 'MI ('*my*') information revolution.' (Figure 3.2). It personalises the concept of privacy for them, therefore makes the promises within the *Information Revolution* real for them.

The Theoretical Issue

Placing the current mindset around informational 'privacy' of the NHS, within the four proposed stages of the 'MI information revolution' model is a stark indication of the need to change. It is pivotal to understand that today's society is at the 'proxy-individualistic' stage (even before the traditional first individualistic stage), where the NHS controls information on behalf of individuals. In most cases where information sharing is for direct care, this is clearly optimal. However, particularly in the case of the sharing of information for indirect care

21 A. Allen, *Uneasy Access: Privacy for Women in a Free Society* (Rowman and Littlefield 1988).

22 See I. Altman, *The Environment and Social Behaviour: Privacy, Personal Space, Territory, Crowding* (Brooks/Cole 1975).

(e.g., for research and audit) this is either one revolution too advanced or behind what we purport to be the optimal point of control – the fourth stage – starting from a sociological viewpoint. This is because consent is often not actively obtained to validate this role, but if consent has been obtained this would be optimal. It is this optimal point which the Alaskan Community Health Aide Program as discussed in Chapter 2 appears to have achieved, in direct contrast to the UK model. Below we consider each stage of the revolution in turn in the context of the UK health model, articulating the issues underlying each.

Stage 1 is not achievable

The typically 'individualistic' starting point (the first stage) is already reversed and therefore not achievable – the NHS is the primary decision maker, in stark contrast to the typical individualised starting point of privacy conceptions. Although this could be viewed positively as the optimal 'sociological' starting point for information sharing, it is largely illegitimate because it is often not underpinned by the consent of individuals. Therefore the individual has no real option to take an individualistic stance. The NHS assumes a duty of confidentiality and appoints itself as a 'proxy-individual' figure, making decisions on behalf of the individual. This is understandable as Schedule 3 to the Data Protection Act 1998 (DPA) does incorporate the concept of medical confidentiality, stipulating that sensitive data 'must be processed with the subjects' explicit consent and/or, if necessary for medical purposes, by a health professional who owes a duty of confidentiality'. The onus on explicit consent could increase if the proposed new Data Protection Directive is implemented.[23] However, it is arguable that without consent, there is no such thing as 'confidentiality' or privacy per se – just control vested almost entirely in the NHS.

As a consequence of the control being balanced in favour of the NHS, the first stage of the 'revolution' – the individualistic starting point – is often unintentionally masked by the NHS. Rights and laws are autonomy-based, but the individual does not have the power to be autonomous due to the NHS's 'proxy-individual' role. Whilst its 'proxy-individual' role can be problematic, the NHS must have some role that reverses the individualistic starting point of typical privacy theories so that it can discharge its safeguarding duties for individuals, to allow them 'positive

23 See European Commission, Brussels, 25.1.2012, COM (2012) 11 final 2012/0011 (COD) Proposal for a Regulation of The European Parliament and of the Council on the protection of individuals with regard to the processing of personal data and on the free movement of such data (General Data Protection Regulation). This is beyond the scope of this paper as it deals with the current state where the ethics of consent is discussed, not the mechanics.

freedom'.[24] This illustrates the complementary nature of 'individual privacy' and 'collective transparency'. Because control or freedom can be viewed as both the opposite of and the same as privacy, this overlap is unsurprising – all concepts arrive at the same point using opposite logic for the balance of power.

The NHS has a positive obligation to engage in activities to secure the effective enjoyment of the fundamental right of privacy, as opposed to the classical negative obligation to merely abstain from human rights violations. Although the European Court of Human Rights (ECtHR) has not extended the NHS's role, rights have been interpreted as *enabling* people to live autonomous lives, rather than *disabling* the state.[25] This contradiction must be addressed and reflected in the balance of power, expanding government whilst promoting autonomy by protecting people from outside interferences to control over their own lives.[26]

An individualised concept of privacy would not acknowledge the social elements of privacy that Leith[27] warns of but in health it is somewhat polarised. Mandatory legal gateways, such as section 8 of the National Audit Act 1983, impose a legal obligation on public bodies to provide relevant information to the National Audit Office. Therefore this 'individualised' view is inherently restricted. Individuals, however, would decide at this stage to keep everything they do have power to decide about to themselves, and not share any information voluntarily.

This theoretical option has been tested recently through the care.data patient information leaflet sent to every household in the UK. This explained that the HSCIC intended to collect information from an individual's GP record but that the individual has a right to tell their GP that they would like to 'opt out' of this. On closer inspection they actually have two opt outs. An individual can:

- opt out of information from their record going to the HSCIC in identifiable form (the option if you don't trust the HSCIC to handle it appropriately); and/or
- opt out of the HSCIC being allowed to further disseminate the information in identifiable form to others for purposes other than direct care (e.g., research, commissioning, audit etc.).

NHS England's care.data Privacy Impact Assessment (PIA) states that, 'whilst it is possible for patients to object to the processing of personal confidential data

24 See C. Ovey and R. White, The European Convention on Human Rights (OUP 2006) 51.

25 K. Moller, 'Two Conceptions of Positive Liberty: Towards an Autonomy-based Theory of Constitutional Rights' (2009) *OJLS* 757.

26 S. Fredman, Human Rights Transformed (OUP 2008).

27 P. Leith, 'The Socio-Legal Context of Privacy' (2006) 2 *Int. J. Law in Context* 105.

under section 10 of the DPA, this new 'code' (referring to a technical IT code the GPs use to register the opt-out request) allows patients to exercise choice more easily, to a large degree: they simply need to ask their GP to enter this code into their GP practice record'. Put simply, patients who are concerned about their privacy can now control the flow of confidential data both out of their GP practices and out of the HSCIC.[28] The PIA seems contrary to the original NHS England guidance to GPs which stated that: 'Section 10 of the DPA does not apply; the right to object has been implemented as a constitutional rather than legal right'. This statement has notably been removed from the newly reissued guidance from NHS England to GPs. If that wasn't confusing enough it doesn't mention that the flows of information from the HSCIC account for only a small minority of data flowing from the GP record for purposes other than direct care. How do individuals get to know about and opt out or object to others?

Then there is the inevitable confusion around terminology. Many are conflating the concepts of 'dissent' (requiring prior consent), 'opt out' and 'objection'. Whether objection is indeed a right is debated, not least within the NHS Constitution. The legal underpinnings are s.10 of the Data Protection Act and Article 8 of the Human Rights Act. Perhaps stronger – and what contributes towards some of the public confusion – was the Secretary of State for Health's 'veto' promise which related only to data flowing to the HSCIC. This begs the question of 'why?' but also 'why does it not apply to hospital episode statistics that have been flowing to the HSCIC for more than 20 years?' a question that has been picked up by the papers.[29] The right to object underpins stage 1 of the theoretical model we propose. It must be otionally sound and at least a 'blanket opt out' of use of information for purposes beyond direct care must be in place before proceeding to further options. A more granular opt-out model can be integrated into options 2 and 3 below.

Stage 2 is enacted by law but is not transparent

The second stage of the 'revolution' –'restricted access' to information in the control of the NHS and the NHS allows the individual to control – is already enacted through legislation which provides permissive legal gateways through provisions such as section 251 of the NHS Act 2006.[30] This Act permits the common law duty of confidentiality to be set aside in limited circumstances,

28 NHS England, care.data Privacy Impact Assessment. www.england.nhs.uk/wp-content/uploads/2014/01/pia-care-data.pdf.

29 Lyn Whitfield HSCIC reviews HES access, ehi: eHealth Insider; www.ehi.co.uk/news/ehi/9364/hscic-reviews-hes-access.

30 Formerly covered in section 60 of the Health and Social Care Act 2001; referred to hereafter as 's. 251'.

enabling the Secretary of State[31] to support and regulate the use of confidential information for 'public good.' This is a transitional measure to provide safeguards while options for improving consent practice and/or introducing anonymisation techniques are pursued.

Current legislation has extended what were very limited exceptions to setting aside the common law duty of confidentiality. In the same legislation controls are placed on organisations to add another governance layer (which doesn't necessarily involve the patient) but restricts sharing. Section 251 of the NHS Act has been used to form an interim legal basis for the use of personal confidential data for commissioning purposes, including the validation of invoices for care and risk stratification[32] despite the findings of Dame Fiona Caldicott's 2013 Information Governance Review that use of personal confidential data in commissioning must have a very strong justification.

A proposed data sharing regulation consultation signified the further use of legislation to regulate the use of data on the following purposes:

- creating new safeguards around information sharing for the purposes of commissioning and understanding population health needs – requiring information to be processed in 'accredited safe havens';
- establishing clear rules around the use of data that might potentially identify individuals disseminated by accredited safe havens and the Health and Social Care Information Centre;
- clarifying the rules on when information about people receiving health or care services, particularly the most vulnerable, must be shared by those providing the care with those who commission it.[33]

The biggest concern here in our view was the use of the term 'accredited safe haven' in a way that was never intended when the concept was created through the Caldicott Review of 2013. The Caldicott Review stated that the Health and Social Care Act 2012 provides primary legislation for the creation of an accredited safe haven, called the Health and Social Care Information Centre.

31 In overseeing these exceptions to confidentiality, the Secretary of State must consult with the independent NIGB (formerly PIAG).

32 See NHS England, Risk Stratification Assurance Statement, CAG 7-04(a)/2013 compliance for CCGs, www.england.nhs.uk/wp-content/uploads/2014/02/rsa-state-02-141.pdf; see also Risk Stratification, www.england.nhs.uk/ourwork/tsd/ig/risk-stratification/.

33 Department of Health, 'Protecting Health and Care Information: A Consultation on Proposals to Introduce New Regulations' (June 2014), www.gov.uk/government/uploads/system/uploads/attachment_data/file/323967/Consultation_document.pdf.

It noted that there may need to be other local ASHs but that they would need their own clear legal basis for processing confidential data. *'Being an accredited safe haven does not necessarily mean that the organisation is receiving personal confidential data, but does mean it can receive de-identified data for limited disclosure or limited access.'*[34]

When translated through a policy lens, personal confidential data was brought into focus. The potential for almost anyone to become an Accredited Safe Haven may allow a person or organisation to link pieces of information to an individual. When read alongside the new legislative framework, it is even questionable whether this is legal. At best it is confusing. The Health and Social Care Act 2012 grants an organisation named the Health and Social Care Information Centre (HSCIC) powers to collect, analyse, publish and share (disseminate) information. It can collect and analyse confidential information but may only be able to publish or disseminate confidential information with another legal basis, although this is open to interpretation. Furthermore, the Care Act 2014 gives the Health Research Authority's Confidentiality Advisory Group (HRA CAG) a role in advising the HSCIC on any releases of pseudonymised data. Is this a hollow provision given that the HSCIC may need a legal basis to release pseudonymised data anyway?

Beyond this debate, the law has never recognised anything other than either 'personal' identifiable data, as protected by the Data Protection Act 1998 or anonymised as defined by standards such as the Information Standards Board (ISB) anonymisation standard. Nothing in between (such as pseudonymised data) has ever been recognised in law before. During the care.data debate the following types of data were differentiated between by NHS England:

- Green 'Anonymised Data', which are to be made accessible to anyone;
- Amber 'Potentially identifiable data', which we are told may 'only be released to approved organisations, and restricted to specific purposes that will benefit the health and social care system' subject to certain controls; and
- Red 'Identifiable data', which will only be disclosed by the HSCIC where there is a legal basis for doing so, e.g., with patient consent, where advised by the Confidentiality Advisory Group, or in a public health emergency.[35]

It is clear that amber or pseudonymised data creates an ambiguity which is not subject to regulation by law. The Confidentiality Advisory Group has therefore either been given a huge and unclear responsibility, or none at all, as outlined above.

---

34 Ibid.

35 www.england.nhs.uk/2014/01/15/geraint-lewis/.

Many campaigners have argued that insufficient information has been provided to citizens about the identities of the third parties that may potentially receive the pseudonymised information, and what they may do with it – most controversially the potential use by commercial organisations such as insurance companies.[36] We assert that it is this category of data – which could be identifiable if linked – which is where the law is not clear but potentially where the concerns of the informed public peak. We propose that 'Stage 2' of the information revolution cannot be enacted transparently, without some major clarifications for the public, which would lead to informed decisions should an individual make a 'Stage 2' choice.

Stage 3 is not supported as individuals are not aware enough to join the debate

In theory, the restricted access provisions outlined above do have the potential to facilitate the third stage of the revolution – which we term as the 'boundaries' concept of privacy. However, the limited transparency outlined above hinders progression towards 'boundary' conceptions of privacy which would allow for flexibility and provides for a more equal starting point for the NHS and the individual. Furthermore, there appears to be limited audit capability within systems that handle confidential data. This means that individuals are not aware enough of how their information is used to play an active part in the debate about decisions made about their data when there is an element of discretion.

Borrowing the elements of 'restricted access' and 'control', Moor's 'control/restricted access' theory[37] is close to this conception, incorporating the flexibility that the elements of choice within the Information Revolution introduces. Although Moor's 'control/restricted access' theory[38] was developed for the information age, health currently falls between Moor's 'naturally'[39] and 'normatively'[40] private situations. In these situations privacy can be lost and violated, respectively, as the NHS's self-imposed proxy-individualistic role means that society is moving from a situation in which legal rights to privacy for the individual existed but were often masked. Therefore, privacy can only be 'lost' initially and not violated, but can further be 'violated' once informed choice is facilitated. Moor's expression of choice

---

36 S. Pritchett, 'Care.data – Why Should We Care?' (2014) 14(4) *P. & D.P.* 14.

37 J. Moor, 'Towards a Theory of Privacy in the Information Age' (1997) 27 *Computers and Society* 3, 27.

38 Ibid.

39 In a naturally private situation, privacy can be lost but not violated or invaded because there are no conventional, legal, or ethical norms which could give rights to be protected.

40 Privacy is also protected by ethical, legal and conventional norms.

through 'informed consent' and the 'publicity principle', which could invite debate around any boundaries to access to information set by the NHS, is largely missing. Such expression of choice would need to be available to move towards the fourth stage.

Stage 4 autonomy relies on disclosure and the opportunity for democracy

To reach the fourth and final stage would require a reversal of the primary control vested in the NHS. This primary control is inherently ironic; whilst the NHS can use legal provisions to bypass consent en masse in the second stage (legitimately for the welfare of society), patients have to *individually* litigate using the Article 10 ECHR right to respect for one's 'private and family life, his home and his correspondence'. This inequality positions the concept of privacy further away from *both* control from a sociological standpoint (Stage 4) *and* the individualised (Stage 1) notion of privacy Leith[41] warns of. This is because in health, disclosure is necessary for autonomy so there needs to be transparency, facilitated by disclosure. This dynamic renders most theories overly simplistic. Even Feinberg's[42] distinction between spheres of personal autonomy and state control falters. To take an example, distinguishing *self-regarding decisions* from *other-regarding decisions* focuses on objective features of concepts that individual behaviour does not have – it has multiple effects.

The Missing Building Blocks

It is therefore clear that when individuals do not have primary control, they must have the power and visibility to make choices and to question the NHS's control of their data (Stages 3 and 4). This is particularly so when the two dimensions of data protection – protection of one's data from the public and from the state – are essentially the same, because the state represents the public. The autonomous right *to* informational self-determination was espoused by the German FCC and is defined in its ground-breaking census judgement in *Von Hannover v Germany*:

> A person who cannot overlook with sufficient security which information concerning him is known in specific areas of his social environment and who cannot somewhat estimate the knowledge of possible contact persons, can be substantially inhibited in his freedom to plan and to make decisions in self-determination … This would … also

41 P. Leith, 'The Socio-Legal Context of Privacy' (2006) 2 *Int. J. Law in Context* 105.

42 J. Feinberg, Harm to Self (OUP 1986) 47.

> (affect) the common good because self-determination is an elementary condition of a free democratic polity which is based on the ability of its citizens to engage in activities.[43]

Here, although to 'overlook' could be interpreted as 'power/visibility', and the spirit of the language, such as use of the term 'engage', suggests a collaborative approach, the court concluded that the right to informational self-determination 'guaranteed ... the right of the individual to decide autonomously about the release and use of his personal data',[44] emphasising that this applied to *all* personal data: *'in times of automatic data processing there exists no "trivial" data'*.[45] Legislation such as the DPA compounds this perception of negative freedom (privacy), neglecting the social considerations surrounding information sharing.[46]

Accordingly, 'privacy' in the NHS must mean the opposite of the 'secrecy' it currently implies – individuals must choose what to disclose. Once issues regarding ownership and power are resolved, this should allow individuals the ability to experience the stages of 'privacy' conceptualisation they have missed out on as a result of the NHS's 'proxy-individual' role. Hence, to establish the changes required to redefine 'privacy' in the NHS, the respective roles of the NHS and of individuals are discussed to examine the starting point for such change. Due to the overly paternal role of the NHS and the resulting limited autonomy of individuals, current theoretical roles of individuals and the NHS do not reflect reality when they are implemented; as a result, mindsets are misinformed. The balance between collective transparency for the welfare of society and individual privacy requires consideration of both by the individual primarily affected. However, this decision is firmly in the hands of the NHS at present.

Role Reversals: Controlling the Law and Technology

The NHS also has primary control of the tools of law and technology, which is ironic, as both are designed to empower individuals. Law is designed to be autonomy-based in order for individuals to enforce individual privacy, but the 'proxy-individual' role of the NHS circumvents this by inadvertently masking the role of the individual. Technical innovation is defined as the technical infrastructure used in the UK in IT systems that hold patient information (technical IG controls). These include systems such as the 'patient administration system' (PAS) which holds demographic details of patients, such

43 *Von Hannover v Germany* (App no 59320/00) (2005) 40 EHRR 1 [50]–[53].

44 Ibid. [43].

45 Ibid. [45].

46 See note 40.

as names and addresses and the IT controls which dictate who has access to such data, depending on their role. These technical controls are also controlled by the NHS at the moment, but are designed for individuals to control access to information about them, and may also empower individuals to decide between individual privacy and collective transparency.

The mindset of the NHS is apparent through its self-imposed role relating to ensuring individual 'privacy'. We can see how this role has arisen as the NHS has traditionally dealt with the direct care of an individual. However, we argue that its legitimate role should also be the consented utilisation of individual data for the 'public good', for the welfare of society en masse, which we term 'collective transparency'. This should be both in terms of the legal definition of 'public good' and the legal definition of 'public interest', specifically when that definition relates to requirements in health. The NHS must employ collective transparency to facilitate exceptions to consent for secondary uses of information, such as performance management or the s. 251[47] process which allows the common law duty of confidence to be set aside for purposes such as research.

As the NHS has moved into the realm of information technology, its unintentional paternal blurring of the distinction between ownership of technical innovation and ownership of information has propelled the 'privacy' myth. Similarly, the NHS's collective transparency role is likely to be criticised, because although the NHS aims to appreciate the social aspects of privacy, it fails to make this commendable process visible. The Health and Social Care Act 2008 established the independent National Information Governance Board (NIGB, abolished[48] through the 2012 Act). The NIGB reviewed applications requesting that the duty of confidentiality be set aside in specific circumstances, e.g., s. 251 for research or management collection of personal information for the public good, established through the NHS Act 2006 with an accountability structure through the Secretary of State. Similarly, the Health Service (Control of Patient Information) Regulations 2002[49] give the UK Health Protection Agency (HPA) permission to collect Personal Identifiable Data[50] under certain conditions, e.g., HIV infection.[51] Such governance should be retained as it is through the Health

47 NHS Act 2006.

48 Department of Health, 'Equality and Excellence, Liberating the NHS' (White Paper, Cm 7881, 2010).

49 The Health Service (Control of Patient Information) Regulations 2002, SI 2002/1438.

50 Patient Identifiable Data.

51 For example the NHS (Venereal Diseases) 1974 Regulations, SI 1974/29, allows patient anonymity to encourage service uptake. The discloser of information for contact-tracing is supported in the case of sexually transmitted diseases. This disclosure can only be by a doctor or someone working on instruction. For example, GPs are not

and Social Care Act, but transparency is required so individuals can see the benefits to the welfare of society. One opportunity to do this has been taken by the Health and Social Care Information Centre (HSCIC) in their leaflet drop[52] which explains the use of information collected by them.

Without transparency one law expressly allows another law to be circumvented as the NHS inadvertently masks the rights of the individual. The NHS's middleman status somewhat invalidates the rights provided by the Human Rights Act as rights of the citizen against the state. Despite the NHS's apparent lack of accountability for leaks shown in *Ackroyd*,[53] the HRA *has* been used to increase the NHS's powers as representative of the wider social impacts of leaks. It is the perception of this as negative that misconstrues 'privacy', invalidating the 'middleman' status of the NHS as 'information guardian' and blocking the legitimate enactment of its duties of safeguarding information to facilitate 'positive freedoms'. *Ashworth*[54] held that duties were owed by two parties who dealt with medical records: the patient and the holder of records (NHS). This was accepted in *Ackroyd*, where '... the hospital was suing to safeguard the respect for the private lives of *all* its patients';[55] hence, 'the Article 8 rights of those individuals require consideration'.[56] Despite being positioned as 'an unwarranted extension of the powers of State bodies such as NHS Trusts',[57] it would be more appropriately placed as a missed opportunity to extend *Z v Finland*,[58] which failed to support the extension of Article 8 to third party (State) sponsored litigation

---

routinely informed, although patients are encouraged to allow this. There was a legal challenge to this practice at the time of the initial HIV outbreak. For reasons of public good it was agreed that patients could not stop reporting of this condition. This has allowed a tracking of the progress of the condition. Likewise, The Health and Social Care Act 2008 allows exemption to consent to be sought through review by the NIGB, for example for a national audit for a disease such as diabetes where without a survey of GP records, an accurate picture cannot be gained from other sources. The survey must be as representative as possible; therefore a s. 251 application would be made.

52 www.hscic.gov.uk/article/3715/Building-confidence-in-the-use-of-information.

53 *Ackroyd v Mersey Care NHS Trust* (No.2) [2006] EWHC 107 97.

54 *Ashworth Security Hospital v MGN Ltd* [2001] 1 WLR 515.

55 *Ackroyd v Mersey Care NHS Trust* (No.2) [2006] EWHC 107 97 (Tugendhat J).

56 Ibid. See also Mr Justice Tugendhat's reference to Hannover *v* Germany (2004) 16 BHRC 545 at [57].

57 R. Sandland, 'Case Comment: Freedom of the Press and the Confidentiality of Medical Records' (2007) *MLR* 405.

58 The relevance of Article 8 of the Convention was shown in *Z v Finland* where it was held that 'the protection of personal data not least medical data, is of fundamental importance to a person's enjoyment of his or her right to respect for private and family life as guaranteed by Article 8 of the Convention'.

in order to 'safeguard' those rights. *Ashworth* also discussed Article 8, holding that 'the protection of personal data, not least medical data, is of fundamental importance to a person's enjoyment of his right to respect for private and family life'. Although *Ackroyd*[59] and *Ashworth*[60] cited *Finland*[61] in support, the ECtHR's comments in *Finland* regarding the protection of health data were about a data subject attempting to prevent disclosure of information protected by *her own* right to privacy.

Case Study: The Importance of the HRA to Privacy

Regardless of case law, the European Convention of Human Rights (ECHR) represent rights of the citizen *against* the state, developed for the individual before the NHS's self-imposed 'information guardian' role masked this important role. Transparency and control must be offered to individuals so that they can exercise their individual rights, as any quasi-vicarious ability the NHS has to safeguard society's rights is only exercisable against individuals. Rougier J in *Ashworth* noted that the hospital owed no vicarious right of confidentiality to anyone besides Brady,[62] and that *Ashworth* was wrongly decided, invalidating the *'proxy-individual'* status of the NHS, despite arguments by theorists such as Fredman regarding 'positive duties' of the state.[63] Leith's[64] logic suggesting that

---

59 See note 52.

60 *Ashworth Hospital Authority v MGN Ltd.* [2002] UKHL29.

61 (1998) 25 EHRR 371.

62 *Ashworth Hospital Authority v MGN Ltd.* [2002] UKHL29 64 (Rougier J) using the concept developed by Lord Woolf in *Broadmoor Special Hospital Authority v* R [2000] QB 775, 26.

63 S. Fredman, Human Rights Transformed (OUP 2008). Its proponents in the philosophical domain are, among others, Ronald Dworkin and Joel Feinberg, and in the legal domain a related understanding of constitutional rights has been advocated by G. Letsas, 'Two Concepts of the Margin of Appreciation' (2006) 26 *OJLS* 705, 717. See also D. Oliver and J. Fedtke (eds), Human Rights and the Private Sphere (Routledge-Cavendish 2007) which provides a comprehensive comparative study of the horizontal effect of constitutional rights. For an argument to the effect that the different doctrinal devices employed in different jurisdictions are actually irrelevant for the substance of constitutional rights protection in the private sphere, see M. Kumm and V. Ferrerez Cornelia, 'What's So Special about Constitutional Rights in Private Litigation? A Comparative Analysis of the Function of State Action Requirements and Indirect Horizontal Effect' in A. Sajo and R. Uitz (eds), The Constitution in Private Relations (Eleven International Publishing 2005) 241.

64 P. Leith, 'The Socio-Legal Context of Privacy' (2006) 2 *Int. J. Law in Context* 105.

the social context of information and the rapidly changing digital environment render privacy expectations redundant and that legislation usually misses the mark[65] could be extended under the justification that the legislation's intention has been skewed by the NHS's self-imposed 'information guardian' role, invalidating individual rights and 'privacy'.

However, patients' confidentiality rights are not absolute, and patients should be made aware of this, because 'if you are going to put other people at risk you are not entitled to confidentiality'.[66] For example, addiction is private but has social implications. Therefore, privacy cannot be the dominant value in society,[67] where disclosure is part of a social process, rendering privacy's status as a 'fundamental right' misleading. Letham J, for example, acknowledged that 'the majority of patients would ... be unconcerned[68] ... and that the courts have paid more attention to the needs of the hypersensitive than theoretical issues'[69] in *R v Department of Health ex p Source Informatics Ltd.*[70] Moreover, proactive groups are uninformed,[71] having limited access to the ICO and limited knowledge of Data Protection Act breaches, with only reactive redress through the HRA or common law. As Wacks[72] highlights, privacy remains undefined as a legal concept;[73] therefore, judicial entrenchment simply reinforces a hollow concept, barring valid communication of information whilst allowing data leaks. This mindset can be reversed by adequately representing the balance of individual

65 Ibid.

66 See National Treatment Agency for Substance Misuse, 'Confidentiality and Information Sharing' (September 2003).

67 B. Moore, *Privacy: Studies in Social and Cultural History* (M E Sharpe 1984) 274.

68 Information Commissioners' Office, 'Who Cares About Data Protection? Data Protection Act: Segmentation Research' (2003) 12. The ICO emphasises privacy concerns but most individuals appear unconcerned. Only 1 per cent of the population alter their behaviour to protect privacy; for example there were only three respondents to the Cabinet Office's consultation on data sharing yet data protection law adversely affects consumers. In medical records, 'privacy' renders intelligence worthless. For example, registration for cancer registry research falling below 95 per cent would make registries worthless.

69 [1999] 4 All ER [185] (Letham LJ).

70 Ibid.

71 L. Bergkamp, 'The Privacy Fallacy: Adverse Effects of Europe's Data Protection Policy in an Information-Driven Economy' (2002) 18 *Computer Law and Security Review* 1.

72 R. Wacks, 'Private facts: Is Naomi Campbell a Good Model?' (2004) 3(1) *SCRIPT-ed* 460.

73 This was established in *Campbell v MGN Ltd* [2004] UKHL 22, [2004] 2 AC 457 where the House of Lords failed to clarify privacy as a legal concept.

privacy versus collective transparency as complementary in nature. The vehicle for this must be considered with a clear view of the inadequacies of the previous vehicle (the NHS as a 'proxy-individual' making decisions on behalf of individuals), recognising that whilst privacy is a personal, subjective concept, the public benefits of disclosure are necessarily objective.

The problem with 'the law'

This has been recognised by the common law, but the common law is almost entirely inaccessible to the average patient on the street. How would they know what takes precedence at any given time? And what can they do about it? There is no certainty about the outcome of a set of circumstances and individuals do not know about it until something goes wrong and their confidentiality is breached. Because of the common law 'mystery', the simple solution for many is to concentrate on the Data Protection Act as it is tangible and comparatively easy to understand. However, it suffers from two issues. The first is that while it is necessary to abide by the Data Protection Act and its principles, doing so may not be sufficient. As a healthcare provider you might not realise that the Act is just one layer of governance. A care provider could comply completely with the Data Protection Act but still breach confidentiality or privacy. The second key issue is around roles and responsibilities imposed by the Data Protection Act. The data subject – the patient – has an almost dormant role, with only the retrospective rights to see what is recorded in the record (a section 7 DPA access to record request) and who has accessed their information (a section 7 subject access request). They can be charged (usually up to £50) for both. Surely this is entirely the wrong starting point. Who actually owns the information about the patient? The key players are the data controller and the data processor. The data controller must register with the Information Commissioner's Office and must determine the purposes for which, and the manner in which, any personal data are, or are to be processed. The data processor, in relation to personal data, means any person (other than an employee of the data controllers) who processes the data on behalf of the data controller. They are not directly subject to the DPA. The Department of Health, GPs and the HSCIC are but a few of those who have been cited as the data controller in the NHS. This leaves an unhelpful gap as to who the data owner is.

Fair processing requirements

The gap is not only around who the data owner is, but also how they are informed about how their information is being processed. The Data Protection Act does not define fair processing notices but principle one dictates their use.[74]

---

74 Personal data shall be processed fairly and lawfully and, in particular, shall not be processed unless (a) at least one of the conditions in Schedule 2 is met, and (b) in

Fair processing notices are presently a precursor to securing the right to object, articulated by the Secretary of State for Health and dubbed 'the veto'.[75] However, there is a danger that the public could be flooded with multiple fair processing notices to the point that they become meaningless. There is therefore a need to establish one place where all fair processing notices – or the information that would be stored within them – are stored. That would mean that the public do not have to wait for information to be given to them about the processing of their information, but that they can proactively seek the information, should they feel the need.

Before disclosing confidential patient information for purposes not directly related to his or her care or treatment, there is currently a responsibility upon health professionals to consult with a patient wherever practicable. The Health and Social Care Act 2012 has diluted that responsibility to consult, at least in relation to any information that the Health and Social Care Information Centre requires health professionals to disclose. This is at odds with other moves to support an individual's involvement in decisions that affect them. Moreover, a responsibility to consult can be shown to be a procedural aspect of the fundamental right to respect for private and family life, as guaranteed by Article 8 of the European Convention on Human Rights.

The scope and nature of a procedural requirement for consultation can be revealed, at least partially, by considering the case law concerning disclosure in the area of criminality information sharing. If the Health and Social Care Act 2012 is to be adequately protected from a challenge for incompatibility with the ECHR, then practicable opportunities to provide information about the intended purposes of processing, and respect for any reasonable objection to information sharing and/or disclosure, must be recognised beyond those explicitly provided for by the 2012 Act. It is promising to see that the HCSIC has taken opportunity in its the Code of Practice on Handling Confidential

---

the case of sensitive personal data, at least one of the conditions in Schedule 3 is also met. This is the first data protection principle. In practice, it means that you must have legitimate grounds for collecting and using the personal data; must not use the data in ways that have unjustified adverse effects on the individuals concerned; must be transparent about how you intend to use the data and must give individuals appropriate privacy notices when collecting their personal data; handle people's personal data only in ways they would reasonably expect; and make sure you do not do anything unlawful with the data.

75 www.pulsetoday.co.uk/your-practice/practice-topics/it/patients-to-be-given-veto-over-their-data-being-shared-from-gp-records/20002754.article.

Information[76] to reassure the public that adequate levels of consultation should be preserved, consistent with proposed changes to the NHS Constitution.[77]

Informational Privacy in the NHS: Information

The Theoretical Ideal

The mindset and cultural issues around privacy highlighted above need to be addressed before moving onto issues relating to the information itself. The framework of privacy options within the 'MI information revolution' model provides us with a baseline upon which to assess the current theoretical role of individuals in protecting the 'privacy' of their information. There are some important roles which the MI information revolution model would potentially designate to the individual, including ownership, consent giving and recipient of recourse from breaches through the invocation of legislation. Theoretically, individuals should have the option to 'own' this information (with legal caveats),[78] and the NHS should use it to varying degrees with the permission of individuals.

The Theoretical Issue Now

Ironically, this theoretical ideal is currently reversed. The NHS has developed proactive technical security/privacy measures – 'IG controls' – which were developed for 'patient choice' – for example, 'sealing' of data items from the view of particular roles. However, they are not transparent enough for individuals to control them. Ironically, individuals are required to pay for access to their information through the Subject Access Request process,[79] as the NHS has interpreted the intent of the Data Protection Act[80] on behalf of all parties

---

76 http://systems.hscic.gov.uk/infogov/codes/cop

77 J. Grace and M. Taylor, 'Disclosure of Confidential Patient Information and the Duty to Consult: The Role of the Health and Social Care Information Centre' (2013) 21(3) *Med. L. Rev.* 20, 13.

78 It is recognised that legally the Secretary of State owns patient records but this prefers 'theoretically' to 'ownership' as control.

79 Subject Access Request processes include technical Information Governance controls that govern access control (Role Based Access Controls (RBAC)), Workgroups (WGs), Legitimate Relationships (LRs), Authentication (Registration Authority\ Smartcards), patient choice (Sealing, locking, s-flagging - whether to have a Summary Care Record (SCR) or not. See NHS CFH, 'Confidentiality' www.connectingforhealth.nhs.uk/systemsandservices/infogov/confidentiality.

80 See section 7 of the Data Protection Act.

involved. We argue that this should be unnecessary and individuals should always have transparent access to their data. In reality, lack of awareness around the ability to access and control health information coupled with stultifying complexity were epitomised in the underuse of HealthSpace, a portal that allowed patients access to their Summary Care Record (SCR). It facilitated some progress towards transparency, yet lack of publicity and high registration complexity[81] were blockers. Of the 150,000 HealthSpace basic account holders in 2010, only 39 completed registrations for the 'advanced account', which allowed access to (not control of) their SCR.[82] It is therefore of great concern that in the Greenhalgh report[83] regarding HealthSpace, information governance was viewed as a 'cumbersome, bureaucratic and intrusive'[84] blocker, causing 'unanticipated administrative workload'.[85]

We argue that ownership – without consent to share information confidentiality – is invalid. Moreover, without awareness or uptake of "read access", data protection through IG controls cannot be achieved, and without the safeguards achieved through IG controls, the NHS cannot claim to keep information 'confidential'. The Article 29 Working Party developed alongside the Data Protection Directive[86] advocates the 'specific' consent these IG controls offer. They sum up the current situation around 'privacy' of health records, stating: 'If (consent) is correctly used, consent is a tool giving the data subject control over the processing of his data. If incorrectly used, the data subject's control becomes illusory and consent constitutes an inappropriate basis for processing.'[87]

This lack of control devalues the DPA in terms of individual privacy protection because individuals lack the ability to detect infringements. Even

81 Ironically registration is an IG control in itself.

82 A. Dickinson, *Qinetiq*, 'A Fine Balance: Privacy in the Digital Society' (2010) (Digital Systems Knowledge Transfer Network) www.v3.co.uk/v3-uk/analysis/2004967/ uk- tougher-privacy-standards/page/1.

83 T. Greenhalgh, et al., 'The Devil's in the Detail: Final Report of the Independent Evaluation of the Summary Care Record and HealthSpace Programmes' (University College London 2010). Final Report' (2008) 6; www.ucl.ac.uk/openlearning/documents/;scrie2008.pdf.

84 Ibid.

85 D. Carlisle, 'IG "Major Block" on IT Projects' *eHealth Insider* (13 April 2011) www.ehi.co.uk/news/EHI/6805/ig-'major-block'-on-it-projects.

86 The Working Party on the Protection of Individuals with regard to the Processing of Personal Data, 'Article 29' Opinion on Consent. WP131 – Working Document on the processing of personal data relating to health in electronic health records (EHR) (13 July 2011), http://ec.europa.eu/justice policies/privacy/wpdocs/2011/wp187_en.pdf.

87 Ibid.

when individuals detect DPA breaches,[88] redress is only available through the ICO,[89] which is limited to ordering monetary sanctions. In '*What Price Privacy*',[90] the ICO lobbies for more powers, but currently, even with increased fining powers of up to £500,000, social engineers who wish to obtain 'private' information from the NHS can easily justify the financial risks that may result from such a breach. Likewise, the NHS could be incentivised not to report breaches as there is currently no single route to report such breaches. Regardless, at present individuals do not have the necessary access to determine how and by whom their data is being used to facilitate a complaint to the ICO until it is too late and a breach has occurred. The onus on explicit consent appears set to increase if the proposed new 'Data Protection Directive' is implemented, but this is still in the preliminary stages.[91] Consequently, secrecy surrounding illegitimate confidentiality (or confidentiality without consent) trumps the DPA in the area of health records. Is 'privacy' therefore lawless, or are individuals protected by the Human Rights Act?

Ironically, overenthusiastic application of the Human Rights Act means societal impacts of privacy have been systematically overlooked. Although on face value it may appear that the HRA provides privacy protection for an individual, its polarised application to protect the 'privacy' of the individual without considering the impact of privacy on society can actually have a negative impact on the individual. Overzealous application of *individual* rights through the HRA overshadows society's and other individuals' rights and societal good as a whole. Even though the autonomy-based HRA was developed for individuals, in this case to control their information, individuals have no power to choose to be autonomous due to the NHS's 'proxy-individual' role. Therefore, in reality, in the absence of the availability of informed choice around information sharing, rights expressed through the HRA have been used reactively to expand

88 Redress is available through the ICO specifically relating to the DPA, but an action can be brought by individuals under the HRA, or the common law duty of confidentiality.

89 Information Commissioner's Office.

90 R. Thomas, 'What Price Privacy: The Unlawful Trade in Confidential Personal Information' (ICO, May 2006), www.ico.gov.uk/news/current_topics/~/media/documents/library/Corporate/Research_and_reports/WHAT_PRICE_PRIVACY.pdf.

91 See European Commission, Brussels, 25.1.2012, COM(2012) 11 final 2012/0011 (COD) Proposal for a Regulation of The European Parliament and of the Council on the protection of individuals with regard to the processing of personal data and on the free movement of such data (General Data Protection Regulation). This is beyond the scope of this paper as it deals with the current state where the ethics of consent is discussed, not the mechanics.

individuals' 'privacy' protections at the expense of the public interest, thereby compromising individual privacy. In breach of confidence cases post the HRA, the test has moved from 'confidential' to 'private',[92] thereby resulting in an imbalance between individual privacy interests and societal interests as a whole. Such 'distortion'[93] of 'privacy' has supported the necessity of an independent tort of privacy.[94] Conversely, the right of individuals to exercise 'privacy' protection (whatever this means to them) can only be obtained through an initial loss of individual 'privacy' on a societal level. A decision needs to be made about what 'privacy' means to each individual. This will in most cases mean some disclosure in the interests of society, which in turn allows others to live autonomously.

Beyond the neglect of society's group 'privacy' interests, other affected individuals have been denied access to information through an overzealous reliance on the ECHR. The reasonable expectation test has broadened individual privacy protection in cases assessing 'best interests'[95] in the right to confidentiality, such as the *A v X*[96] ruling that disclosure of a non-party's confidential medical data would only be made in very exceptional situations. In *A v X*, Morland J stated that disclosure of genetic predispositions to a psychiatric condition would interfere with the third party's right to privacy under Art. 8 (HRA), which '… enables English judges to do justice in a way which was not previously open to (them)'. However, these words of Brooke LJ in *Cachia v Faluyi*[97] contrast with

92 T. Aplin, The Development of the Action for Breach of Confidence in a Post-HRA Era' (2007) IPQ 19. Courts no longer analyse the action for breach of confidence in the terms of the three-limbed test of Coco v Clark (Coco v A N Clark (Engineers) Ltd [1969] RPC 41). Rather, the key question is whether the information is 'private' and, if it is, an obligation of confidence arises. Courts will then engage in a balancing exercise between Article 8 and 10 of the ECHR.

93 See J. Caldwell, 'Protecting Privacy Post Lenah: Should the Courts Establish a New Tort or Develop Breach Of Confidence?' (2003) 26 *UNSWLJ* 90, 121; See also J Morgan, 'Privacy in the House of Lords, Again' (2004) 120 *LQR* 563; See R. Mulheron, 'A Potential Framework for Privacy? A Reply to Hello!' (2006) 69(5) *MLR* 679, 686.

94 Support includes: the emphasis on whether information is 'private' as opposed to 'confidential'; the falling away of the second requirement of Coco v Clark (Coco v A N Clark (Engineers) Ltd [1969] RPC 41). See R. Singh and J. Strachan, 'Privacy Postponed' (2003) *EHRLR* 11, 19.

95 See P. Sparks, 'The Impact of the Human Rights Act for Patients and Accident Victims' (2008) *JPIL* 97.

96 *A v X (Disclosure: Non-Party Medical Records)*[2004] EWHC 447, QBD.

97 [2001] EWCA Civ 998.

Lord Woolf's warning in *Daniels v Walker*[98] against overzealous reliance on the ECHR. We argue that such overzealous reliance has been replicated in cases of conflicting rights when divulging data about contagious diseases,[99] assessing the duty of confidentiality owed to a child,[100] and sharing medical records with health professionals when such sharing leads to mental distress,[101] all favouring the individual's privacy rights. Not only does individual privacy take precedence over an individual with a personal interest, in cases of societal interest, the identity of those infringing upon the privacy of other individuals is concealed by 'privacy'. When two 'social goods' are balanced, subjective assessment of the social good of freedom of the press[102] appears to override the social good of disclosing the sources of leaked health information. Therefore, journalists can legitimately leak medical records because public interest in the confidentiality of medical records is not 'sufficiently great'.[103] The Court of Appeal upheld the decision of the High Court[104] in *Ackroyd v Mersey Care NHS Trust (No.2),* the sequel to the High Court,[105] Court of Appeal[106] and House of Lords[107] decisions in *Ashworth v* MGN, involving the leaking of medical records to the *Mirror* by Ashworth hospital's patient records. When MGN disclosed the journalist's name rather than the initial source of the leak, Ashworth brought a further action, requiring 'A' to reveal his sources,[108] but at the trial, Tugendhat J held that public interest in favour of 'A' disclosing his source was not sufficiently compelling.

Therefore, when balancing two public interests (the media versus the public, whose health records are at risk) 'privacy', which is fiercely protected on an individual level, is diminished when it might affect the entire population's

98 [2000] 1 WLR 1382.

99 See London Borough Council v Mr and Mrs N (foster carers of the Child) (1), P (A Child by her Guardian Pauline Bennett) [2005] EWHC.

100 The duty of confidentiality owed to a child has also been decided in favour of the individual's privacy. See R (on the application of Axon) v Secretary of State for Health [2006] EWHC 37. See also Gillick v West Norfolk and Wisbech AHA [1986] AC 112.

101 Cornelius v De Taranto [2001] EWCA Civ 1511, QBD.

102 Through Articles 10 and 12 of the ECHR.

103 R. Sandland, "Freedom of the Press and the Confidentiality of Medical Records" (2007) *MLR* 400.

104 [2006] EWHC 107.

105 [2000] WL 3354.

106 [2001] 1 WLR 515.

107 [2002] UKHL 29.

108 [2007] EWCA Civ 101 at [4].

privacy. Lord Woolf in Ashworth[109] referred to the ECtHR's decision in *Goodwin v United Kingdom,*[110] where 'an overriding requirement in the public interest'[111] was deemed necessary to restrict press freedom. Therefore, the presumption is against disclosure of the source, the burden of proof is on those seeking disclosure, and the affected parties (society) would never know enough about the matter to seek it. If revealing the source of leaked medical data is not a pressing social need[112] when balanced against the rights of the press, one questions whether there is any understanding of the implications of individualistic interpretations of privacy in the courts.

Judicial priorities are further illustrated in the overruling of Rougier J's societal considerations in *Ashworth at first instance,* when discouraging further leaks was considered 'the most important'[113] reason for ordering disclosure.[114] Although theoretically this would not be a problem if technical IG 'access monitoring' controls revealed the source, *Ashworth*[115] and *Ackroyd*[116] highlight how such controls are not applied through business processes which are fit for purpose for individual privacy. Moreover, the mix of electronic and paper records, coupled with inadequate audit and access controls, could mean that potential sources cannot be effectively restricted, even to the 200 originally quoted.[117] To resolve related issues, Dame Fiona Caldicott's 2013 *Information*

---

109 *Ashworth Security Hospital v MGN Ltd* [2001] 1 WLR 515 38.

110 Goodwin *v* United Kingdom (1996) 22 EHRR123, 39.

111 See note 108.

112 *Ashworth Security Hospital v MGN Ltd* [2001] 1 WLR 515 29. Per Lord Woolf in Goodwin *v* United Kingdom (1996) 22 EHRR 123 at [62] 'The "necessity" for any restriction of freedom of expression must be convincingly established, there must be a "pressing social need" for disclosure, and any order must be proportionate to its aim.'

113 *Ashworth Security Hospital v MGN Ltd* [2001] 1 WLR 515 35.

114 Even in 2010 Sheik felt it necessary to emphasise the need for vigilance in accessing, storing and discussing PID. See A. Sheikh, 'Confidentiality and privacy of patient information and records: a need for vigilance in accessing, storing and discussing patient information' (2010) 16(1) *MLJI* 2.

115 *Ashworth Security Hospital v MGN Ltd* [2001] 1 WLR 515. In February 2007, the Court of Appeal upheld the decision of the High Court in Robin Ackroyd *v* Mersey Care NHS Trust (No.2).

116 Ackroyd *v* Mersey Care NHS Trust (No.2) [2006] EWHC 107. This case is the sequel to the decisions of the High Court, Court of Appeal and House of Lords in Ashworth v Mirror Group Newspapers *(MGN).*

117 The Department of Health, 'NHS Information Governance, Guidance on Legal and Professional Obligations' (September 2007).

Governance Review made the following recommendation in the report of April 2013,[118] but the ability to implement it was doubted by the government in their response of September 2013.[119] Therefore, at present the role of the individual in controlling information appears to be overlooked, when in fact this should be the driving force which shapes the complementary role of the NHS. However, continued emphasis on the NHS's responsibilities in consultations[120] contradicts the *Information Revolution's* goals to move away from

- information belonging to the system;
- patients merely receiving care;
- top-down information collection; and
- a culture in which information has been held close and recorded in forms that are difficult to compare.[121]

Informational Privacy in the NHS: Innovation

The Theoretical Ideal

The ideal use of innovation – or technology - would be for the NHS to put a secure infrastructure in place and for the patient to directly control the use of it. This would mirror what the Spanish government has started to do for access to patient information and that which the Alaskan state government has extended for the benefit of the community, as we have discussed in the previous chapter. Much like legislation, innovation should be a tool which is used as a vehicle for individuals to transparently see and exercise their rights through.

The Theoretical Issue Now

Conversely, innovation is currently used by clinicians on behalf of individuals, while most individuals remain unaware of this process. Technical IG controls

118 The Department of Health, 'Information: To Share or Not to Share? Government Response to the Caldicott Review' September 2013 www.gov.uk/government/uploads/system/uploads/attachment_data/file/251750/9731-2901141-TSO-Caldicott-Government_Response_ACCESSIBLE.PDF

119 Ibid.

120 See for example Department of Health, Liberating the NHS: An Information Revolution (2010), http://consultations.dh.gov.uk/information-revolution/information revolution.

121 Ibid.

are not necessarily what the patient would expect. Even if EHRs were fully implemented, insights from case law show us that practical application of IG controls is not always intuitive. For example even if individuals give consent for their records to be used by people with 'legitimate relationships', they may not expect that this translates to 'access control', allowing access for the figure of 200 (including support staff[122]) considered acceptable in *Ackroyd*.[123] If individuals were informed about this and decided to use their 'patient choice controls' to 'lock and seal' sensitive data about an embarrassing condition, the team who diagnosed the condition would seemingly already have access. The patient may have to suffer the further embarrassment of asking for the data to be 'locked', only to find that every clinician who attempted to access the record in question would be alerted to the fact that the patient had 'locked' medical information and may subsequently ask the patient for access. This would be less concerning if the 'access monitoring controls' were in operation, because if a patient did not consent to share information with a particular clinician and that clinician accessed the record, an alert would be raised to flag this to an IG officer, and it would be visible on audit trails. However, the original Care Record Guarantee (CRG)[124] commitment 11 which stipulated audit and alert functionality has subsequently been diluted to exclude legacy IT systems.[125]

However, back in the real world, operational functionality is dependent on business processes and information collected and analysed, as opposed to technical functionality. This invalidates IG controls somewhat, because the NHS does not have the power to mandate business processes, technical innovation

---

122 See A. Sheikh, 'Confidentiality and Privacy of Patient Information and Records: A Need for Vigilance in Accessing, Storing and Discussing Patient Information' (2010) 16(1) *MLJI* 2. Sheikh notes that 'There are at least 101,272 non-medical personnel working in NHS acute trusts in Britain that have access to confidential medical records' (p. 4). For further details of the IG controls see NHS CFH, 'NHS CFH IG Controls' www.connectingforhealth.nhs.uk/systemsandservices/infogov/confidentiality/choices

123 Ackroyd *v* Mersey Care NHS Trust (No.2) [2006] EWHC 107.

124 The CRG sets out the rules that govern how patient information is used in the NHS and what control the patient can have over this. It is based on professional guidelines, best practice and the law and applies to both paper and electronic records. Whilst it is not a legal document, the Guarantee can be used as the basis for a complaint.

125 CRG commitment 11 was termed: 'We will keep a record in the newer electronic record systems of anyone who has accessed a health record or added notes to it' until the 2011 version which has added 'Some of the older computer systems will only record who has accessed a record where they have made changes. Paper records only include where people have made notes in the record and not when someone looks at the record. See further NIGB, 'Care Record Guarantee', www.nigb.nhs.uk/pubs/nhscrg.pdf

and implementation features, whilst simultaneously the NHS's self-imposed 'information-guardian' role blurs accountability lines in these areas.

Conclusions

We argue that there must be a change of mindset around 'privacy', moving privacy from an individualistic concept to a concern for society. The balance required between 'individual privacy' and 'collective transparency' reflects this. Information within health records must be standardised and understandable and information must be controlled by the patient to the extent that they choose to do this. Online records are required to facilitate this. Likewise innovation needs to be used by the patient as an impartial vehicle to deliver this control – allowing the individual to control their own information and to use the autonomous laws as intended. At present technical controls within NHS information systems are designed for control by patients but are controlled by clinicians. The principle behind this is that when individuals have the choice of control they will be empowered to think of privacy in the correct way. They can make their own informed decisions by controlling information through innovation appropriately. It is purported to be self-propelling as individuals will see the societal benefit of sharing. It is suggested that it is the current secrecy surrounding 'privacy' that makes people suspicious of information sharing.

Chapter 4
The Practical Problem
Historical Role Reversal: Law and Technology as Vehicles with the Wrong Drivers

Introduction

In Chapter 3 we argued that there must be a change in the mindset around 'privacy', moving privacy from a proxy-individualistic concept to a concern for society. The crucial balance required between the focus on 'individual privacy' we see in the European Union and focus on 'collective' transparency' we see in the US approach reflects this. In this chapter we focus on the practical problem and highlight the historical role reversal, where law and technology are used as vehicles with the wrong drivers as a result of the role reversal.

We will discuss the irony inherent within the *Information Revolution* publications.[1] Even though they promise choice and control to patients, they do not consider repositioning the control of information by individuals as an enabler. We suggest that although the privacy framework per se is fit for purpose, the way in which information is governed renders it unfit for purpose. Therefore, the roles of the individual and NHS need to be reconsidered.

Symptomatic of the need to change mindsets is the fact that the government has released the publication entitled *An Information Revolution*[2] but articulated the revolution purely in terms of the choice and control of treatment and care. Underpinning the choice and control of treatment and care is the choice that patients should be able to exercise about who their health information is shared with. The patient could then see the societal value of sharing (controlling) their health information, which can help inform other people's choices about their care and can improve that care based on their experiences and reactions to medications and treatments.

---

1 The consultation period ran from 18 October 2010 to 14 January 2011and the Department of Health received 742 responses; www.gov.uk/government/uploads/system/uploads/attachment_data/file/216664/dh_129580.pdf.

2 Department of Health, Liberating the NHS: An Information Revolution (2010), see www.dh.gov.uk/en/Consultations/Closedconsultations/DH_120080.

This could extend to a personalised model for treatment, medication and aftercare, personalised by condition, thereby incidentally achieving the aim of the *Information Revolution*. For example, 'AW' a 45 year old man with diabetes and asthma, living in the south east of England, with allergies to steroids could share information about his doctor, change of medication – both preventative and reactive – and share details of recovery time and benefits so that other men in his age range with a similar condition and allergies can look at AW's experience alongside hundreds of others to see what statistically would provide the best outcome for them.

This chapter illustrates that the legal and policy framework to enable this choice and control in a practical sense is fit for purpose. It is the way that it is governed by the NHS in practice that renders it unfit for purpose. This essentially highlights two fundamental issues: Firstly, the NHS assumes a paternal 'proxy' individual role which means the role of the individual is masked so they cannot enforce autonomy based laws; and secondly, 'confidentiality' is the ruling concept which governs the legal processing of health data, but it is not currently always underpinned by the consent of the patient so is often illegitimate. In our view, these two points are intertwined and would benefit from a full exploration of the role of consent in confidentiality. This chapter places this argument into real life examples by outlining the technical information governance controls designed for individuals, which are being exercised by the NHS through technology in systems that contain patient information. The laws and policy direction that underpin the information governance controls are also outlined.

Inherent Irony of the Information Revolution

Fully informed express consent, whereby the person is given full information and their agreement is written down is ideal. However, in reality, this is not common practice. While 'express or explicit consent' should be fairly apparent, the notion of 'implied consent' arises from interpretation of an action indicating at least concurrence if not active endorsement. In a clinical setting, rolling up one's sleeve in response to being asked about an injection would not be an explicit consent, but would be reasonable grounds for implied consent to having an injection. But what exactly is *informed* consent? We argue that to be fully informed, it is necessary to:

- have been given all relevant information about the options: purpose of use, consequences of exercising the option or of not exercising that option; further or subsequent options that may be possible; whether one can change one's mind and, if so, what the consequences will be (it may not be possible to undo the sharing of information after permission is given);

- have understood all the information given;
- apply that information in one's own circumstances;
- decide which option is the best in whatever terms one uses to make the decision (being as selfish or altruistic as one wants to be);
- communicate that choice, and any caveats or conditions to whomever presents the choice, by language, signs, or actions;
- be sure that the choice has been communicated effectively; and
- have some record or remembrance of the event/choice for the future.

Even if we accept informed consent should be a desirable goal, pragmatic reasoning stresses the circumstantial difficulties of fully respecting autonomy in clinical situations.[3] Being able to give consent also depends on the individual being competent and this is much easier to judge in a human relationship than online. Consent can only be given where a person is competent to do so – they may be unconscious, mentally disturbed (either temporarily or permanently), or lack sufficient awareness and understanding to be able to make a proper decision in their own best interests – this will apply to younger children. In an emergency, a clinician is expected simply to act in the patient's best interests, though not against their previously expressed wishes, unless there is some indication that their wishes might have changed. The Mental Capacity Act 2005 sets out some principles around capacity which must be applied to decisions around whether an individual can control their information:

- A person must be assumed to have capacity unless it is established that she or he lacks capacity.
- A person is not to be treated as unable to make a decision unless all practicable steps to help her or him to do so have been taken without success.
- A person is not to be treated as unable to make a decision merely because she or he makes an unwise decision.
- An act done, or decision made, under this Act for or on behalf of a person who lacks capacity must be done, or made, in her or his best interests.
- Before the act is done, or the decision is made, regard must be had to whether the purpose for which it is needed can be as effectively achieved in a way that is less restrictive of the person's rights and freedom of action.

---

3 M. Kottow, 'The Battering of Informed Consent' (2004) 30 *J. Med. Ethics* 565–569; see also M.D. Kirby, 'Informed Consent: What Does It Mean?' (1983) 9 *J. Med. Ethics* 69–75.

However, the Mental Capacity Act 2005 illustrates that the legal test for 'lacking capacity'[4] and for 'best interests' of the patient is heavily biased towards the autonomous decision making of individuals who are deemed to be capable of expressing choice. Ironically, the Act does not give a clear definition of 'best interests', it instead outlines the factors that need to be considered when you are trying to make a decision on behalf of someone else. These factors (known as the statutory checklist and outlined in section 4 of the Act)[5] try to bring together all the relevant information that will enable you to make the best decision for the

---

4 Section 2 of the Mental Capacity Act 2005: for the purposes of the Act, a person lacks capacity in relation to a matter if at the material time he is unable to make a decision for himself in relation to the matter because of an impairment of, or a disturbance in the functioning of, the mind or brain. It does not matter whether the impairment or disturbance is permanent or temporary. A lack of capacity cannot be established merely by reference to (a) a person's age or appearance, or (b) a condition of his, or an aspect of his behaviour, which might lead others to make unjustified assumptions about his capacity. In proceedings under the Act or any other enactment, any question whether a person lacks capacity within the meaning of the Act must be decided on the balance of probabilities.

5 Section 4 of the Mental Capacity Act 2005: in determining for the purposes of this Act what is in a person's best interests, the person making the determination must not make it merely on the basis of (a) the person's age or appearance, or (b) a condition of his, or an aspect of his behaviour, which might lead others to make unjustified assumptions about what might be in his best interests. The person making the determination must consider all the relevant circumstances and, in particular, take the following steps: He must consider (a) whether it is likely that the person will at some time have capacity in relation to the matter in question, and (b) if it appears likely that he will, when that is likely to be. He must, so far as reasonably practicable, permit and encourage the person to participate, or to improve his ability to participate, as fully as possible in any act done for him and any decision affecting him. Where the determination relates to life-sustaining treatment he must not, in considering whether the treatment is in the best interests of the person concerned, be motivated by a desire to bring about his death. He must consider, so far as is reasonably ascertainable (a) the person's past/present wishes and feelings (and any relevant written statement made by him when he had capacity), (b) the beliefs and values that would be likely to influence his decision if he had capacity, and (c) the other factors that he would be likely to consider if he were able to do so. He must take into account, if it is practicable and appropriate to consult them, the views of (a) anyone named by the person as someone to be consulted on the matter in question or on matters of that kind, (b) anyone engaged in caring for the person or interested in his welfare, (c) any donee of a lasting power of attorney granted by the person, and (d) any deputy appointed for the person by the court, as to what

person. It seems odd that in health this information gathering is not facilitated, even when the individual is competent.

In a similar vein of contradiction, the law, society, and many mental health professionals generally presume that children,[6] by virtue of their age, lack competence to make information sharing decisions. However, the *Oxford Radcliffe Confidentiality Guidelines* contradict this:

> The parental right to determine whether or not a child below the age of 16 will or will not have medical treatment terminates if and when the child achieves sufficient understanding and intelligence to enable him to understand fully what is proposed. We urge the reader to note that 'Gillick competence' relates to the particular child and the particular treatment, and there have been cases where a 17-year-old has been found insufficiently competent to refuse medical treatment, while in other cases much younger children have been deemed sufficiently competent. In addition, where a child is 16 or 17 either parent or child can consent to treatment independently (though neither can override the other or exercise a veto). The court can, however, override the wishes of both where treatment is vital to the child's welfare.[7]

The *Access to Health Records Act 1990* complicates the picture further by allowing a child under 16, deemed 'Gillick competent' by a doctor, to veto the parent's access to medical information held by that doctor, even though the parent can consent to treatment which the child cannot reject. However, it is for the doctor to decide whether or not an individual child is 'Gillick competent' or not. The courts are generally reluctant to do so. To add to the complexity, there

---

would be in the person's best interests and, in particular, as to the matters mentioned in subsection (6). The duties imposed by subsections (1) to (7) also apply in relation to the exercise of any powers which (a) are exercisable under a lasting power of attorney, or (b) are exercisable by a person under this Act where he reasonably believes that another person lacks capacity. In the case of an act done, or a decision made, by a person other than the court, there is sufficient compliance with this section if (having complied with the requirements of subsections (1) to (7)) he reasonably believes that what he does or decides is in the best interests of the person concerned. 'Life-sustaining treatment' means treatment which in the view of a person providing health care for the person concerned is necessary to sustain life. 'Relevant circumstances' are those (a) of which the person making the determination is aware, and (b) which it would be reasonable to regard as relevant.

6 G.P. Koocher, and P.C. Keith-Spiegel, P.C., *Children, Ethics, and the Law: Professional Issues and Cases* (University of Nebraska Press 1990).

7 Oxford Radcliffe Confidentiality guidelines; http://confidential.oxfordradcliffe.net/Gillick; Gillick v West Norfolk and Wisbech AHA (1986) AC112 HL.

are the Fraser guidelines,[8] which are concerned only with contraception and focus on the desirability of parental involvement and the risks of unprotected sex.[9] These three subjective assessments of competency to give consent for information sharing highlight the practical problems which need to be addressed in any type of online consent or objection management tool such as the MI Information Revolution Model we have suggested in Chapter 3.

However, regardless of the capacity to provide consent, the Department of Health's Confidentiality Code of Practice[10] includes the strap line 'no surprises', which on face value is commendable. Patients must be made aware that the information they give may be recorded, shared in order to provide them with care, and used to support clinical audit and other work to monitor the quality of care provided. If patients would be surprised to learn that their information was being used in a particular way, then they are not being effectively informed. This is quite subjective and varies from person to person, so we argue that this information needs to be readily available to the public, rather than placing a duty on all caregivers. To provide an indication of the onerous and subjective nature of the 'no surprises' requirement, the list below provides an indication of what staff must do in order to inform patients properly.

- Check, where practicable, that information leaflets on patient confidentiality and information disclosure have been read and understood. These should be available within each NHS organisation.
- Make clear to patients when information is recorded or health records are accessed.
- Make clear to patients when they are or will be disclosing information with others.

---

8 The Fraser guidelines refer to the guidelines set out by Lord Fraser in his judgement of the *Gillick* case in the House of Lords.

9 See R. Wheeler, "Gillick or Fraser? A Plea for Consistency over Competence in Children' (2006) 332 *BMJ* 807; R. Taylor, 'Reversing the Retreat from Gillick? R (Axon) v Secretary of State for Health' (2007) 19(1) *CFLQ* 81–97; see also S.P. DeCruz, 'Parents, Doctors and Children: the Gillick Case and Beyond' (1987) *J. Soc. Welfare L.* 93–108; Children's Legal Centre, 'Landmark Decision for Children's Rights' (1985) 22 *Childright* 11–18.

10 Health and Social Care Information Centre, 'Code of practice on confidential information, Good practice guidance for organisations collecting, analysing, publishing or otherwise disseminating confidential information concerning, or connected with, the provision of health services or adult social care in England' (December 2014), http://systems.hscic.gov.uk/infogov/codes/cop.

- Check that patients are aware of the choices available to them in respect of how their information may be disclosed and used.
- Check that patients have no concerns or queries about how their information is disclosed and used.
- Answer any queries personally or direct the patient to others who can answer their questions or other sources of information.
- Respect the rights of patients and facilitate them in exercising their right to have access to their health records.

When viewed in the similar context, 'fair processing'[11] is another important, yet onerous requirement, which the *Caldicott Review* recommended as one of the three key issues that need to be improved across the health and social care system.[12] We argue that if in 2015 Dame Fiona Caldicott still needs to emphasise the requirement for these to be carried out properly, a fundamental shift is required – one that ensures that people are not left helpless waiting to be drip fed how their information might be used but instead that they can proactively log onto a system to see for themselves which notices they are interested in.

This all amounts to a need for processes to allow control and choice directly for individuals about the sharing of their information. We argue that 'opt-in' or 'opt-out' processes administered by the NHS do not allow real control for the individual. 'Opt in' or 'opt out' is an unnecessary governance

11 The Data Protection Act 1998 requires that 'Personal data shall be processed fairly and lawfully' – In determining for the purposes of the first principle whether personal data are processed fairly, regard is to be had to the method by which they are obtained, including in particular whether any person from whom they are obtained is deceived or misled as to the purpose or purposes for which they are to be processed [therefore the emphasis is on 'not deceiving' as opposed to simply 'informing']; and: (a) the identity of the data controller, (b) if he has nominated a representative for the purposes of this Act, the identity of that representative, (c) the purpose or purposes for which the data are intended to be processed, and (d) any further information which is necessary, having regard to the specific circumstances in which the data are or are to be processed, to enable processing in respect of the data subject to be fair unless: (a) that the provision of that information would involve a disproportionate effort, or (b) that the recording of the information to be contained in the data by, or the disclosure of the data by, the data controller is necessary for compliance with any legal obligation to which the data controller is subject, other than an obligation imposed by contract.

12 See also: ICO: (2002) Use and Disclosure of Health Data; http://cryptome.org/use-and-disclosure-of-health-data.pdf.

layer that circumvents the true intention of privacy laws. An 'opt-in' consent process means that no action (or only some default action) will be taken unless a person positively agrees. In the case of 'opt-out' consent processes, the suggested action will take place unless the person actively objects. The latter is sometimes treated as 'implied consent', which we argue has no place outside of information sharing for direct care. There is a key question of what the consequences are for those who express no choice: Is the result likely to be beneficial? Having an 'opt-in' system might deprive people of benefits that might otherwise ensue – which may be worse than the possible sense of outrage felt by a few key campaigners. Meanwhile, having an 'opt-out' system could deprive those other than the most informed of the control of their information. Despondently, this is a point of ethics that often doesn't enter into the equation.

In legal terms, there is only definitively 'consent' where the person has made some indication of their choice – if they are told inaction will result in a certain option being applied, then their consent might be implied by inaction as a reason for proceeding, but is not defensible in court. 'Implied consent' is not recognised in law. In practical terms this will end up being a decision based on a balance of interest. However, when it is left in the hands of the NHS, the clinician or NHS manager, with the best will in the world they cannot always take into account the individual's choice. In today's geographically mobile community, they often do not know enough about the individual in question to make that decision.

Information Governance Controls

We therefore currently have the less than optimal situation where technical information governance controls designed for individuals are being exercised by the NHS through technology in systems that contain patient information. The foundations are therefore in place and they reflect the law and commitments to patients, so they are an asset waiting to be optimised by the public.

However the task of converting this to something the public can consume should not be underestimated. The onset of the use of technology to store and share information whilst other sharing parties still use paper records makes this complex. Coupled with the application of the overlapping laws and legislation, this creates a difficult situation. It has resulted in an issue that clinicians or managers need to apply a layer of interpretation by controlling technical controls. Therefore they make the real time decisions and have control of the technical audit trail. However, clinicians and managers are not expected to be legal experts so how do they ensure they have a legal basis for their information sharing choices? They have one tool – 'the IG Toolkit' which pulls together the relevant laws, policies and professional obligations necessary for organisations to show they are compliant with 'information governance' controls. The length of this list[13] illustrates how overwhelming the different laws and obligations can be to a professional or clinician who needs to be aware of all of these and then make an information sharing decision, taking into account the wishes of the individual.

Ethics plays a big part in the decision making process. When combining something so subjective with a technical 'command' it is difficult to use the 'apply to all' logic that technical rules demand. Nonetheless, there is a set of technical IG controls that are designed to enforce the laws, policies and rights of individuals in relation to privacy. The technical controls applied to systems that hold patient information include 'legitimate relationships', 'access control', 'authentication' and 'patient choice'. They implement the Human Rights Act, Article 8 right to a private life and reflect the Data Protection Act Principles and Care Record Guarantee. Each will be discussed below, but Table 4.1 aims to contextualise them at a high-level.

It should be noted that 'Information Governance' and the controls[14] to protect patient information require a mixture of the triad of security qualities: confidentiality, integrity and availability. This means ensuring the information is available at the point of care, that integrity is maintained so that the content can be relied upon to make clinical decisions and ensuring that it is kept confidential, so that only those with a need to know can see the data. It is important that in practical terms none of these three elements are undermined. Real life tragic examples help to illustrate their impact in isolation, similarly the impact of elements of all three being undermined can be catastrophic.

Breaching confidentiality would most likely result in a lack of trust between the doctor and patient, which might result in a monetary fine or striking off of the professional register for a clinician. More importantly it could lead to a breakdown in the 'confiding' relationship between a patient and their clinician which might mean that vital pieces of information are not disclosed due to fear

---

13 There is a range of complex legal and professional obligations that limit, prohibit or set conditions in respect of the management, use and disclosure of information and, similarly, a range of statutes that permit or require information to be used or disclosed. It is beyond the scope of this book to provide a comprehensive list of all the laws and regulatory obligations that has to be followed. See Department of Health, NHS Information Governance Guidance on Legal and Professional Obligations (September 2007), www.gov.uk/government/uploads/system/uploads/attachment_data/file/200702/NHS_Information_Governance_Guidance_on_Legal_and_Professional_Obligations.pdf.

14 There are separate leaflets, explaining more about each of these 'IG controls'.

Table 4.1 Technical information controls

Real-life question aimed at clinicians	IG control
Am I who I say I am?	Registration and Authentication (Smartcard)
What types of clinical data may I access and can I update it?	Role Based Access Control (RBBAC)
Can I access Mrs Smith's clinical data?	Legitimate Relationships and Workgroups
Can Mrs Smith prevent her clinical data being shared outside her local GP?	Consent and Dissent to data sharing
Can Mrs Smith not have a Summary Care Record?	SCR Consent (including permission to view)
Can Mrs Smith protect parts of her clinical data from the view of other clinicians?	Patient 'sealed envelope'(also clinician sealed envelope), sometimes known as sealing and locking
Can I find out if someone has accessed Mrs Smith's records inappropriately?	Audit and Alerts

of them being repeated. This could have a negative impact upon an individual's safe and effective care. It could also mean that vital pieces of information needed to assess the quality of treatment for others are also missing. Breaking the integrity of the data can be equally as detrimental to safe and effective care. If a database holding patient data was hacked, an organisation/individual with malicious intent could change the medication dosage or type on a vulnerable person's prescription. The impact of this could be as serious as instant death. Similarly, a break in availability of the information could be tragic. If a patient presented at an accident and emergency unit was unable to communicate their allergies or medication for example, and the system that stored their patient record was not available, they could be given medication which they are allergic to and again this could result in (avoidable) death.

As these three elements are essentially about the importance of timely access to accurate information, there are some controls which can be applied at the technical front end to control access. These controls should regulate the availability elements in terms of which job roles the information should be available to – collectively known as 'access control'. To monitor that only those who should see the information are seeing it, there is a group of controls termed 'access monitoring'. Finally there is a set of controls named 'patient choice' which in theory allows patients to decide who can see which part of their record. Conversely, the majority of individuals are unaware of these controls, as they are controlled by clinicians on behalf of the individual. We therefore assert that these are excellent provisions that have been put in place by the NHS; but, the communication of these provisions to the public should be improved. This should take the pressure off clinicians who have to administer them in an already constrained time slot when providing care is the clinician's priority.

The Care Record Guarantee[15] contains these rights for the individual and outlines the IG controls which should support the rights. We assert that this is an excellent tool to use for wider awareness and communication. Below we have provided an overview of the three areas of IG controls to outline just how Effective they could be, if the roles of the NHS and the individual were reversed so that the individual can control the technical controls, should they wish to. The current reversal is magnified by the use of technology as a solution in itself instead of being used as a vehicle to facilitate a solution to be administered by an individual.

Access Control

The end point of any information sharing decisions culminates in 'access control' identifying who can see what part of the care record. The term 'legitimate relationship' is used in the NHS both as a concept and as a technical control. Its significance as an important concept for validating information sharing decisions in direct care settings was reinforced in the *Caldicott Review*. Indeed, recommendation 2 of the report states: '*For the purposes of direct care, relevant personal confidential data should be shared among the registered and regulated health and social care professionals who have a legitimate relationship with the individual.*'[16]

The types of legitimate relationships in the NHS care record system IT applications which apply to clinicians or healthcare support workers (termed 'user' throughout) allocated to a particular work group include:

- Patient Referral Legitimate Relationships
- Patient Self-Referral Legitimate Relationships
- Patient Registration Legitimate Relationships
- General Practice Registration Legitimate Relationships
- Subject Access Request Legitimate Relationships
- Patient Complaint or Litigation Legitimate Relationships
- Expressed Patient Consent to Access Legitimate Relationships and
- Court Order or Other Legal Demand Legitimate Relationships.

---

15 'The Care Record Guarantee, Our Guarantee for NHS Care Records in England' (NIGB January 2011), http://webarchive.nationalarchives.gov.uk/20130513181011/http://nigb.nhs.uk/pubs/nhscrg.pdf.

16 Department of Health, 'Information: To Share or Not To Share? The Information Governance Review' (March 2013).

Two types of Legitimate Relationship enable a single NHS care record system user to gain access to a patient clinical record:

- Self-Claimed Legitimate Relationships and
- Colleague-Granted Legitimate Relationships.

'Access control' is underpinned by both the duty of confidence owed to a patient which invokes the common law duty of confidentiality and the Data Protection principles.[17] This is of course laudable and necessary but not necessarily sufficient. Although such controls can be underpinned by static Data Protection Principles, the Human Rights Act right to a private family life is much more subjective and multi-dimensional, so must therefore be underpinned by choices of the individual.

Patient Referral Legitimate Relationships

When a patient is referred, for example from a GP to an outpatient service in a hospital, it implies that a relationship exists between the patient and those staff providing the outpatient service, which justifies access to the patient's clinical record. When a referral like this is recorded within the NHS care record system, a 'Patient Referral Legitimate Relationship' will be created between the patient and the workgroup of staff providing the outpatient service. Patient Referral Legitimate Relationships are created automatically by the NHS care record service as a result of many different types of referrals and service requests, such as

- a referral between consultants in a hospital;
- a request for a laboratory test;

---

17 Principle 1: Personal data shall be processed fairly and lawfully and, in particular, shall not be processed unless (a) At least one of the conditions in Schedule 2 is met, and (b) In the case of sensitive personal data, at least one of the conditions in Schedule 3 is also met. Principle 2 Personal data shall be obtained only for one or more specified and lawful purposes, and shall not be further processed in any manner incompatible with that purpose or those purposes. Principle 3 Personal data shall be adequate, relevant and not excessive in relation to the purpose or purposes for which they are processed. Principle 5 Personal data processed for any purpose or purposes shall not be kept for longer than is necessary for that purpose or those purposes. Principle 7 appropriate technical and organisational measures shall be taken against unauthorised or unlawful processing of personal data and against accidental loss or destruction of, or damage to, personal data.

- booking an appointment for a patient from a radiology service;
- an admission to a hospital ward; and
- a referral made by a social worker to a community mental health service.

A Patient Referral Legitimate Relationship can be applied in any situation where a member of staff requests a service from another member of staff or team on behalf of a patient (or service user).[18] The *Caldicott Report* found evidence that these types of referrals to support direct care are generally expected by patients and they would be surprised if they did not happen.

Example scenario

An IT application accepts referrals on behalf of the oncology unit in a hospital. The oncology unit has been configured as an application artefact into the application under the name 'Oncology Unit'. The application has also been configured with the workgroup 'Oncology WG' mapped to 'Oncology Unit' for Legitimate Relationship creation purposes. The IT application receives a referral for Mrs White through the Choose and Book appointment making IT system. It puts Mrs White on its patient list for 'Oncology Unit' and creates a referral LR between Mrs White and 'Oncology WG' so that when she arrives at the Oncology Unit the staff can treat her properly as they will have access to her record.

Mr Green, Mr Blue and Mrs Pink have previously been referred into the unit and also been recorded in a similar manner by the IT application. Mr Black, a consultant on the oncology team has been made a member of 'Oncology WG'. This workgroup is therefore recorded in his User Role Profile.

Mr Black logs onto the application and attempts to access the patient list, which consists of the patients identified above. The application can now make the single inference that all of the patients on the list have an LR with Mr Black as follows: It knows that each of the patients has an LR with 'Oncology WG' because when they were put on the patient list for 'Oncology Unit', it created an LR for each of them with 'Oncology WG' that was appropriate for their treatment during the period they are on the list. It knows that Mr Black is a member of 'Oncology WG' because this workgroup is identified in Mr Black's current logon user role profile. Therefore Mr Black has a legitimate relationship with each of the patients on the list through their referral Legitimate Relationships with 'Oncology WG'.

We suggest that this is an appropriate IG control for the clinician or care worker to administer but that the patient should see that it exists and be able to check all legitimate relationships periodically as a way to verify and validate their information sharing choices.

---

18 Below is a simple example of how this would work in operation: An application accepts referrals on behalf of the oncology unit in a hospital.

Patient Self-Referral Legitimate Relationships

When a patient attends an accident and emergency service, this can be considered a self-referral. In normal circumstances, a patient is registered by the accident and emergency service as soon as they enter the department. A clerk will record the patient's identifying details, such as name and address, and try to find the record for the patient. Recording the accident and emergency attendance causes the NHS Care Record System to automatically create a Self-Referral Legitimate Relationship with the patient, and that enables the clinical staff (such as the doctors and nurses) to view the patient's clinical record. In an emergency situation, where a patient has lost consciousness, a self-referral is implied, and so the same type of Legitimate Relationship can be created. This is the type of IG control where we assert that it is firmly in the best interests of the patient for this to be administered on their behalf.

There are other circumstances where patients can self-refer to a service, and this is where the patient's control of their records can result in better care. For example, when attending a walk-in clinic, a sexually transmitted disease clinic, or the birth of a new baby, which are all considered examples of a self-referral, a Patient Self-Referral Legitimate Relationship can be created automatically by the NHS Care Record Service between the patient and a group of staff providing the service. Here the patient should be able to activate this if they wish and to see who can see which part of their record and for what reason.

Patient Registration and General Practice Registration Legitimate Relationships

When a patient registers with a new general practitioner, a General Practice Registration Legitimate Relationship between the patient and the practice is created. For the period that the patient stays registered with the practice, the GPs and nurses who are members of the Workgroup for the practice will be entitled to access relevant parts of the patient's clinical records by using the Legitimate Relationship that was created when the patient registered. There are times when administrators working in a general practice need access to limited clinical information about the patient, and so the Legitimate Relationship created at registration must enable access to the whole practice team (workgroup). For example, a practice manager will make use of the Legitimate Relationship when issuing a repeat prescription because this requires access to a limited set of clinical information within the record of the patient receiving the prescription.

The average patient might not pre-empt this, but also may not object given the rationale, so in line with the 'no surprises' principle there should be an active campaign to make individuals aware of this. This would, for example, allow them to decide whether they would like administrative staff to have access to order repeat prescriptions or whether they would like to do this through the Electronic Prescription Service. We know that society will give up a considerable amount of privacy for convenience or incentives when we examine the number of people willing to have their behaviour tracked in exchange for a Tesco Clubcard,[19] for example.

Patient Registration Legitimate Relationships will be applied in the NHS Care Record Service to other situations such as registration with NHS dentistry, preventative health services, screening, and other situations where patients are added and removed from a well-defined, and long-term, registered service. The behaviour of these Patient Registration Legitimate Relationships will be equivalent to those created for general practice. We see no reason why, in the interest of transparency, the patients should not be offered the control to administer this themselves, should they wish to, but we assert that sharing information for this direct care purpose is the least controversial.

Subject Access Request Legitimate Relationships

Earlier we suggested that subject access requests should not be necessary as patients should be able to see what data an organisation holds on them without requesting it from a third party. Under the Data Protection Act 1998, a person, or someone acting for a person, is entitled to submit a 'subject access request' to an organisation that maintains 'personal data' about the person. The organisation receiving the subject access request must process the request within a set period of time and provide the subject of the request with a copy of all the personal data held within their record. A patient therefore may apply to their general practice, or other NHS organisation, and expect to be sent a copy of their record. In order to provide this, the organisation must be able to gain access to the patient's record through a Legitimate Relationship. In a general practice setting, this normally would be achieved through an existing Patient Registration Legitimate Relationship, but if the patient has left the practice, that Legitimate Relationship will have expired, and so a Subject Access Request Legitimate Relationship would be created. In a hospital setting, there may be a specific team of people who process subject access requests. That team would be defined as a Workgroup within the NHS Care Record Service, and a Subject Access Request Legitimate Relationship would be created automatically with that Workgroup whenever a subject access request is received. This Legitimate

19 Jason Turner, *Do Tesco Customers Exhibit a Social Type of Loyalty towards Tesco and Tesco Clubcard? A Critical Analysis of the Nature and Type of Tesco Customer Loyalty* (VDM Publishing 2011).

Relationship gives the Workgroup access to the patient's record for just long enough to process the request. We argue that this is unnecessary in most cases and a waste of scarce NHS resources. Patients should be able to access their record online themselves in line with government commitments.

Patient Complaint or Litigation Legitimate Relationship

An example of where this would be extremely helpful to a patient is in the unfortunate circumstances when they have reason to complain. When a patient complains or begins litigation with respect to some aspect(s) of the service that they receive from an NHS organisation, their complaint must be investigated. In many cases, patients submitting complaints or beginning litigation against an NHS organisation do so because they are unhappy with the clinical care that they have received. This type of complaint can only be investigated properly if it is possible to see relevant information within that patient's clinical record. When such a complaint is received and recorded within the NHS Care Record System, a Patient Complaint or Litigation Legitimate Relationship will be set up automatically between the patient and the Workgroup processing the complaint until the case is closed when the NHS Care Record Service will terminate the Legitimate Relationship.

This type of Legitimate Relationship will also be used to enable authorised investigations. If a member of staff becomes concerned that a colleague is not practising good clinical care, they may raise the issue with someone who has responsibility for clinical governance. That person will then have a duty to investigate the problem. This may require access to one or more patient records so that an assessment can be made of whether patient care was provided according to agreed standards. Access to the patients' records will be enabled through 'Patient Complaint or Litigation Legitimate Relationships'. A complainant might be happy with this, but they would have to be asked before, even if this is to ask generally if they would consent to their information being used to monitor performance. On the other hand the very subject of an individual's complaint might be about confidentiality so the individual might choose to compile the evidence themselves; the patient/complainant should at least be given the tools to exercise this option – primarily access to the audit trail of their data.

Court Order or Other Legal Demand Legitimate Relationship

We accept that there will be times when it is not appropriate for the individual to control such access. A court may demand information from a patient's clinical record. It is a relatively rare occurrence, but it will require someone from an NHS organisation to access the patient's clinical record. In these cases, a 'Court Order or Other Legal Demand Legitimate Relationship' will be established within the NHS Care Record Service between the patient and the Workgroup, thereby allowing relevant information to be accessed and extracted from the patient's record in order to satisfy the court. It may be necessary to gain access to the patient record for other legal reasons, although the need for this will be extremely rare.

Self-Claimed Legitimate Relationships

As the Legitimate Relationships above illustrate, the NHS Care Record Service Legitimate Relationships have laudably been designed to work 'behind the scenes', triggered automatically by patient events such as referrals. Occasionally, a care professional using the NHS Care Record Service may be denied access to the patient record because they have no existing Legitimate Relationship. However, they may have an urgent need to view the patient record and, if they have sufficient authorisation, they will be able to gain access to the patient's record through the creation of a 'Self-Claimed Legitimate Relationship'. This type of Legitimate Relationship expires after a few days.

Where a user of the NHS Care Record Service self-claims a Legitimate Relationship, they must justify their actions, and this justification will form part of an alert which is sent to the organisation to which the NHS Care Record Service user is accountable. The alert is sent to deter NHS Care Record Service users from self-claiming a Legitimate Relationship with a patient that they have no relationship with (and thus abusing their access privileges). If a member of staff self-claims a Legitimate Relationship without good reason, they will face disciplinary action, including possible dismissal. Only people in certain types of jobs will be entitled to create 'Self-Claimed Legitimate Relationships'. We assert that this is acceptable practice, but that the patient's access to the alert and audit trail, where appropriate, might help to break the suspicion around 'privacy' as a concept.

Colleague-Granted Legitimate Relationships

In some circumstances, a care professional might want to ask a colleague for a second opinion about a patient, rather than make a full referral, and will agree this with the patient. If the colleague is a member of the same Workgroup, then no new Legitimate Relationship need be created within the NHS Care Record Service. However, if the colleague works in a different Workgroup, he or she is unlikely to have a Legitimate Relationship with the patient. In such circumstances, the patient's doctor can create a 'Colleague-Granted Legitimate Relationship' to provide the colleague with access to the patient's clinical record. The Legitimate Relationship created will last for a short period only and will be between the patient and that colleague only (not the Workgroup the colleague belongs to) so that an audit trail is easy to investigate.

The care professional granting the relationship will only be able to do so if they already have a Legitimate Relationship with the patient, and that relationship must not have been self-claimed. This rule prevents a user of the NHS Care Record Service using their access privileges to self-claim a Legitimate Relationship in order to grant access to a colleague. It is reassuring to have this level of assurance and accountability but without the transparency for patients to know of this, due diligence it is wasted.

It would therefore be confidence-inspiring for the public to know that most types of Legitimate Relationship are created as a result of routine patient related events being recorded within the NHS Care Record Service, such as referrals and GP registrations. As the relationship between the patient and Workgroup providing a service to the patient changes, the status of the Legitimate Relationship changes. When a patient is discharged, the Legitimate Relationship is nearing its end, although the relationship does not end immediately. When a patient is discharged, the Legitimate Relationship remains active for a period of time to allow the patient's record to be updated, and then becomes inactive for a further period of time just in case there is any follow-up care by the care professional.

Authentication (Registration Authority/Smartcards)

There is further due diligence apparent when identifying healthcare professionals. In order to access national health IT systems and applications, healthcare professionals must be registered on 'the Spine'[20] (a set of national services used by the NHS CRS) and be issued with a 'Smartcard'.[21] The service responsible for managing and administering this process is known as the 'Registration Authority'.[22] The Registration Authority is responsible for identifying and granting appropriate access rights or profiles to users via their sponsors and issuing Smartcards to users.

Expressed Patient Consent to Access Legitimate Relationships

Moving away from direct care and into the indirect care domain we approach territory where we feel that there is most opportunity for patient control.

---

20 The Spine is part of the NHS Care Records Service www.bcf.nhs.uk/dl/8263_3711303609.pdf/as/.

21 Healthcare professionals and workers are required to use Smartcards for accessing NHS Care Records Service (NHS CRS) compliant applications.

22 Each NHS Trust has a Registration Authority (RA) that is responsible for ensuring that all aspects of Smartcard registration services and operations in the Trust are performed in accordance with Department of Health/NHS Policy, Procedure and Information Governance requirements, www.this.nhs.uk/our-services/registration-authority-smartcards/.

Researchers are able to gain access to anonymised patient information within the NHS Care Record Service through the Secondary Uses Service. Occasionally, research requires access to identifiable patient information ('Patient Confidential Data' or PCD) including clinical data. Access to NHS Care Record Service clinical records will be granted for research purposes if the patient has given explicit consent. When the patient's consent is recorded within the NHS Care Record Service, a new 'Expressed Patient Consent to Access Legitimate Relationship' will be set up between a patient and the Workgroup carrying out the research. These Legitimate Relationships last for the period of research or the period of consent granted by the patient (whichever is the shortest). This type of Legitimate Relationship can also be applied to other situations such as epidemiology and financial audit. We assert that individuals should be given the option to make informed decisions on all secondary uses at a time and place that suits them, rather than it being administered by a professional on their behalf.

Access Monitoring

As we have seen above, access controls are necessary for the successful control of the health service. We see scattered amongst the access control provisions, audit and alert provisions which allow for the transparency this book is calling for. The issue is that they are not yet visible to the public. Audit and alert tools are available when organisations are using the NHS Care Records Service so that they can meet the obligations identified in the NHS Care Record Guarantee. Every organisation is responsible for ensuring these commitments are adhered to. Several commitments are particularly relevant to audit and alert functionality. Although electronic tools have been developed to support the delivery of these commitments, it should be noted that the NHS Care Record Guarantee recognised that records are both electronic and manual and the Guarantee extends to all health records.

NHS Care Record Service Information Governance Alerts

NHS Care Record Service Information Governance Alerts are automatic messages that are generated in association with potentially inappropriate accesses to elements of the NHS Care Record Service patient information. They may be generated by clinicians or care staff accessing local IT applications, the Summary Care Record Application and other system suppliers that have integrated the Summary Care Record into their functionality. For example, alerts are generated whenever a clinician self-claims a legitimate relationship or overrides a patient's preference to dissent to share their information. When an alert message is received an email notification can be sent to an individual with the appropriate Role Based Access Control (RBAC) activity in their User Role Profile (URP).[23]

Whenever an unusual access is made to a patient's record in the NHS Care Record Service, a special message (an 'IG alert') is sent to an Information Governance Officer, who is responsible for checking such accesses are appropriate. They will review all such accesses. If it turns out that NHS staff have misused the access, then disciplinary action will be taken against them, and the individual to whom the data relates should be informed. However, we argue that this is too passive and an individual should know about this in real time by having access to their data. Examples of such unusual accesses include:

- self-claiming a Legitimate Relationship in order to access medical records;
- 'breaking a seal' to view information a patient has asked to be 'sealed' (kept protected from immediate view from NHS staff); and
- accessing a person's Summary Care Record without their permission (for example in the case of an emergency admittance to hospital).

In each case, the user is doing something unusual, but usually for a good reason, such as with the patient's permission. Otherwise it might be in an emergency or where legally required to do so. However, it needs to be checked that the circumstances justify this access. Therefore, an IG Alert does not necessarily mean that something has gone wrong, only that something out of the ordinary has taken place which should be investigated. A balance must be found between making an individual's record available when it is needed to provide treatment, and preventing access to anyone who does not have a good reason to look at it. IG Alerts help with this but this needs to be made visible to the patient to have maximum value.

Patient Choice

In the NHS Care Record System there are various aspects which support patient choice already. However, disappointingly, the patient does not control these – the clinician does. Examples include:

- whether to have a Summary Care Record (SCR): an electronic summary of the patient record, containing information about the medicines a patient takes, allergies they suffer from and any bad reactions to medication a

23 The email notification contains no patient or user identifiable information; it only states that an alert has been triggered and has been recorded in the TES for investigation.

patient has had. Having this information stored in one place makes it easier for healthcare staff to treat patients in an emergency setting or when a GP practice is closed) or not;

- whether or not to be asked at every point for permission to view the Summary Care Record;
- whether to prevent detailed care records from being shared (subject to other controls);
- whether to 'seal' or 'seal and lock' particular elements of a record from the view of users such as clinicians;
- whether to restrict the display of location-related details available through the Personal Demographic Service (PDS, 'S-flagging');
- to give express consent for particular groups to access their records for specific purposes (Express Patient Consent to Access 'Legitimate Relationships (LRs)'); and
- to opt out of use of their medical records for purposes other than direct care.

There are so many choices to be made it could be somewhat overwhelming if communicated without any context and there is no one place to communicate this.

Another feature of the consent system is the introduction of 'Sealed Envelopes'[24] to protect parts of a patient's record that the patient may feel are particularly sensitive and should not be shared outside the immediate clinical team. The patient could request this if they have conditions or a background that they do not want everyone to see, for example a HIV status. There may be statutory reasons for refusing a seal. A record is kept of sealing requests and refusals, so that a clinician can see any past history to help them fully understand the situation when dealing with a request.

An interesting and complex question arises around sealing of parts of children's or vulnerable adults' records and with it comes a whole new raft of ethical issues which we assert could be somewhat addressed through online interaction that provides information in a child-friendly or vulnerable adult-friendly way so that decision making can be shared or, depending on competency and age, the child can make their own information sharing

24 M. Oswald, 'Sealed Envelopes Briefing Paper: "Selective Alerting" Approach' (NHS 206), CfH document NPFIT-FNT-TO-IG-PRGMJT-0035, December 2006, at www.connectingforhealth.nhs.uk/crdb/sealed envelopes briefing v2 0.doc; Sealed Envelopes – Guiding Principles Document, NHS CfH document NPFIT-FNT-TO-REQ-DEL-0139, December 2006, at www.connectingforhealth.nhs.uk/crdb/sealed envelopes guidingprinciplesv1-0.doc.

decisions. Currently parents or guardians may request the sealing of a child or incompetent adult's record, but the decision is primarily the clinician's based on the patient's best interests. Depending on the version of the GP application, patients may be able to choose:

- whether to have a Summary Care Record or not;
- whether to have a full GP Summary uploaded or not (initially just current medication and allergies); and
- exactly what goes into the GP Summary – while few GP systems have any concept of 'sealing', the doctor can choose to omit items from the GP Summary, though this is a manual exercise.

The rationale for the Summary Care Record (SCR) is that a basic subset of the patient's health records is available to support unscheduled care (Accident and Emergency, Out-of-Hours, Walk-in Centres, etc.). While this is generally deemed a good idea, some people either have specific concerns about their records or have a more general fear of 'national databases', either from a surveillance viewpoint or from security concerns. While having an SCR should be good for the quality of care for a patient, it is not entirely necessary for unscheduled care – and often in the case of accidents, it may not be that helpful.

As more people have SCRs, clinicians will find it more useful and may change their practice to rely more on the presence of an SCR. This may mean that, while not having an SCR now may not offer much of a risk to most individuals, in the future it may delay treatment or mean that poorer treatment may be provided. That is to say the risks and benefits will change over time. The decision as to whether to have a Summary Care Record or not still persists without sufficient knowledge of how useful it might or might not be in the future. There is still some argument as to whether this is a legal right as opposed to a patient choice granted by the NHS; and hence as to whether opt in or opt out is appropriate. Some could invoke DPA section 10 (asserting that it is causing distress) to ask that it be removed, but one could argue that dislike of government databases is not 'distress' – however, the Information Commissioner would probably not find that having an SCR was necessary – albeit a good idea.

The Article 29 Data Protection Working Party consider that having an EHR is so important that one cannot freely consent to having one so it needs explicit support in law, which is sometimes quoted by campaigners as to why opt in is needed. It is understood that ETP (Electronic Transmission of Prescriptions) data is considered part of the SCR. There is a specific leaflet with a form for those considering opting out but we argue that these should not be issued in isolation and a portal looking at all options holistically might go some way to resolving this.[25]

Permission to View Summary Care Record

Scotland and Wales have chosen to have an explicit 'consent to view' model for their summary/emergency care records, which has been followed for the SCR, except that it is called 'permission-to-view' – partly because the NHS do not consider that it is a legal right, so 'consent' is not an appropriate a term. The Access Control Service (ACS) technical flag by default requires users to seek the patient's permission to view the SCR – they may seek permission for just themselves in this encounter or may seek permission for the team to view the record as part of a wider episode of care – but it needs to be reasonably clear to the patient what is the scope of the permission in terms of who can access and until when. This could be time periods such as 'while at the hospital' or 'while we are treating you', not generally a specific timescale, such as 'two days'.

Some patients may well get frustrated at being asked or are so comfortable with the concept of an SCR, so that they would prefer not to be asked again. Their flag can then be set to 'express consent' to indicate that they give this broad consent for any authorised care person to access their record when needed. They can also request that this be changed back to 'always ask' but this would surely be made easier if they could see this in real time and change it themselves online. The default for accessing the SCR is that the patient should be asked for permission before the SCR is accessed. Clearly if patients have chosen not to have an SCR, then the choice will not apply. However, it is also possible for patients to choose the option of 'never to be asked' – that is, they consent to any necessary access. This is equivalent to the original 'default' position under 'implied consent', except that now no presumption is made.

As discussed earlier, there are, however, occasions when it is not appropriate to seek permission, for example:

- when the access would occur anyway because of statutory or legal requirements;
- when the patient is unconscious or incompetent and so cannot make a valid choice; and
- in an emergency, when it is not practicable to seek permission.

25 See HSCIC, 'Summary Care Records (SCR)', www.connectingforhealth.nhs.uk/systemsandservices/scr/documents/noscr.pdf.

These circumstances have been made clear to the public as part of the Public Information Programme (PIP),[26] which we assert could have been more effective if facilitated by allowing some control to the individual and if all of this information was available in one place, online.

Under the previous 'consent model', access to a patient's record could be made without seeking a patient's permission – unless they had 'dissented' when access would only be for 'legal reasons' or with a patient's temporary permission (for that user alone). With the introduction of permission-to-view for the SCR, it was necessary to identify occasions when access was made without the patient's permission, because of an emergency (so that it was not viable to seek the patient's permission) which is a significant step forward for transparency.

Example scenario

An elderly lady, Mrs A, is brought into the casualty department and is incoherent. The receptionist who sets up the Legitimate Relationship with the casualty department usually requests permission to view on behalf of the team. Mrs A cannot be asked for permission to view, and the receptionist cannot press the emergency view button because their smart card does not allow this level of access.

Mrs A is then seen by the triage nurse who assesses the patient. The nurse has access rights to the emergency button and, by using the emergency button, accesses the Summary Care Record and uses the information to inform the history for the team. The nurse has acted in the best interests of the patient and is accountable for his or her action. The nurse records the justification in free text in the Summary Care Record application. One week later the privacy officer checks the alerts report and sees the alert raised by accessing Mrs A's record. The privacy officer checks the audit trail and reads the justification recorded. If necessary the local records can also be checked. There are many opportunities for manual error in this scenario and we suggest that the lack of transparency could add to the suspicion and fuel the privacy myth.

For the purpose of sharing data across organisations, the Patient Demographic Service Consent flag covers the choice as to whether to permit or prevent data sharing between NHS organisations asking whether they want their records to be shared for integrated care. Even where the person has dissented, medical records can be shared on a referral letter basis, so that the bare minimum information is provided as part of the referral process on an as-needed basis, and possibly with the explicit agreement of the patient to cover any sensitivities.

Once a patient is made aware that they can dissent to sharing across organisations, alerts can be triggered if the record for such a patient, who has dissented from data sharing across organisational boundaries (as indicated in

26 http://systems.hscic.gov.uk/scr/gppractices/communicating/index_html.

the Patient Demographic Service Consent flag), is actually accessed despite warnings that an alert would be raised. This override could be for legal or other reasons or because the patient had given temporary permission for access. There is a specified dialogue for dissent override and the user must choose from the following reasons:

- access made in the public interest;
- access required by statute;
- access required by Court Order; or
- temporary patient permission for access.

According to the findings of Dame Fiona Caldicott's *Information Governance Review* in 2013, most people would not object to the sharing of information between organisations treating them. However, there is a very important but under-publicised move from technology being used to control access to information for direct care purposes for clinicians and other professionals to others for indirect care purposes. This brings into sharp focus the potential of information being used for purposes other than the direct care of an individual. This information should be anonymised according to rule 3 of the Confidentiality Guide issued by the Health and Social Care Information Centre (HSCIC), an organisation which will be carrying out such processing as a 'safe haven'.

Taking this move towards the use of information for indirect care and the focus on 'big data'[27] the use of technology and rights invoked must now move from data protection concerns and the obligations of the data controller and towards transparency, confidentiality and consent management. One complication is that the law draws a 'bright' line between identifiable and non-identifiable data and does not capture the subtleties of de-identified information or 'anonymised in context' data as outlined in Chapter 3.[28]

Technology for Opt In and Opt Outs for Sharing Information

The use of technology and rights invoked through the use of technology have been forced to move towards transparency, confidentiality and consent management as the Health and Social Care Act 2012 appointed the HSCIC as 'the Safe Haven'. This means that it will be the mechanism through which

27 www.gov.uk/government/uploads/system/uploads/attachment_file/data/389095/Horizon_Scanning_-_Emerging_Technologies_Big_Data_report_1.pdf.

28 We have discussed the categories identified in the Caldicott Review in Chapter 3.

confidential information will be collected in identifiable form, de-identified, linked with other data, analysed, published and disseminated. The first phase of this is for GP data to be sent to the HSCIC in identifiable form. The HSCIC can then distribute that data to others for purposes other than direct care. A publicity campaign was initiated in 2014 at the request of the Information Commissioner's Office. Each household in the UK has received a leaflet explaining that they can opt out of two information flows; these are

- confidential information flowing to the HSCIC from a GP practice;
- confidential information flowing from the HSCIC to other organisations for purposes other than direct care.

This opt out revolves around HSCIC (a legally constituted safe haven) as the 'Accredited Safe Haven'. The concept of an 'Accredited Safe Haven' was created through the Caldicott Review: '*the linkage of personal confidential data, which requires a legal basis, or data that has been de-identified, but still carries a high risk that it could be re-identified with reasonable effort, from more than one organisation for any purpose other than direct care should only be done in specialist, well-governed, independently scrutinised and accredited environments called 'accredited safe havens*'.[29] These accredited safe havens are able to process 'weakly pseudonymised data' and operate primarily to support care service provision.[30]

Linking of data items must take place within an accredited safe haven. This is a particularly challenging area from a privacy perspective. Effective linkage of data sets must ensure that data for the same individual is brought together from two or more data sets. This usually requires personal data. The *Data Sharing Review* stated that 'safe havens' 'should be developed as an environment for population based research and statistical analysis'.[31] The linkage of personal

29 The 2008 Data Sharing Review recommended the creation of 'safe havens' and, more recently, Dame Fiona Caldicott's 'Information: To Share or Not to Share? The Information Governance Review' (*Caldicott Review*) called for the establishment of 'accredited safe havens'. See R. Thomas and M. Walport 'Data Sharing Review' (2006), www.connectingforhealth.nhs.uk/systemsandservices/infogov/links/datasharing review.pdf; F. Caldicott, 'Information: To share or not to share? The Information Governance Review' (2013), www.gov.uk/government/publications/the-information-governance-review.

30 F. Caldicott F, 'Information: To Share or Not To Share? The Information Governance Review' (2013) www.gov.uk/government/publications/the-information-governance-review.

31 R. Thomas and M. Walport, 'Data Sharing Review Report' (Ministry of Justice, UK July 2008), http://webarchive.nationalarchives.gov.uk/+/http:/www.justice.gov.uk/docs/data-sharing-review.pdf.

confidential data from more than one organisation for any purpose other than direct care, should only take place in specialist, well governed, independently scrutinised accredited environments ('accredited safe havens'). The Review Panel concluded that where de-identified data for limited access is processed, assurance of the data stewardship component could be achieved in a number of ways, including but not necessarily limited to

- establishing the receiving organisation as an accredited safe haven;
- using the facilities of an accredited safe haven; and
- volunteering for an audit from the Information Commissioner's Office.

The Health and Social Care Act 2012 provides primary legislation for the creation of an accredited safe haven, called the Health and Social Care Information Centre. The amount of data linkage required by the new health and social care system may be beyond the resources of the Information Centre as currently envisaged. Additionally, much of this linkage may be required at a local level, which is at odds with the Information Centre's national focus. This gives rise to the question of whether further accredited safe havens will be required to support the health and social care system.

The Caldicott Review Panel has found there are plans for at least 20 accredited safe havens. These include safe havens within Royal Colleges, National Clinical Audit contract holders, approximately ten Data Management Integration Centres, Public Health England and the Clinical Practice Research Datalink service of the MHRA. These accredited safe havens will need a clear legal basis to link data. Being an accredited safe haven does not necessarily mean that the organisation is receiving personal confidential data, but does mean it can receive de-identified data for limited disclosure or limited access.

Classifications of Data: The Grey Area

The use of Accredited Safe Havens to process data that is not anonymous necessitates consideration of the classifications of data as the law only recognises confidential and anonymous data but nothing in between (the 'grey area'). The 'grey area' is therefore articulated as 'anonymous' in context following the definition of 'de-identified data', which refers to personal confidential data, that has been through anonymisation in a manner conforming to the ICO 'Anonymisation Code of Practice'.[32] There are two categories of de-identified data:

32 Information Commissioner's Office, Anonymisation: managing data protection risk code of practice (November 2012).

- de-identified data for limited access: this is deemed to have a high risk of re-identification if published, but a low risk if held in an accredited safe haven and subject to contractual protection to prevent re-identification; and
- anonymised data for publication: this is deemed to have a low risk of re-identification, enabling publication.

However data ceases to be personal and confidential when it has been anonymised. In those circumstances, publication is lawful and actively encouraged. Data, which has been anonymised but still carries a significant risk of re-identification or de-anonymisation, may be treated either as personal and confidential or as anonymised depending on how effectively the risk of re-identification has been mitigated and what safeguards have been put in place.

De-identified data for limited disclosure or access is the data that has been through a process of anonymisation such as removing formal personal identifiers, or using coded references or pseudonyms in their place, or by aggregating data together so it is not possible to identify individuals. However, it could be relatively straightforward for a third party to re-identify individuals or de-anonymise the data, especially if it is combined with other data. This represents the 'grey area' of data. This data should only be disclosed in accordance with the ICO Anonymisation Code of Practice.[33] The disclosing and processing of this data must always have safeguards for limited access that have two components, a contractual agreement and a set of data stewardship functions.[34] The contractual agreement mitigates the risk of re-identification and sets out as a minimum the justification for the data flow, the purposes to which the data can be put, the penalties and liabilities and how the public are informed. The data stewardship functions should include, but not be limited to, the technical and organisational security arrangements for security, human resource policies such as contractual obligations, any training requirements and data retention policies. A key challenge is establishing conformance to the data stewardship functions, while enhancing a vital research and innovations community.

As the law only recognises anonymised information and confidential information and nothing in between ('the grey area'), the NHS has implemented technology to bring the 'grey area' data within the legal definition of confidential. This is at the heart of the media debate about invasion of privacy. Pseudonymisation at source is a process that replaces identifiers in a data set with a coded reference or pseudonym so information about an individual can

33 Ibid.

34 H & SCA only allows HSCIC to release anonymised information but using the ICO code of practice this includes de-identified data in certain contexts.

be distinguished without their 'real life' identity being revealed. If the process of pseudonymisation is 'enterprise wide', meaning it is standard across the whole health and social care system, it is then possible for it to be safely linked with another data set and the identity of the individual protected. There is evidence to suggest that the health and social care system should adopt a single mechanism to pseudonymise data at the source where it is collected and consider seriously an enterprise-wide pseudonymisation at source, in theory allowing improvements in linkage, protection of data and the use of information for activities such as service improvement.

The Caldicott Review Panel heard evidence that the banking and card payment industry have a duty of care to protect the identity and sensitive data of clients. Following significant investment, a Banking and Payment Card Industry Data Security Standard was adopted in 2010. The health and social care system has a similar duty of care and could consider adopting a similar single standard. However, there is a lack of clarity as to the costs, risks and benefits involved in adopting such a system for the whole of health and social care. The Review Panel concluded that there should be an evaluation of benefits, costs, risks and management issues of adopting such a system (or systems).

The implementation of audit trail functionality was also a key recommendation from the *Caldicott Review*. It recommended that an audit trail of everyone who has accessed a patient's personal confidential data should be made available in a suitable form to patients via their health and social care records. This is an excellent step forward, particularly the following commitment: 'patients themselves (and any other people they have given access to their record) should be treated in exactly the same way as staff and be captured on the audit trail'.[35] However the government response that followed was not encouraging and took a defeatist attitude to taking this forward.

Conclusions: The Need for a Technical Consent Recording Mechanism

In this chapter we have identified that the technical IG controls designed to protect the privacy of an individual's record are already in place. However, they are complex and are controlled by clinicians so an individual would never

35 33: Recommendation 1: People must have the fullest possible access to all the electronic care records about them, across the whole health and social care system, without charge. An audit trail that details anyone and everyone who has accessed a patient's record should be made available in a suitable form to patients via their personal health and social care records. The Department of Health and NHS Commissioning Board should drive a clear plan for implementation to ensure this happens as soon as possible.

know of their existence under normal circumstances. The proposed solution effectively comes down to the need for an individual to be able to give consent to share or not to share information about them. However, there is no one consistent approach to consent recording, flags and codes which makes it very difficult for a patient to be fully informed. Some approaches appear complex and subject to significant variation in use. This may have major consequences for integration projects aiming to share information appropriately between health and social care settings and the implementation of the 'Caldicott 2' recommendations. It is time to reframe the debate. It is time to hand the choice of control of the technology over to the individual whose privacy rights are being exercised through the technical controls. We assert that this is more of a communication and education issue than a technical issue and by no means an easy task. However, we assert that other sectors have already handed control over to the individual, including the banking sector and social media sites such as Facebook. Facebook is so widespread, spanning across the generations, that this interface would lend itself to reuse in health.

Although this would move the role from the clinicians and NHS managers over to the individual, in exchange the technical experts within the NHS would take on a new role to develop the technical systems to a point that they are able to interoperate with all other technical systems, send standard messages and use code that is standard throughout the health system.

It is of course, unrealistic to expect perfection in any system. However, appropriate electronic sharing is difficult, if not impossible, if there is not a consistent approach to recording, flags and codes so that the appropriate conditions associated with sharing carry forward, and the system prevents exporting/extracting where this is the individual's wish. Clinical systems have a consistent approach to the Patient Demographic Service and GP extractions, although it is not clear that these approaches (business processes) are consistently applied. As such flags and coding for integrated care (often complex direct care) require health and social care systems to be interoperable for these flags/codes. This is currently not possible. We found that guidance on explaining the codes and flags to individuals appears to be non-existent. The social care-based forms are slightly easier to explain in terms of how consent decisions are recorded and shared for direct care. But they do not deal with system functionality and transmission to the HSCIC and others.

At the time of writing, it appears that concern has been expressed about informing and seeking consent to the Summary Care Record and care.data and then effectively recoding decisions in systems to support compliance with individuals' wishes. The implications for integration pioneers (integrating health and social care data) and other integration projects are likely to be significant and possibly not yet clearly articulated. The Secretary of State for Health's commitment that 'objections' to the use of data will be treated as dissent could be jeopardised if resolution to these issues is not delivered in a timely fashion. The government, in its response to Caldicott 2 recommendation,[36] has argued that by following the common law duty of confidentiality some IT systems that hold care records already provide tools for managing consent decisions.[37] One aspect that has become increasingly clear is that the Department of Health is committed to work with NHS England to develop a consent management standard that is applicable to all such systems and across the whole health and care system including the research sector. It will further consider how best to enable the implementation of mechanisms for sharing the decisions of individuals between different systems. However there is a general sense of acceptance that it will be some time before old systems could be either upgraded or replaced.

NHS England committed to include the proposed new standard on consent management within the Technology Strategy.[38] We argue that such a 'standard' and associated guidance would need to address a range of risks and issues. It would need to be fit for the whole system and all relevant purposes, not just health or secondary uses. The main organisations with responsibilities in this area may have limited knowledge or experience relating to the social care domain. There is no dedicated, funded programme for development of social care systems to be able to comply with common standards within health systems. There is potential for confusion between consent for direct care, consent for personal confidential data to flow to the HSCIC, consent or restrictions relating to specific uses after it is received by the HSCIC, and consent related to the Summary Care Record. There will be additional challenges regarding consent related to research uses of information. In the following chapters we will examine a suggested solution to this problem.

---

36 Recommendation 8: Consent is one way in which personal confidential data can be legally shared. In such situations people are entitled to have their consent decisions reliably recorded and available to be shared whenever appropriate, so their wishes can be respected. In this context, the Informatics Services Commissioning Group must develop or commission: guidance for the reliable recording in the care record of any consent decision an individual makes in relation to sharing their personal confidential data; and a strategy to ensure these consent decisions can be shared and provide assurance that the individual's wishes are respected. See Department of Health, 'Information: To Share or Not to Share? The Information Governance Review' (April 2013), www.gov.uk/government/publications/the-information-governance-review.

37 Department of Health, 'Information: To Share or Not to Share? The Information Governance Review' (April 2013), www.gov.uk/government/publications/the-information-governance-review.

38 Department of Health, 'Information: To Share or Not to Share Government Response to the Caldicott Review' (September 2013), www.gov.uk/government/publications/caldicott-information-governance-review-department-of-health-response.

Part III

THE PROPOSED SOLUTION

Chapter 5
The Theoretical Solution

Introduction

In this third and final section of the book, we argue that the solution must be twofold. The first element is the theoretical solution discussed in this chapter, which provides a framework for options of varying levels of control over information to allow the patient to address those issues outlined in Chapter 3. The second element is the practical solution,[1] which applies technology as an impartial vehicle to deliver the solution. We argue that both the theoretical framework and the vehicle of technology are essential to actually achieve the balance we propose. The practical, or technological, solution has the ability to provide every user with controls adjusted for the balance of privacy and accessibility they seek.

Technological and societal changes have modified the era. In terms of utilisation of information, the meaning of protection that has in political circles won individual control over the revelation and utilisation of particular data has progressively lost its remarkable quality.[2] In Chapter 3, we explored the theoretical underpinning of the problem, concluding that there are three issues which necessitate change – first, the 'mindset' around informational privacy; second, the quality and control (currently termed as 'ownership' in some countries) of information; and third, the use of innovation. The key question we try to answer in this chapter is 'In theory what might a step in the right direction be?' In order to answer this question, we looked at NHS England's care.data initiative and the varied public reaction it has provoked. The aim of care.data is to link together coded records from general practice with data from other national data systems, starting with linkages to existing 'Hospital Episode Statistics' made accessible to researchers and private companies.[3] The plan is

---

1 As discussed in the next chapter.

2 Kenneth A. Bamberger and Deirdre K. Mulligan, 'Privacy in Europe: Initial Data on Governance Choices and Corporate Practices' (2013) 81(5) *Geo. Wash. L. Rev.* 1529, 1529–1663.

3 In 2011 David Cameron, Prime Minister of the UK, announced that every NHS patient would henceforth be a 'research patient' whose medical record would be 'opened up' for research by private healthcare firms. He added that 'this does not threaten privacy, it doesn't mean anyone can look at your health records, but it does mean using anonymous data to make new medical breakthroughs'. See, for example,

to provide 'linked data that will eventually cover all care settings, both in and outside of hospital.[4]

As we have discussed before, the NHS uses various methods of de-identification (e.g., anonymisation and pseudonymisation) to distance data from personal identities.[5] The key question is: How robust must de-identification be in order to 'liberate' data from the throes of privacy legislation? That's not a question that anyone except the individual should be able to answer. However, the NHS has insisted that patient data will usually only be shared in an anonymised or 'pseudonymised' form, with any releases of identifiable data subject to strict privacy safeguards and a public interest test.[6] Under the powers of the Health and Social Care Act 2012, the Health and Social Care Information Centre (HSCIC) can, under certain circumstances, require personal confidential data from GP practices without seeking patient consent. The Health and Social Care Act creates a statutory obligation for GP practices to disclose the data to the HSCIC. This has resulted in 'polarisation between those who think they can use pseudonymised data to meet all of their activities and those who say, equally vehemently, that it is impossible'.[7] On the other hand, once the data become anonymous or are processed, an individual ceases to have control over the processing of that data. Although we agree that 'effective' anonymisation in accordance with the HSCIC/ISB standard may well be adequate,[8] 'pseudonymisation' (replacing identifiers with codes) is not, unless of course, the individual has been asked. Although anonymisation is not always an adequate tool for protecting confidential information,[9] our argument is that it depends upon a decision taken by the individual which balances the risks of using the data. Anonymised information always carries some risk of re-identification; however, many of the most pressing privacy risks exist only if there is a reasonable likelihood of re-identification. We suggest the benefits to

---

'Everyone "to be research patient", says David Cameron', BBC News (5 December 2011), www.bbc.co.uk/news/uk-16026827.

4 www.hscic.gov.uk/article/3525/Caredata.

5 See W. Kuan Hon, Christopher Millard and Ian Walden, 'The Problem of "Personal Data" in Cloud Computing—What Information is Regulated? The Cloud of Unknowing' (2011) 4(1) *IDPL*. 211–228.

6 Almost all data about an individual person offers a risk of identification even where it does not include any explicit identifiers.

7 Jennifer Trueland, 'Patient Records: Too Much Information?' (2014) 123(6391) *Health Service J.* Suppl. 10-1.

8 www.isb.nhs.uk/library/standard/128.

9 Paul Ohm, 'Broken Promises of Privacy: Responding to the Surprising Failure of Anonymization' 57 *UCLA Law Review* 1701.

the community (communicated transparently to the individual) should normally be perceived to outweigh the risks but this is a decision each individual must take.

Effective pseudonymisation and/or anonymisation processes depend upon robust information governance. However, questions remain on how to decide when to allow anonymous transactions and when 'pseudo-anonymity' would be sufficient, but there are concerns about re-identification of de-identified data and the loss of trust in confidential relationships.[10] It is possible for an individual to object to the extraction of personal confidential data from the GP practice. This type of objection will prevent the identifiable information held in a GP record from being sent to the HSCIC. Individuals can also object to any information containing data that identifies them from leaving the HSCIC. This includes information from all places at which one receives NHS care. If the individual does not object, information that identifies that individual will leave the HSCIC in limited circumstances where there is special legal approval – for example, for medical research. The Health and Social Care Act 2012 demonstrated the will of parliament to allow the HSCIC to provide 'directions' to extract people's data from a GP practice with no mention of consent. At the launch of the second *Caldicott Report* in 2013, the Secretary of State for Health announced the right of an individual to 'veto' this data flow – effectively, to object. This has not necessarily been followed through, and the mixed messages were not missed by the public.[11]

This has triggered a campaign to empower people to completely 'opt out' of the new care.data system by telling their GP that they do not want their health records uploaded to it. The problem is that 'opting out' will undermine both the new system and existing national statistics and will also play into the hands of the private sector. However, campaigners are concerned that the pharmaceutical industry and health insurance companies will simply be 'given' the data.[12] *Section*

---

10 Anita L. Allen, 'Privacy Law: Positive Theory and Normative Practice' (2013) 126 *Harv. L. Rev. F.* 241.

11 Mark J. Taylor and Natasha Taylor, 'Health Research Access to Personal Confidential Data in England and Wales: Assessing Any Gap in Public Attitude between Preferable and Acceptable Models of Consent' (2014) 10 *Life Sciences, Society and Policy* 15.

12 On 23 February 2014 an article in *The Daily Telegraph* newspaper described how the records of hospital patients in the UK were sold to insurance companies. Despite being anonymised, the records contained information such as postcode, length of visit, disease and treatment information. This information was then combined with lifestyle data held by credit scoring company Experian in order to enable the insurance companies to revise their premium structure, and increase premiums for some groups. Donnelly, Laura, 'Hospital Records of All NHS Patients Sold to Insurers' *The Daily Telegraph* (London, 24 February 2014), www.telegraph.co.uk/health/healthnews/10656893/Hospital-records-of-all-NHS-patients-sold-toinsurers.html.

251 of the NHS Act 2006 requires entities to state what uses will be made of data and how they will be stored securely. They will also have to answer similar questions from the Health and Social Care Information Centre's Data Access Advisory Group. Applicants do not 'own' the data but can use them. This still raises serious questions about how the purposes for which the data will be used can be restricted[13] and the extent to which analyses may be subsequently sold. There is still no clarity or transparency about the ownership or control of the data and how the data will or will not be accessed and used by the private sector. We argue that legislative measures such as the Health and Social Care Act 2012 and Care Act 2014 are inadvertently moving in the wrong direction when providing more control to government bodies without balancing this with increased control to individuals.[14]

The direct and indirect care distinction has undoubtedly thrown up issues as people have conflated the two purposes, so that the implied consent broadly accepted as the legal basis for direct care is being extended to cover indirect care purposes, such as for payment of some treatments. Caldicott principles[15] state that *access should be on a need-to-know basis*. This principle applies to the use of Personal Confidential Data for secondary or indirect care purposes.

Theoretically, there are four phases of what 'privacy' can be conceptualised as to an individual, and the decisions individuals make should inform their role and the role of the NHS in managing health information. We argue that there must be a change of mindset around privacy, moving privacy from an 'individualistic' concept to a 'concern for society'. The balance required between 'individual privacy' and 'collective transparency' reflects this. Information within health records must be standardised, and information must be controlled by the patient to the extent they choose to do so. Online records are required to facilitate this. Likewise, innovation needs to be used by the patient as an impartial vehicle to deliver this control – allowing the individual to control their own information and to use the autonomous laws as intended. At present, technical controls within NHS information systems are admirably designed for control by patients but are, in fact, inevitably controlled by clinicians.

---

13 Although Care Bill [HL 93] 2013-14, Commons Amendments (13.03.2014), paragraph 45 suggests that data could only be disclosed by the Health and Social Care Information Centre '(a) for the purposes of the provision of health care or adult social care, or (b) the promotion of health'.

14 For discussion of privacy expectations and the relationship with control see Mark. J. Taylor, *Genetic Data and the Law: A Critical Perspective on Privacy Protection* (CUP 2012) Ch. 2.

15 The Caldicott Committee. 'Report on the Review of Patient-Identifiable Information' (Department of Health 1997).

In this chapter, we analyse the theoretical framework for the solution we are proposing. We have phrased this as a 'MI Information Revolution', which serves to invalidate the current 'proxy-individual' role of the NHS to allow individuals to exercise autonomy-based law. The theoretical element binds the first two issues – 'mindset' and 'information' – by creating a framework of choice of varying levels of control of information, which individuals may choose based on their individually chosen definition of privacy. This will validate the concept of 'confidentiality' by the act of patients consenting to the current role of the NHS who exercise 'proxy-individual' control or by patients accepting varying levels of control.

The theoretical choices are informed by well established privacy theory. We argue that there is no reason why traditional privacy theory should not apply to the management of health information. This chapter integrates traditional privacy theory with the differing conceptions of privacy used in health in Europe and the USA. A common contrast between EU and US privacy law is that the sectoral laws of the USA typically permit consumers to consent to disclosures of personal information by default, simply by not affirmatively 'opting out'.[16] In contrast, EU protection of privacy, including personally identifiable medical information, is based on a 'human right to privacy' and relevant directives,[17] with the presumption of privacy for sensitive health records.[18]

In the USA, the legal framework for healthcare privacy is a combination of constitutional, statutory, and regulatory law at the federal and state levels.[19] However, at one point in time, healthcare privacy was almost entirely regulated by common law[20] and disconnected state laws and regulations, which proved to be inconsistent and inadequate.[21] As we have discussed in Chapter 2, the

16 See note 10.

17 Data Protection Directive 1995 and the 2002 Directive Concerning Personal Data and the Protection of Privacy in the Electronic Communications Sector. The 1995 Data Directive created an Article 29 Working Party that, in 2007, issued a working document on the processing of personal data in electronic health records.

18 Common law historically aimed to protect natural and human privacy rights. See Anita L. Allen, 'Natural Law, Slavery, and the Right to Privacy Tort' (2012) 81 *Fordham L. Rev.* 1187.

19 Lior Strahilevitz, 'Toward a Positive Theory of Privacy Law' (2013) 126 *Harv. L. Rev.* 2010.

20 Jana Sutton, 'Of Information, Trust, and Ice Cream: A Recipe for a Different Perspective on the Privacy of Health Information' (2013) 55 *Ariz. L. Review* 1173, 1180, 1171–1200; Ilene N. Moore, et al., 'Confidentiality and Privacy in Health Care from the Patient's Perspective: Does HIPAA Help?' (2007) 17 *Health Matrix* 215, 219–227; see, e.g., *Doe v Cmty. Health Plan–Kaiser Corp.*, 268 A.D.2d 183, 186–87 (N.Y. App. Div. 2000).

21 See note 20: Sutton.

Health Information Privacy and Accountability Act of 1996 was aimed at solving some of these shortcomings. The provisions were intended to provide the necessary privacy and security framework for administrative simplification and to improve the efficiency and effectiveness of the healthcare system.[22] HIPAA, however, introduced a number of new problems. It failed to make patients' own health information available to them[23] and focused almost entirely on ensuring consumer confidence by restricting access to information instead of granting access to information.[24] Similarly, the High Court of Australia in *Breen v Williams,* which involved a patient's access to her own medical records, expressed that it 'is only in a loose metaphorical sense that any knowledge as such can be said to be property'.[25] HIPAA's Privacy Rule was then expanded by the Health Information Technology for Economic and Clinical Health Act 2009 to provide a better connection between patients and their own health information and stronger consequences for any breach of HIPAA's Privacy Rule.[26] 'Even with this new found focus on patient access to health information, the direction that Congress has taken with information privacy, particularly in the health care context, seems to be paternalistic; it is to restrict, protect, and enforce.'[27] Privacy law gives patients the right to control access to their medical information, and to inspect, copy,

---

22 Bob Brown, 'New Technologies Have Created New Threats to Electronic Protected Health Information' (2009) 11 *Journal of Health Care Compliance* 35, 35.

23 See note 20: Sutton.

24 See note 20: Sutton.

25 *Breen v Williams* (1996) 186 C.L.R. 71, 128 (Austl.) (quoting *Fed. Comm'r of Taxation v United Aircraft Corp.* (1943) 68 C.L.R. 525, 534 (Austl.)); see also John R. Christiansen, 'Why Healthcare Information Isn't Property—And Why That Is to Everyone's Benefit' (2009) 27 *Health L. Dig.* 3, 5–6 (noting that the law 'does not give patients exclusive ownership rights in this information. Nor does the law grant exclusive property rights in patient data to other parties to have access to this information'); Adelle A. Waller and Oscar L. Alcantara, 'Ownership of Health Information in the Information Age' (1998) 69 *J. Am. Health Information Management Assoc.* 28, 28–29 ('[T]he traditional concept of "ownership" is not a useful construct when applied to patient-identified information ... [since] no one person or entity can be truly said to "own" patient-identifiable information.'). See generally Mark A. Hall and Kevin A. Schulman, 'Ownership of Medical Information' (2009) 301 *JAMA* 1282.

26 Anna L. Spencer, 'Responding To Challenging Aspects of HITECH's Modifications to HIPAA' in *Recent Developments With HIPAA: Leading Lawyers on Interpreting the New HIPAA Laws, Developing Effective Compliance Strategies, and Responding to Recent Enforcement Actions* (Aspatore Books 2010) 129, 132.

27 See note 20: Sutton.

and correct their medical records. While these privacy and access rights can be enforced in ways similar to property rights, properly characterised, they are not actually property rights.[28]

Our analysis in Chapter 2 suggests that there is an internal coherence to privacy attitudes across different jurisdictions, and it therefore may be worth reframing existing privacy doctrines around these unifying principles. It is argued that we should take the concept of ownership from the EU and the concept of choice, along with the principle of notice from US statutes and regulations, and the concept of 'explicit' consent as mooted at the EU level. We should integrate this into traditional privacy theory to develop four theoretical options: individualistic control, restricted access, boundaries, and sociological theories of privacy regarding individual control of health data. The objective is to maximise the total benefits of healthcare services, regardless of who receives those benefits.

Privacy as a Multidimensional Construct: Four Major Shifts

The importance of protection of privacy of healthcare data cannot be underestimated. With the development and implementation of information technology in healthcare, we have managed to streamline and amplify the collection and analysis of healthcare data, as well as its use in decision making. The problem for us is how privacy can be conceptualised in a way that ensures a balance between individual and societal interests.

We argue that privacy is best understood as a cluster of concepts covering multiple privacy dimensions.[29] As Allen argues, 'there is no definitive taxonomy'[30] of privacy. It appears to provide a panacea of observation, analysis, prediction, and control for those who wish to reduce uncertainty and unpredictability. We

28 See *Estate of Finkle*, 395 N.Y.S.2d 343, 344–45 (N.Y. Sur. Ct. 1977) (listing cases where courts permitted patients to inspect but not possess their records).

29 P.R. Burgoon, J.K.M. Burgoon et al., 'Privacy Between Physicians and Patients: More Than a Matter of Confidentiality' (1989) 29 *Soc. Sci. Med.* 1381–1385; see Chapter 3 for a detailed discussion. See Robert S. Laufer, Harold M. Proshansky and Maxine Wolfe, 'Some Analytic Dimensions of Privacy' in R. Kuller (ed.), *Architectural Psychology: Proceedings of the Lund Conference* (Dowden, Hutchinson & Ross 1974). See also Robert S. Laufer and Maxine Wolfe 'Privacy as a Concept and a Social Issue: A Multidimensional Development Theory' (1977) 33(3) *J. Social Issues* 22–42; Naveen Farag Awad and M.S. Krishnan, 'The Personalization Privacy Paradox: An Empirical Evaluation of Information Transparency and the Willingness to Be Profiled Online for Personalization' (2006) 30(1) *MIS Quarterly* 13–28.

30 Anita Allen, *Unpopular Privacy: What Must We Hide?* (OUP 2011) 4, 30.

question the argument that the current conceptions of privacy as they occur in law and legal theory are too weak as to their normative and descriptive evaluation and distinction potential to capture problems relating to healthcare data.[31] As we have mentioned previously, in an information society, those who send information and those who filter information have economic control, and they have the power to influence and shape and most likely will ultimately control the privacy of individuals.[32] But this has also created vulnerability. This vulnerability is manifested as a lack of clarity regarding classification of information that is making the management of information more complicated. In the context of healthcare and privacy, this vulnerability is also blurring the distinction between implied consent for direct care and explicit consent for indirect care.

The economic and social significance of privacy in the information society is dependent on how much people value their privacy. The earliest economic analyses of privacy focused on the efficiency of markets for personal information. Almost all developed countries have grappled with the trade-offs between open access to information, which enables economic efficiency, and an individual's right to privacy. There is the argument that market-oriented mechanisms based on individual ownership of personal data may enhance personal data protection.[33] If 'personal data markets' were allowed to function more effectively, there would be less privacy invasion. Under the traditional economic model, competitive market forces generally deliver an economically efficient outcome. Hence, an efficient amount of information sharing will occur up to the point where the economic benefits of information sharing are balanced against associated costs. Specifically, if the economic value created by information sharing exceeds the value derived from privacy, the theory maintains that the economically efficient outcome would be to share information. In contrast, if the economic value generated by private parties from access to information does not exceed the benefit from privacy, then economic efficiency dictates that information is not shared.[34] Simultaneously,

---

31 Vedder, A.H., 'Medical Data, New Information Technologies, and the Need for Normative Principles other than Privacy Rules' in M. Freeman and A. Lewis (eds), *Law and Medicine: Current Legal Issues* (Vol. 3. OUP 2000) 441–459.

32 T. Buchanan, C.B. Paine, A.N. Joinson and U.-D. Reips, 'Development of Measures of Online Privacy Concern and Protection for Use on the Internet' (2006) 58(2) *J. Am. Soc. Information Science and Technology* 57–165.

33 K. C. Laudon, 'Markets and Pprivacy' (1996) 39(9) *Commun. ACM* 103.

34 See Hal R. Varian, 'Theory of Markets and Privacy' in *Privacy and Self-Regulation in the Information Age* (Washington, DC: US Department of Commerce, June 1997), www.ntia.doc.gov/reports/privacy/privacy_rpt.htm.

disclosure or non-disclosure of personal information is also subject to what is called the 'calculus of behaviour',[35] which means an individual considers future consequences an important determinant when considering the disclosure of personal information.[36] An individual who perceives potential future (negative) consequences to be minimal will be more willing to disclose personal information.[37] In other words, individuals will exchange personal information as long as they perceive that adequate benefits will be received in return – that is, benefits which exceed the perceived risks (economic or social benefit outweighs the risks)[38] of information disclosure as they view them.[39] We argue that there must be a shift in the balance between the need to protect information and the benefits of disclosure. At present, there is not enough transparency around the benefits of sharing, so individuals are naturally suspicious. If individuals knew how many lives had been saved via research, some might feel differently.

However, individuals have varying degrees of privacy concerns. As we have discussed before, the traditional starting point for privacy is Warren and Brandeis' individualistic conception of privacy,[40] whereby 'protection of society comes through recognition of the rights of the individual'.[41] They were the first to discuss privacy as a property and personal right.[42] Conversely, this 'hierarchical' relationship

---

35 Robert S. Laufer and Maxine Wolfe, 'Privacy as a Concept and a Social Issue: A Multidimensional Development Theory' (1977) 33(3) *J. Social Issues* 22–42.

36 May O. Lwin and Jerome D. Williams, 'A Model Integrating the Multidimensional Developmental Theory of Privacy and Theory of Planned Behaviour to Examine Fabrication of Information Online (2003) 14(4) *Marketing Letters* 260, 257–272.

37 Ibid.

38 George R. Milne and Mary Ellen Gordon, 'Direct Mail Privacy-Efficiency Trade-Offs within an Implied Social Contract Framework'(1993) 12(Fall) *J. Public Policy and Marketing* 206–215.

39 See Alessandro Acquisti and Jens Grossklags, 'Privacy Attitudes and Privacy Behavior: Losses, Gains, and Hyberbolic Discounting' in Jean Camp and Stephen Lewis (eds) *The Economics of Information Security* (2004), available at www.heinz.cmu.edu/~acquisti/papers/acquisti_grossklags_eis_refs.pdf.

40 We have referred to this individualist starting point as stage one. See Chapter 3.

41 S. Warren and L. Brandeis, 'The Right to Privacy' (1890) 4 *Harv. L. Rev.* 193, 195, 196.

42 It is important to realise that the point of Brandeis's article was not to offer a definition of privacy but to argue that common law protections of privacy need to be distinguished from common law protections of property. The argument that rights to privacy are just property rights in disguise is misplaced because our interests in privacy can justify forms of collective as well as private property. However, Lever argues 'while our interests in privacy justify some forms of differences and of inequalities,

between privacy and property is criticised[43] for lacking legal grounding,[44] even though this individualistic definition of privacy has provided the underpinning for privacy legislation across the world.[45] For example, conceptual and normative individualism of the European Data Protection Directive[46] reflects the current widely held ideas about informational privacy amongst legal and ethical theorists.[47] However, it is submitted that this account of privacy fails because it prioritises a single interest at the expense of others. Nevertheless, in our theoretical model, it must be offered as an option as part of the thought processes an individual must experience to understand the risks and benefits of each option.[48]

We further argue that the unlimited interaction which the information society has managed to create necessitates a move from an individualistic starting point towards models based upon 'restricted access' to information within an individual's control and 'boundaries'[49] for the types of information an individual can control. There is a far more positive influence from an individual perspective when privacy is defined as being in control over (the accessibility of) personal information,[50]

---

they provide no justification for claims to monopolize valuable social or economic assets': Annabelle Lever, 'Privacy: Restrictions and Decisions' (2013) 12(1) *Philosophy and Law* 1–7; see Judith Thomson, On Privacy (Routledge 2011).

43 R.A. Posner, *The Economics of Justice* (Harvard University Press 1981).

44 R. Bork, *The Tempting of America: The Political Seduction of the Law* (Simon and Schuster 1990).

45 K. Sheehan, 'Towards a Typology of Internet Users and Online Privacy Concerns' (2002) 18(1) *The Information Society* 21–32.

46 A.H. Vedder, 'Medical Data, New Information Technologies, and the Need for Normative Principles other than Privacy Rules' in M. Freeman and A. Lewis (eds), *Law and Medicine: Current Legal Issues* (Vol. 3, OUP 2000) 441–459.

47 See Anita Allen, *Uneasy Access: Privacy for Women in a Free Society* (NJ: Rowman and Littlefield 1988); H. Nissenbaum, 'Protecting Privacy in an Information Age: The Problem of Privacy in Public' (1998) 17 *Law and Philosophy* 559–596.

48 See P. Regan, 'Privacy as a Common Good in the Digital World' (2002) 5(3) *Information, Communication and Society* 382–450. See also D.J. Phillips, 'Privacy Policy and Pets: The Influence of Policy Regimes on the Development and Social Implications of Privacy Enhancing Technologies' (2004) 6(6) *New Media & Society* 691–706.

49 Stages 2 and 3 in our three stages of Informational Privacy, see Chapter 3.

50 See W.A. Parent, 'Recent Work on the Concept of Privacy' (1983) 20 *Am. Philos. Q.* 341–356; S.I. Benn, *A Theory of Freedom* (Cambridge 1988) 264–305; J.L. Johnson, 'Privacy, Liberty and Integrity' (1989) 3 *Public Affairs Q.* 15–34; A.H. Vedder, 'Medical Data, New Information Technologies, and the Need for Normative Principles other than Privacy Rules' in M. Freeman and A. Lewis (eds), *Law and Medicine: Current Legal Issues* (Vol. 3, OUP 2000) 441–459.

which tends to advocate in favour of protective measures in terms of safeguarding an individual's control and consent over the dispersion of personal information.[51] Schwartz concludes that conventional wisdom seeks to place the individual at the centre of decision making regarding the use of personal information by conceiving of privacy as a right of control over data use.[52] Hence, starting from the same individualistic viewpoint yet accepting more control represents the 'restricted-access' conceptions which are defined as 'not simply an absence of information about us in the minds of others; rather, it is the control we have over information about ourselves'.[53] However, 'restricted access' often confuses privacy with secrecy.[54] This seems counter-intuitive. However, it is interesting to note that Tavani and Moor have also argued that 'the concept of privacy itself is best defined in terms of restricted access, not control. Privacy is fundamentally about protection from intrusion and information gathering by others. Individual control of personal information, on the other hand, is part of the justification of privacy'.[55] Bok[56] makes no bones about where he stands with respect to 'restricted access', arguing that the 'restricted access' concept of privacy protects individuals from unwanted access by others. Even though not considered from the present starting point of NHS control,[57] the restricted access theory does exclude 'protection of individual autonomous choice from governmental interference', terming it a liberty of decisional privacy emphasised throughout legal concepts.

---

51 A.H. Vedder, 'Medical Data, New Information Technologies, and the Need for Normative Principles other than Privacy Rules' in M. Freeman and A. Lewis (eds), *Law and Medicine: Current Legal Issues* (Vol. 3, OUP 2000) 441–459.

52 Paul M. Schwartz, 'Privacy and Democracy in Cyberspace' (1999) 52 *Vand. L. Rev.* 1607, 1659. Similar views have also been expressed by others. See A. Michael Froomkin, 'The Death of Privacy?' (2000) 52 *SLR* 1461, 1463 (describing privacy as the ability to control the acquisition or release of information about oneself); see also Fred H. Cate, 'Protecting Privacy in Health Research: The Limits of Individual Choice' (2010) *Faculty Publications,* Paper 235.

53 C. Fried, 'Privacy' in Schoeman, F.D. (ed.) *Philosophical Dimensions of Privacy* (CUP 1984); J. Rachels, 'Why Privacy is Important' (1975) 4 *Philosophy and Public Affairs* 323–333.

54 H. Tavani, 'Philosophical Theories of Privacy: Implications for an Adequate Online Privacy Policy' (2007) 38(1) *Metaphilosophy*, 1–22; see Klemens Kappel, 'Epistemological Dimensions of Informational Privacy' (2013) 10 *Episteme* 179–192.

55 H. T. Tavani, and J.H. Moor, 'Privacy Protection, Control of Information, and Privacy-Enhancing Technologies' (2001) *Computers and Society* 8.

56 S. Bok, *Secrets: On the Ethics of Concealment and Revelation* (Pantheon 1982).

57 Anita Allen, *Uneasy Access: Privacy for Women in a Free Society* (Rowman and Littlefield 1988).

Tavani and Moor acknowledge that such individual control has limits, but focus on the issue that 'the management of privacy requires controls beyond individual control that will ensure restrictions in access',[58] but, more importantly, 'being able to control must be understood as being allowed or supposed to control'.[59]

As an alternative, Tavani suggests a theory that he describes as 'restricted access/limited control'.[60] It contains elements from the control theory and the restricted access theory.[61] 'Privacy is understood in terms of restricted access to information about a person in a particular situation, but also in terms of some limited control that the person has over information about himself or herself. The emphasis is on the individual context.'[62] Although Tavani's theory is useful for understanding privacy issues arising in the healthcare context, we argue Tavani is insufficiently sensitive to what we might call the value of 'collective transparency'. Here, we think Westin[63] provides better insight. He considers decisional autonomy as an aspect of privacy, and he stressed the fact that 'the individual's desire for privacy is never absolute, since participation in society is an equally powerful desire'. In addition to this, Parent, while defining privacy,[64] emphasised that he is defining the 'condition of privacy' as opposed to the 'right to privacy'. He argues that people can and do choose to give up privacy for many reasons: 'to see why, consider the example of a person who voluntarily divulges all sorts of intimate, personal, and undocumented information about herself to a friend. She is doubtless exercising control, in a paradigm sense of the term, over personal information about herself, as well as over (cognitive) access to herself. But we would not and should not say that in doing so she is preserving or protecting her privacy'.[65]

The conception of privacy that played a very influential part in this debate could perhaps be best characterised as a conception of decisional privacy or an autonomous conception of privacy. In this approach, Mill[66] has described the link that decisional privacy provides to the public/private distinction as 'the appropriate realm of governmental authority',[67] as opposed to the 'realm

58 See note 55.

59 Beate Rossler, *The Value of Privacy* (Polity Press 2005) 71,72.

60 H.T. Tavani, 'Philosophical Theories of Privacy: Implications for an Adequate Online Privacy Policy' (2007) 38(1) *Metaphilosophy* 1–22.

61 Ibid.

62 Anders Nordgren, 'Personal Health Monitoring: Ethical Considerations for Stakeholders' (2013) 11(3) *J. Information, Communication and Ethics in Society* 165, 156–173.

63 Westin, A., *Privacy and Freedom* (Atheneum 1970).

64 W.A. Parent, 'Privacy, Morality and the Law' (1983) 12(4) *Philosophy and Public Affairs* 269.

65 Ibid.

66 J.S. Mill, *On Liberty* (Longman, Roberts and Green 1869).

67 Ibid.

reserved for self-regulation'. This provides the transition to the next key theoretical progression – Altman's[68] privacy as 'boundaries'. Altman[69] regards privacy as a dynamic, changeable boundary – a regulatory process of 'selective control of access to the self or one's group'. Although he has challenged current thinking to make privacy a social phenomenon, theorists still have not approached the starting point of privacy as 'social'.[70]

However, one of the most important alternative motivations for privacy goes beyond the value of privacy to the individual and sees privacy as a social good necessary for the functioning of a democratic society. Representative of this paradigm shift was the so-called 'census-verdict' of the German federal constitutional court (Bundesverfassungsgericht) in 1983, which extended the existing right to privacy of the individual (Persönlichkeitsrecht) with the right to *self-determination over personal data* ('informationelle Selbstbestimmung').[71] This concept of self-determination over personal data constitutes an important part of modern privacy legislation with respect to ensuring the autonomy of the individual. First, it extended classical data protection principles with a participatory approach that would allow the individual to decide beyond a 'take it or leave it' choice over the collection and use of his or her personal information. Second, it framed privacy protection no longer only as an individual right, but, rather, emphasised its positive societal role.[72] Miller encapsulates the point of such control: 'the basic attribute of an effective right of privacy is the individual's ability to control the circulation of information relating to him'.[73] We suggest that through choice *and* control, 'sociologically-based' privacy is achievable at the final stage of the 'revolution', where privacy represents control over information about oneself,[74] the value that accords one the ability to control the access others have to them,[75] or a set of norms necessary to control[76] access and

68 I. Altman, 'Privacy Regulation: Culturally Universal or Culturally Specific?' (1977) 33(3) *J. Social Issues* 66.

69 I. Altman, *The Environment and Social Behaviour: Privacy, Personal Space, Territory, Crowding* (Brooks/Cole 1975).

70 P. Leith, 'The Socio-Legal Context of Privacy' (2006) 2 *Int. J. Law in Context* 105.

71 Marc Langheinrich, 'Privacy in Ubiquitous Computing' in John Krumm (ed.), *Ubiquitous Computing* (Chapman & Hall/CRC Press 2009) 11.

72 Ibid.

73 Miller (1971) *The Assault on Privacy: Computers, Data Bases and Dossiers* (Ann Arbor, University of Michigan Press 1971).

74 Parent: see note 64.

75 R. Gavison, 'Privacy and the Limits of Law' (1980) 89 *Yale L. J.* 421; see also Anita Allen, note 57; A. Moore, 'Privacy: Its Meaning and Value' (2003) 40(3) *Am Philos. Q.* 215.

76 Schoeman, F., *Privacy and Social Freedom* (CUP 1992).

enhance choice.[77] Our account of privacy leans heavily on Margulis' conception of privacy as 'control over transactions between person(s) and other(s), the ultimate aim being to enhance autonomy and/or minimise vulnerability'.[78] The power required for such control in healthcare requires societal input through 'collective transparency', which is reflected in 'control' interpreted as social power[79] and personal control.[80] We argue that the distinction between primary and secondary personal control[81] over 'privacy' illustrates the social nature of control, drawing on perspectives of selves, others and organisations through primary (voluntary disclosure of information for a benefit) and secondary information markets (information used by organisations unknown to or unforeseen by the individual), recognising that control to release power can enhance autonomy and/or minimise vulnerability. Perhaps paradoxically, even though control can be confused with autonomy and is 'counter to the way we ordinarily perceive privacy',[82] we argue that autonomy illustrates the complementary nature of individual privacy and collective transparency.

The Individual's (MI) Information Revolution: Freedom of Choice

Legal frameworks all over the world continue to emphasise consent, or individual control, as a fundamental principle of privacy law. In the United States, 'notice and choice' have been the central axes of privacy regulation for more than a decade.[83] In the EU, consent remains the most commonly used basis to legitimise data processing under Article 7 of the Data Protection

77 J. DeCew, *In Pursuit of Privacy: Law, Ethics, and the Rise of Technology* (Cornell University Press 1997).

78 S. Margulis, 'Privacy as a Social Issue and Behavioral Concept' (2003) 59(2) *J. Social Issues* 243, 259.

79 P. Kelvin, 'A Social-psychological Examination of Privacy' (1973) 12 *Br. J. Social and Clinical Psychology* 248.

80 C. Johnson, 'Privacy as Personal Control' in Carson, D. (ed.), *Man–Environment Interactions: Evaluations and Applications* (Washington, DC: Environmental Design Research Association 1974) 83.

81 Ibid.

82 H.T. Tavani, 'Privacy Security' in Langford, D. (ed.), *Internet Ethics* (Macmillan Press 2001); see also J. Rachels, Why Privacy is Important' (1975) 4 *Philosophy and Public Affairs* 323.

83 Omer Tene and Jules Polonetsky, 'Big Data for All: Privacy and User Control in the Age of Analytics' (2013) 11 *Nw. J. Tech. & Intell. Prop.* 260.

Directive.[84] Relying upon consent to satisfy a legal condition of privacy can also be challenging due to the requirement that consent relates to 'specific' purposes. This has been interpreted and implemented in different Member States in different ways. The UK has permitted broad consent, but that is not a position universally adopted across the EU and is arguably inconsistent with the position articulated by Article 29 of the Working Party.[85] However, consent itself cannot achieve the separate aim of privacy protection.

The narrow focus of this section is on 'choice'. We argue that this theoretical solution would replace the need for all of the new legislation which restricts the sharing of information by organisations on behalf of individuals. While the laws governing the use of patient data – principally, the Data Protection Act 1998, the Human Rights Act 1998, and the common law duty of confidentiality – remain fundamentally the same, changes in the structure of the NHS with the development of the 'integrated care agenda', the volume of information being recorded, and the manner in which people wish to use it mean that the landscape has been radically altered. A report by the All Party Parliamentary Groups on Global Health[86] recently argued that patient empowerment is now widely recognised as 'a fundamental pillar of healthcare for the twenty-first century',[87] with self-management and individual responsibility an important aspect of managing the pressure placed on modern healthcare.

It is evident from the 2012 *Care and Support White Paper*[88] that information sharing is critical in support of the integration of services, and Clause 3 of the

84 Council Directive 95/46, 1995 OJ (L 281) 31 (EC); 'Working Party, Opinion 15/2011 on the Definition of Consent', Article 29 (13 July 2011), available at http://ec.europa.eu/justice/policies/privacy/docs/wpdocs/2011/wp187_en.pdf. The European Data Protection Regulation would significantly tighten the requirements for consent, effectively permitting only explicit consent and thereby presumably narrowing the scope of consent-based processing: Council Directive 95/46, 1995 OJ (L 281) 31 (EC).

85 Article 29 'Working Party, Opinion 15/2011 on the definition of consent', WP187, Brussels, 13 July 2011 and Article 29 'Working Party, Working Document on the processing of personal data relating to health in electronic records', WP131, 15 February 2007.

86 All Party Parliamentary Groups on Global Health, HIV/AIDs; Population, Development and Reproductive Health; Global Tuberculosis; and Patient and Public Involvement in Health and Social Care.

87 All Party Parliamentary Group (APPG) on Global Health, 'Patient Empowerment: For Better Quality, More Sustainable Health Services Globally' (15 May 2014).

88 www.gov.uk/government/publications/caring-for-our-future-reforming-care-and-support.

subsequent *Care Bill* sets out the duty of local authorities to promote the integration of care and support with health services. The *NHS Constitution* commits to rights to privacy and confidentiality and to the NHS's responsibility for keeping patients' confidential information safe and secure. In the 2013 update of the *NHS Constitution*,[89] the government included a new right for patients to request that their confidential information is not used beyond their own care and treatment and to have their objections considered, and where their wishes cannot be followed, to be told the reasons, including the legal basis.[90] Although there is the argument that individuals may not always have enough information to know what approach to choose, we argue that the choice of control over treatment has a direct co-relation to choice of control over information; they are complementary.

The privacy problem can be dealt with by arguing that most people are not concerned about the physiological data of individuals when properly authorised personnel are the sole recipients of this data. It is the potential for foul play by parties who are capable of obtaining this data that causes patients to be wary of technology that facilitates the sharing of information, for example. The difficulty in healthcare resides in the fact that one must address both privacy and data longevity.[91] The problem for us is that the idea of 'informed' choice will sometimes raise difficult, normative and conceptual problems. Usually, patient information is collected for the primary purpose of providing healthcare for a specific episode. Any secondary usage must be in accordance with and governed by patient consent. It has been argued that patients should be aware of all of the systems collecting their information and should be able to specify how this information can be used.[92] However, this assumption, especially in the field of bio-informatics, where there is no strict boundary between information needed for research and for clinical care, does not hold true. It could be the case where the health records of participating patients in a single study data set may be invaluable in the support of investigations and analyses by the same and by other research teams, but this value was not foreseen when the original consent was obtained.

---

89 www.gov.uk/government/publications/the-nhs-constitution-for-england.

90 Department of Health, 'Information: To Share or Not to Share, Government Response to Caldicott Review' (September 2013).

91 Bob Mungamuru, Hector Garcia-Molina and Christopher Olston, Configurations: Understanding Alternatives for Safeguarding Data (Technical Report. Stanford 2005). See B. Mungamuru, H. Garcia-Molina and S. Mitra, *How to Safeguard Your Sensitive Data* (Stanford InfoLab Technical Report, 2006).

92 E.H.W. Kluge, 'Informed Consent and the Security of the Electronic Health Record (EHR): Some Policy Considerations' (2004) 73(3) *In. J. Med. Informatics* 229–234.

Health information is used for a spectrum of purposes ranging from those for which the results of that use directly impact upon the patient personally (such as clinical care) to those for which the potential benefits are to populations of patients in the future (such as drug discovery). Hence, in this section, using the 'MI Information Revolution' decision framework as a starting point, we examine the future role of the NHS in facilitating the *Information Revolution.*[93] It also examines the corresponding role of the individual to reveal the complementary nature of these roles. Because this is underpinned by the change of mindset that the previously identified blockers illustrate, this is considered a first step, shortly followed by the complementary roles and responsibilities surrounding the sharing of information. This is made real by the use of 'innovation' through an internet portal as a vehicle in the final part of the proposed solution (Chapter 6).

We have previously highlighted that the NHS's 'proxy-individual' role in reality significantly limits the choice of the individual because the health and social care system is designed to promote an asymmetrical relationship. Addressing the 'mindset' blocker that individuals have no power to choose to be autonomous due to the NHS's 'proxy-individual' role, the 'MI Information Revolution' model asserts that the NHS must be allowed to legitimately enact safeguards and realise collective transparency to facilitate positive freedoms and minimise vulnerabilities, so that individuals can exercise autonomy-based rights and laws. Equally, the NHS must facilitate individual 'control' of information by removing its self-imposed paternal 'proxy-individual' role and providing a framework of options for 'control' by the individual, thereby placing the NHS in an information user role.[94] At the same time, individuals must accept their role as information owners and either abdicate this role completely to the NHS or accept varying degrees of responsibility, hence defining their individual concept of privacy.

We argue that the current privacy framework has the capacity to emphasise access and transparency. For us, the objective should be to explore how individuals can be empowered with enhanced transparency and control. We argue that if individuals were provided with access to and control of their data, the quality and the value of the data would increase, which would not only benefit the NHS, but also individuals. This represents a significant departure from the traditional approach which the NHS follows, as individuals themselves

93 Department of Health, 'An Information Revolution: A Consultation on Proposals' (2010), www.dh.gov.uk/prod_consum_dh/groups/dh_digitalassets/@dh/@en/documents/digitalasset/dh_120664.pdf.

94 K. Caine and R. Hanania, 'Patients Want Granular Privacy Control over Health Information in Electronic Medical Records' (2013) 20 *J. Am. Med. Informatics Assoc.* 7–15.

would be able to define the policies that control third party access to their personal health information.[95] The change is necessary because healthcare organisations are linking their systems to enable interoperability, increasing the potential for unauthorised access. Since there is a myriad of individual scenarios, circumstances and relationships, the access control framework must be flexible and highly expressive to ensure that an individual's chosen access policy can be recorded and enforced in a manner that mirrors their understanding of whom they want to have access and whom they don't want to have access.[96]

There appears to be asymmetry in public perceptions when it comes to the NHS's handling of information; in particular, it appears to be paternalistic. This paternalistic use of information should require special justification that is transparent to the individual. It would need a legal basis – a statutory gateway, either permissive or mandatory – which means that the information can or must be shared. What must the NHS do to complement individuals' 'MI Information Revolution' choices? Before connecting information and innovation, the NHS must take some precursory actions to shift the mindset around 'privacy' of health records towards a 'societal welfare' mindset facilitated by collective transparency.[97] This can be achieved by educating patients and explaining the NHS's past usage of information, undoing entrenched behaviour, and rendering data usage more transparent going forward. This process should encourage a cultural change that exposes the privacy myth through informed consent. This transitional role of educating, informing, and guiding individuals towards their roles is necessitated by the *Information Revolution's* aims. Clinical rights to access health record information should primarily be on the grounds of direct care provision, where a legitimate relationship with the patient is declared. These rights are normally applied to a clinical team involved in the provision of care to patients and frequently extend to non-clinical personnel directly supporting care providers. Unfortunately, the definition of this extended care team is not consistent.

We argue that sharing personal information effectively is a key requirement of good information governance, and cultural changes in the health and social

---

95 J. Reid, I. Cheong, M. Henricksen and J. Smith, 'A Novel use of RBAC to Protect Privacy in Distributed Health Care Information Systems' in *ACISP'03: Proceedings of the 8th Australasian Conference on Information Security and Privacy* (Springer-Verlag, 2003) 403–415.

96 Ibid., 406.

97 See P. Case, 'Confidence Matters: the Rise and Fall of Informational Autonomy in Medical Law' (2003) 208 *MLR* 1. The autonomy, control and 'social good' balance within NHS medical records has been long debated but action is now necessary due to rapidly changing demographics – an ageing more geographically mobile population – coupled with limited funding for the NHS.

care system are key to achieving this. The *Information Revolution* proposals are 'evolutionary, not revolutionary'. However, they must be revolutionary in empowering patients by letting go of institutional control. This important goal may have been lost in the splitting of the two elements of *Liberating the NHS*[98] into the *Information Revolution* and *Greater Choice and Control*, when they are in fact mutually dependent in the same way that 'individual privacy' and 'collective transparency' are dependent upon one another. The *Information Revolution's* aspirations of 'accurate records available electronically with information to serve patients'[99] will empower 'greater choice and control'.[100] Together, they could reconceptualise 'privacy'. The NHS must balance individual privacy whilst increasing its collective value by encouraging innovation designed to protect information and enhancing the 'welfare of society mindset' to position individual privacy and collective transparency as complementary. To expose this collective transparency, the NHS must actively obtain consent to share particular elements of information and must also transparently and consistently justify why it does not need to obtain consent due to existing 'public good' exceptions for all options. The implied consent or public interest defence to breach of confidentiality should be re-articulated to reposition current thinking that imputed/implied consent eradicates 'privacy'. Patients must know that what is recorded about them will be shared across organisational boundaries – even if some information is out of their 'primary' control and is utilised under implied/imputed consent.[101] Imputed consent, as defined by the NHS LifeHouse Project, assumes that 'if we were to tell you what we do with the data, we are sure that you would agree to its use'.[102] This paternalistic form of 'consent' for collective transparency requires no active consent process or comprehensive review prior to the provision of information. Implied consent, which is attracting most of the debate, is defined as follows: 'If a patient goes for treatment to a doctor other than the one with whom he is registered, he is impliedly consenting to the doctor having access to details of his previous treatment'(emphasis added).[103] Sometimes, this concept of direct care

98 Department of Health, Liberating the NHS: greater choice and control. A consultation on proposals (2010) www.dh.gov.uk/en/Consultations/Liveconsultations/DH_119651.

99 Department of Health, 'An Information Revolution: A Consultation on Proposals' (2010), www.dh.gov.uk/prod_consum_dh/groups/dh_digitalassets/@dh/@en/documents/digitalasset/dh_120664.pdf 1, Pg.4.

100 See note 98, para 2.2, p. 6.

101 K. Doran, 'Medical Confidentiality: The Role of the Doctrine of Confidentiality in the Doctor–Patient Relationship' (1997) 3 *MLJI* 21.

102 Department of Health, 'NHS Lifehouse Project 9' (2001).

103 J. McHale, *Medical Confidentiality and Legal Privilege* (Routledge 1993) 32.

and the 'legal basis' of 'implied consent' are conflated with indirect care purposes, which therefore denies the individual the right to consent to indirect purposes in direct contrast to the EU's approach to 'explicit consent'.

Despite obvious advantages to disclosure for research purposes[104] stemming from 'imputed' consent, the General Medical Council (GMC)[105] has historically required express consent for use in registries.[106] It is becoming far more challenging to ensure that all confidential health information disclosures have been expressly consented to, particularly as there are potential health service providers who will access the information for purposes for which consumers have not expressly given their consent.[107] Disconcertingly, historically guidance issued by other professional organisations validates 'implied' consent. The British Medical Association (BMA)[108] has advised that 'health professionals must make reasonable efforts to ensure patients understand that their data may be used in research unless they exercise their right to object'.[109] The Medical Research Council (MRC)[110] has agreed that information may justifiably be disclosed without express consent for research if the likely benefits to society outweigh the implications of loss of confidentiality.[111] Research could suffer from the less liberal approach of the GMC, and the brunt of these disadvantages would be borne by patients, as medical advances would likely stagnate when research capacity slows down, as 'anecdotal evidence from the US already suggests that the

104 J.G. Hodge, 'Health Information Privacy and Public Health' (2003) 31(4) *J. Law, Medicine and Ethics* 663–671.

105 General Medical Council. See www.gmc-uk.org/.

106 Paragraph 27 of GMC, 'Confidentiality: Protecting and Providing Information' (September 2000). The relevant provision reads as follows: 'The automatic transfer of personal information to a registry, whether by electronic means or other means, before informing the patient that information will be passed on, is unacceptable save in the most exceptional circumstances. These would be where a court has already decided that there is such an overwhelming public interest in the disclosure of information to a registry that patients' rights to confidentiality are overridden; or where you are willing.'

107 See note 95.

108 British Medical Association. See www.bma.org.uk.

109 BMA, 'British Medical Association Guidance: Confidentiality and Disclosure of Health Information' (14 October 1999).

110 MRC. 'Personal Information in Medical Research' 2000, at para 2.2.2.

111 Ibid. 'When consent is impracticable confidential information can be disclosed without consent only if: the likely benefits to society outweigh the implications of the loss of confidentiality, so that it is clearly in the public interest for the research to be done; there is no intention to feed information back to the individuals involved or take decisions that affect them, and; there are no practicable alternatives of equal effectiveness.'

regulatory requirements due to HIPAA have had an adverse effect on the conduct of medical research'.[112] 'Consent bias' may also arise, as individuals could refuse permission to disclose their information due to the 'privacy myth'. Conversely, data procured with consent is 'richer' and therefore more valuable because it includes additional background detail, facilitating genetic knowledge and comprehensive 'journeys' through the healthcare system.[113] The process that does not require consent through statutory provisions such as s. 251 must be visible to patients by communicating the benefits to medical research and the measures taken to anonymise or pseudonymise patient information. This transparency would give patients 'secondary'[114] control as observers who know and understand how their data are being used and why (alongside the opportunity to object) – facilitating joint decision making processes as envisioned in the *White Paper*.[115]

However, such 'collective transparency' also requires a framework of principles, as Lord Hailsham in *D v National Society for the Protection of Children from Cruelty*[116] suggested, in which 'categories of public interest are never closed and must alter from time to time whether by restriction or extension'. Individuals must be aware of this critical consideration. This constitutes judicial recognition that 'public interest' is inherently sociologically relative to the context of the inquiry. Consequently, authorities who address public interest exclusions deal with specific, identifiable, and immediate risks to the public rather than potential risks, such as those posed by not pursuing medical

112 A. Appari, and Eric Johnson, M., 'Information Security and Privacy in Healthcare: Current State of Research' (2010) 6(4) *Int. J. Internet and Enterprise Management* 279–314; see J. Kaiser, 'Patient Privacy: Rule To Protect Records May Doom Long-term Heart Study' (2006) 311(5767) *Science* 1547–1548. It is reported that nearly 68 per cent of researchers felt that HIPAA made medical research 'highly difficult' and only about 25 per cent believed that it has increased patients' confidentiality or privacy. More importantly, about 39 per cent of researchers believed that HIPAA had increased research cost by a 'great deal', especially owing to additional compliance-related administrative cost and about 51 per cent of researchers believed HIPAA enforcement led to delays in research. See R.B. Ness, 'Influence of the HIPAA Privacy Rule on Health Research' (2007) 298(18) *JAMA* 2164–2170.

113 G. Turnbull, 'Cancer Registries Say Informed Consent is Unworkable' (2001) 18(2) *Br. J. Healthcare Computing and Information Management* 11.

114 C. Johnson, 'Privacy as Personal Control' in Carson, D (ed.), *Man–Environment Interactions: Evaluations and Applications: part 2* (Washington, DC: Environmental Design Research Association 1974) 83.

115 Department of Health, 'Equality and Excellence, Liberating the NHS' (White Paper, Cm 7881, 2010).

116 [1978] AC 171 at 175.

advances via research. Similarly, the public interest defence enumerated in *W v Edgell*[117] does not support access for research,[118] advocating only for a limited duty to patients who pose a specific direct threat to individual safety.

Conversely, although *R v Department of Health ex parte Source Informatics*[119] was not argued based on a public interest defence, Brown LJ supported the use of Patient Identifiable Data (PID) for 'thorough research and management ... whether because it falls within the public interest defence or, as is perhaps the preferable view, because the scope of confidentiality is circumscribed to accommodate it'.[120] We support the latter, in appreciation of the social nature of confidentiality.

Breach of confidentiality claims in justified 'public good/interest' cases should fail due to the difficulty of proving 'detriment' that appears to be non-existent or superficial, per Rose J in *X v Y*.[121] By contrast, Lord Keith in the *Attorney General v Guardian Newspapers (No 2)*[122] said that if detriment were required, unwanted disclosure was generally sufficient.[123] English law's emphasis on individual privacy, epitomised by Brown LJ's statement that 'the concern of the law [regarding confidentiality] is to protect the confiders' personal privacy',[124] suggesting that the 'social' approach of *Seager v Copydex*[125] is outdated.[126] The NHS has a duty to move the mindset of society through an entire revolution in order to reinstate this, identifying individual control as an alter ego of privacy.

To alter the individual's mindset towards power and away from 'privacy', individuals must be empowered to decide whether they choose to accept control

---

117 [1990] Ch 359.

118 *W v Edgell* [1990] Ch 359 361. After first of all stating that the public interest in preserving confidence was a public health issue, Scott J continued to explain that W, a schizophrenic with convictions for manslaughter, was not in the position of an ordinary member of the public. His past conduct meant that Dr Edgell had a duty to the public at large. W was consequently owed a duty of confidence less extensive than the duty that would be owed by psychiatrists to ordinary members of the public.

119 [2001] QB 424 at [444].

120 Ibid. at [443].

121 [1988] 2 All ER 648 at [653].

122 [1990] AC 109.

123 *Attorney General v Guardian Newspapers (No 2)* [1990] AC 109 at [256]. See Jones, M., 'Medical confidentiality and the public interest' (1990)6(1) *PN* 16, where the view of Lord Keith is supported.

124 *R v Department of Health ex parte Source Informatics* [2001] QB 424 (Brown LJ). See also *Douglas v Hello! Ltd* [2001] QB 967.

125 [1967] FSR 211, 220.

126 Privacy occupied only a residual role in legal protection at the time.

or abdicate such control to the NHS to ensure confidentiality. This depends on acceptance of the assertion that control over both/either dimensions of privacy, identified by the Supreme Court[127] as information about oneself (individual privacy) and information to make important decisions (collective transparency), can form the alter ego of privacy. Both dimensions are considered in the decision over which party primarily controls the risk versus benefits equation to allow access, as well as which party provides 'secondary'[128] approval. Currently, individuals provide neither, but because a sociological viewpoint must be considered in the primary equation, only an entity with a view of society – the NHS – can make the 'primary' decision. Through transparency, individuals can be empowered to 'approve/oversee' access. The tool for this transparency is suggested as a portal named the 'WIi Fit'. The individual would enter a contractual situation within the 'primary information market'.[129] We argue that the process would require individuals to be educated about the collective value of transparency of information retained for the 'public good' in order to make a balanced decision. This would illustrate that anything straying into the 'secondary information market'[130] without transparency would be cause to complain to the Information Commissioner (IC), because under the Data Protection Act, individuals should be allowed sufficient visibility to foresee each future use of information.[131] Such transparency would allow individuals to consider the sociological implications and review the options that are underpinned by the various theoretical concepts of 'informational privacy'. Consequently, individuals could choose at which point in the cycle of uptake they choose to participate.

Although total transparency should be available to all, some will lack the competence or interest in making important disclosure decisions autonomously. However, they must be granted the access required for the 'individualistic'

127 *Whalen v Roe*, 429 U.S. 589, 1977.

128 See A. Froomkin, 'Regulation of Computing and Information Technology. flood Control on the Information Ocean: Living with Anonymity, Digital Cash and Distributed Databases' (1996) 15 *J. L. & Com.* 396.

129 C. Johnson, C., 'Privacy as Personal Control' in Carson, D. (ed.), *Man–Environment Interactions: Evaluations and Applications* (Washington, DC: Environmental Design Research Association 1974) 83.

130 Ibid.

131 In line with Principle 2 of the DPA 1998: 'Personal data shall be obtained only for one or more specified and lawful purposes, and shall not be further processed in any manner incompatible with that purpose or those purposes' and Principle 3 DPA 1998 – 'Personal data shall be adequate, relevant and not excessive in relation to the purpose or purposes for which they are processed'.

standpoint to be an option, thereby negating the 'proxy individual' role the NHS now assumes. There must also be an option for caregivers to control an individual's care and information, and existing options must remain in acknowledgement of the standard curve of innovation uptake. The required transparency, facilitated by the intended application of European style data protection rules, combined with the benefits of legislation and self-regulation,[132] would provide individuals with a vehicle through which to exercise individual control in an informed way, effectively redefining individual 'privacy'. Consequently, it would provide a measure of the relative importance of privacy and disclosure as intermediate (for themselves) and final[133] 'goods' (for society). This mindset would be facilitated by individuals who are empowered to take on the roles of both information 'owner' and innovative user. The 'informed' knowledge that accompanies individual control should solve the privacy myopia[134] and allow legislative protection to be applied as intended – by the individual.

The concept of privacy by consent has potential, but it also has some limitations, and it does not always equate with privacy. A consent-based system without legally enforceable limits would unfairly shift the burden for protecting privacy to individuals. The result may be less protective of privacy and confidentially. However, we argue that by changing the mindset, there would be greater incentive for electronic healthcare record providers to design systems with stronger technical privacy and security protections. Allen notes[135] that privacy is a foundational human good, and it is at least sometimes permissible to protect, promote, or even mandate this value by following a paternalistic approach, similar to the self-imposed 'information guardian' role of the NHS. Allen offers support by noting that individuals are often poor decision makers, prone to bias, procrastination, lack of self-control, and information deficiency. Moreover, the very overabundance of choices can be a form of tyranny, much like information overload. Allen notes that in some cases, the best way to promote the dignity, autonomy, and self-worth of individuals is to paternalistically limit the choices, goals, and projects of otherwise competent and peaceful adults. However, we argue that the NHS is also susceptible to these characteristics. More importantly, one could argue that when the NHS makes bad policy, by incorrectly mandating privacy or using the wrong legal instruments, for example, the consequences for individual autonomy, self-respect, and dignity can be profound.

---

132 R. Marsh Jr, 'Legislation for effective self-regulation: a new approach to protecting personal privacy on the Internet' (2009) 15 *Michigan Telecommun. Technol. L. Rev.* 543.

133 See note 128.

134 See A. Froomkin, 'The Death of Privacy?' (2000) 52 *SLR* 1461.

135 Anita Allen, *Unpopular Privacy: What Must We Hide?* (OUP 2011).

The NHS as Information Users: Less Governance and More Transparency for Individuals

The proposed solution is driven by our belief that individuals should be increasingly empowered to play a critical role in defining how their healthcare data can be collected, used, and shared across various providers.[136] We argue that when exchanging medical information across systems under different administrative domains, traditional privacy models are reinforcing patient privacy preferences. To address this challenge, we propose 'control' based on 'choice' that is focused on the individual and that offers a consent-based access control solution across medical information systems. Privacy suffers not only when individuals are *unaware* of data practices, but also when they are uninterested or disengaged.[137] As an information user, the NHS must consider the role it can legitimately assume regarding IG by supporting individuals as information controllers. This means undertaking fewer IG tasks directly on behalf of the individual, while empowering individuals to use IG controls and promoting their use. Although it has been asserted that 'confidentiality' currently has no meaning in relation to medical records, it is acknowledged that IG controls can 'stop things becoming worse',[138] but only if controls are publicised and consent is obtained.[139] However, existing approaches that address consent do not provide the adequate concepts to express, in an unambiguous manner, an individual's wishes with respect to the access and management of their health

136 A. Khan and I. McKillop, 'Privacy-centric Access Control for Distributed Heterogeneous Medical Information Systems' *ICHI 2013* (Proceedings of the 2013 IEEE International Conference on Healthcare Informatics, Philadelphia, PA, 9–11 September, 2013) 297–306.

137 In 2010, the Obama Administration announced the 'Blue Button', a web-based feature through which patients can easily download their health information in usable format and share it with healthcare providers and trusted third parties. To make the information more useful, the initiative challenged developers to create applications that build on the Blue Button by helping consumers use their data to manage their own health. See Aneesh Chopra, Todd Park and Peter Levin, '"Blue Button" Provides Access to Downloadable Personal Health Data' *White House Blog* (7 October 2010), www.whitehouse.gov/blog/2010/10/07/bluebutton-provides-access-downloadable-personal-health-data.

138 M. Perez-Carceles, J. Pereniguez, E. Osuna and A. Luna, 'Balancing confidentiality and the information provided to families of patients in primary care' (2005) 31 *J. Med. Ethics* 531.

139 N. Sirc, 'Data Protection and the NHS: Putting Patients First?' (2005) 2(5) *D.P.L & P* 6, www.e-comlaw.com/dplp/archive/volume_2_issue_5.htm.

data.[140] Because information ownership, access, control, and accountability are confused in the handling of health records, the NHS must make multiple leaps to ensure that information is fit for purpose for the *Information Revolution*. The closest the law comes to establishing ownership, i.e., through the health professional's control of medical records,[141] is complicated by the process of distinguishing the information conveyed to a doctor and the doctor's conclusions. However, doctors are not the only ones to view medical records – non-medical staff access invalidates this logic.[142]

It is therefore difficult to understand how 'control' can be envisaged when ownership and access are still being debated. Common law has answered some questions about patient access to medical records, but in our opinion, now that information will be more widely shared, patients must be empowered to control medical records. Therefore, access must first be determined but ownership seems to be a red herring with 'data controllers' having all the power from a legal perspective. *McInerney v McDonald*[143] raised the issue of patient access to medical records without a doctor's prior approval,[144] and La Forest J held that the records belonged to the clinic, not to the patient. This rejected the contractual approach to access within common law.[145] *McInerney* concluded that information within medical records remained one's own, 'for the individual to communicate or retain as he sees fit',[146] following *Halls v Mitchell*,[147] where Duff J held that medical records were the patient's property subject to the patient's control, stating that 'personal privacy and access to medical information are interchangeable rights'.[148]

---

140 C. Pruski, 'e-crl: A Rule-based Language for Expressing Patient Electronic Consent' (International Conference on eHealth, Telemedicine, and Social Medicine 2010).

141 If the data controller is not a health professional, then the data controller needs to consult with the appropriate health professional. See L. Brinn, 'Ownership of Electronic Health Information Must Be Addressed' (2009) www.fuqua.duke.edu/news_events/releases/schulman_jama_health_info.

142 Big Brother Watch UK, 'Broken Records: the Worrying Lack of Security Around Your Medical History, and How It Could Be Changing for the Worse' (2010), www.bigbrotherwatch.org.uk/brokenrecords.pdf.

143 [1993] DLR 415.

144 B. Dickens, 'Medical Records – Patient's Right to Receive Copies – Physician's Fiduciary Duty of Disclosure: *McInerney v. McDonald*' (1994) 73 *Can Bar Rev.* 234.

145 Westin, A. *Computers, Health Records, and Citizen's Rights* (NBS Monograph 157, United States Department of Commerce 1976).

146 *McInerney v McDonald* [1993] DLR 415 422.

147 *Halls v Mitchell* [1928] SCR 125.

148 Ibid. 127 (Duff J); and Knoppers, B., 'Confidentiality and accessibility of medical information: a comparative analysis' (1982) 12 RDUS 431.

To achieve the vision inspired by the *Information Revolution*, active control rather than passive access must become the interchangeable right with regard to privacy. We argue that a judicial leap is also required, because this endorsement of patient access to medical records by the Canadian Supreme Court was rejected by English courts in *R v Mid-Glamorgan FHSA and South Glamorgan Health Authority, ex parte Martin.*[149] Popplewell J held that even if a common law right of access existed, it would be conditioned on whether there is no risk to the patient's mental or physical health, thereby defeating the objective of privacy and access as interchangeable rights. Conversely, control would solve this problem through visibility of use, as patients would have immediate access to information about them and to see who was using it. Popplewell J dismissed the fiduciary relationship used in *McInerney*[150] to justify patient access to medical records on the basis of the interchangeability of patient privacy and access rights, on the grounds of clinical, not NHS, paternalism. Referencing *Sidaway v Bethlehem Hospital,*[151] he incorporated the fiduciary duty into the doctor's obligations to ensure that clinicians acted in the patient's best interests.[152] In the Australian case of *Breen v Williams,*[153] Kirby P observed: 'The most that can be derived from *Regina v. Mid Glamorgan* is that it is an indication, at a high level of the English courts and outside the obligations of statute, that an assertion by a medical practitioner of absolute ownership and control of "his" medical records concerning a patient, is unacceptable to the common law of England.' But *Mid Glamorgan* fails to provide the conceptual explanation, by reference to a known legal classification which will support the conclusions expressed in a way that is coherent and convincing in terms of legal principle.[154] We argue that this legal endorsement of medical 'best interest'[155] paternalism based on the potential for detriment has been criticised but was nonetheless embedded into the Data Protection Act,[156] and it should also be transparently

149 [1993] 137 SJ 153 (QBD).

150 *McInerney v McDonald* [1993] DLR 415.

151 *R v Mid-Glamorgan FHSA and South Glamorgan Health Authority, ex parte Martin* [1993] 137 SJ 153 (QBD) 415 (Popplewell J) referring to *Sidaway v Bethlehem Hospital* [1984] I All ER 1018 1020.

152 For example, avoiding a threat to patient's physical or mental health in the doctor's opinion.

153 [1994] 35 NSWLR 522.

154 [1994] 35 NSWLR 541. See also Michael D. Kirby, 'A Patient's Right of Access to Medical Records' (1996) 12 *J. Contemp. Health Law and Policy* 93, 98.

155 Feenan, D., 'Common law access to medical records' (1996) 59 *MLR* 101.

156 Rights of access to personal data are central to the DPA. However, if the personal data concerns physical or mental health or condition, the provisions are

embedded into controls. This will enable the NHS to enact its duties to facilitate 'positive freedom' in order to support autonomy and minimise vulnerabilities. Movement in the direction of a less paternalistic approach to the disclosure of information culminated in the pivotal Australian case of *Rogers v Whitaker*.[157] In this case, the High Court unequivocally established a doctor's obligation to provide comprehensive information to patients as part of his or her overall duty of care. The court determined that while treatment standards are a matter upon which expert professional opinion is critically reliant, the question of whether a patient has been given sufficient information upon which to base a medical decision regarding treatment is a matter to be determined by the circumstances of the case, including the unique needs of the individual patient.

These circumstances underscore that when empowering patients and 'letting go'[158] of the central control that manifests itself in the debates outlined above, the true intentions of IG controls and choice are empowered. Therefore, transparent safeguards surrounding information must be established by the NHS. Historically, IG controls have been adapted to the environment in which they were born – where awareness was low due to significant complexity, and where intermediary involvement was high, so uptake was low. The individual's direct control would allow for the potential of transparent audit trails, which would in turn facilitate visibility of leaks and illegitimate access. The layered governance of the NHS, where each healthcare organisation is registered with the Information Commissioner's Office (ICO) as a 'Data Controller', would lend itself to this, as the NHS would be identified more easily and would be held accountable via visible fines from the ICO.[159] However, this layered governance also means that each organisation can collect and store information in its own way. This requires standardisation, because the NHS has a role in facilitating

---

modified by the Data Protection (Subject Access Modification) (Health) Order 2000, SI 2000/214. See in particular Article 5 'Exemptions from section 7': Under the Data Protection Act 1998 there are certain circumstances in which the record holder may withhold information. Access may be denied, or limited, where the information might cause serious harm to the physical or mental health or condition of the patient, or any other person, or where giving access would disclose information relating to or provided by a third person who had not consented to the disclosure. It is in these circumstances the NHS must foresee this and exclude it from the 'MIi' and 'Wii Fit' portals in order to safeguard patients and allow them to exercise positive freedoms.

157 *Rogers v Whitaker* (1992) 175, 479, Commonwealth Law Report.

158 C. Newdick, 'NHS Governance after Bristol: Holding On, or Letting Go?' (2002) *MLR* 111.

159 For an existing guide see ICO, Health http://ico.org.uk/for-organisations/health.

autonomy by freeing up information in a transparent way. For this reason, such information must have consistent meaning and must be able to be used for transparent intelligence creation. By setting standards for data collection and reporting, the NHS can create mandatory information standards to facilitate clinical safety,[160] accuracy, and comparability.

Conclusion

In this chapter we have created a framework of choices of varying levels of control of information which individuals may choose based on their individual definition of privacy. The normative implications of operating with such a concept of privacy are evaluated through the foundational argument that we take forward which suggests that the concept of privacy is too individualistic in the NHS. It is conceptualised and operationalised principally through the idea of secrecy developed around the idea of the NHS being the 'proxy-individual', controlling healthcare data on behalf of the individual. This is at the centre of the problem of achieving the ethical and effective management of healthcare data. We argue that privacy requires a different interpretation from the one which tends to dominate in the UK, it needs to move towards a more optimal sociological conception of control. The theoretical model based on critique of relevant privacy literature developed in this chapter offer individuals to choose what privacy means to them. 'MI Information Revolution' provides that theoretical justification. The four conceptions outlined here show the alternative conceptions and the respective arguments for and against adoption of each. The premise of this argument rests on each conception being constituent parts of a 'whole'. The 'whole' is the mindset change of 'sociological conceptions of privacy as control'. This allows them to see the impact of their decision on society generally and therefore puts them in control and in turn empowers choice over healthcare as it facilitates information sharing and healthcare choices. We argue although the law is correct but the role of the NHS as a 'proxy-individual' inadvertently circumvents the laws, which are autonomy-based, and this compounds negative concepts of privacy and subsequently it exacerbates the problem.

Therefore the solution is purported to be staring us in the face. The legislative framework is in place, it is just not visible to the public, who should be able to invoke it directly. From a substantive perspective, we are asserting

160 Department of Health, 'Building a Safer NHS for Patients: Implementing an Organisation with a Memory' (2007) para. 52.

that a restrictive regulatory measure would be counter-productive. Although this chapter is written from a UK perspective, focusing on the NHS, given the comparability of approach in other countries, readers outside the UK may find equivalent laws apply in their own countries. The theoretical framework is clearly applicable beyond the borders of the UK. It is critical to create a theoretical structure that balances the obligation to provide social benefits with the need to respect and protect patient autonomy and wishes. In other words, balance must be achieved between the positive rights of society and the right of a patient to privacy and confidentiality. We strongly argue that rather than conscious and explicit disclosures, prospective disclosures based on defined roles and access privileges are preferable. This creates an environment of controlled access instead of controlled disclosure. Records should be created, processed, and managed in a manner that optimally guarantees the confidentiality of their contents and legitimate control by patients in terms of how they are used. The communication of health record information to third parties should take place only with patient consent, unless emergency circumstances dictate that implied consent can safely be assumed. Kluge[161] argues that the global integration of patient healthcare information is creating a record that functions as the patient analogue in medical decision-making space: it affects what is done to the patient and how others relate to the patient. We believe that accountability to the individual in patient data management is crucial, from both a practical as well as an ethical perspective. This requires involvement at the collective and individual levels. There should be involvement in mechanisms that provide checks and balances regarding the use of the statutory gateways allowing the sharing of identifiable patient data in the *Health and Social Care Act 2012*, which develop patient IG policy and practice, and which monitor and regulate patients who should be fully able to dissent to such disclosure practices.

There is evidence which suggests that the public is becoming more reconciled to the benefits of electronic systems against the potential risks involved, probably through greater exposure to the internet. In the early 1990s, when uncertainty over the internet was greatest, there seemed to be considerable concern about electronic records – towards the turn of the century, fears have been replaced by firmer expectations, and perhaps surprise that health systems are so poorly advanced. Clearly, such adjustments in thinking are mainly occurring amongst the younger or economically privileged, who have the greatest exposure to online facilities. There are four overarching conclusions. Firstly, patients strongly believe that their information should be shared only with people involved in their care. Secondly, patients identify with the need for information sharing

161 E.H. Kluge, 'Patients, Patient Records, and Ethical Principles' in Greenes, R.A. et al. (eds), (*Medinfo* 8, Pt 2 1995) 1596–1600.

among physicians, although HIV patients are less likely to approve sharing of their health information. Thirdly, many patients who agree to information sharing among physicians reject the notion of releasing information to third parties, including employers and family members. Finally, the majority of patients who have undergone genetic testing believe that patients should bear the responsibility for revealing test results to other at-risk family members.[162]

In the next and final chapter of this book we look to the future, to offer a pragmatic approach to building a strategy for control of patient data based on the 'art of the possible'. In order to allow individuals to own and control their information a technical interface is suggested that allows for the NHS to be transparent in its use of information, and for individuals to exercise their choice in information sharing decisions.

---

162 P. Sankar, S. Moran, J.F. Merz and N. L. Jones, 'Patient Perspectives on Medical Confidentiality: A Review of the Literature' (2003) 18 *J. Gen. Intern. Med.* 659–669.

Chapter 6

The Choice of Control: Putting the Solution into Practice

Introduction

This book began as an investigation into whether the NHS is balancing the critically important informational relationship between individual privacy and collective transparency and whether its approach is fit for purpose. We made a provocative argument that the NHS's 'proxy-individual' role could inadvertently mask individuals' intended roles, effectively circumventing autonomy-based laws by limiting the power of individuals to be autonomous. We have identified three issues – first the prevailing 'Mindset' (the 'M') of 'privacy', which is viewed as individualistic, resulting in an overpowering concept of confidentiality; second, the quality and control of Information (the first 'I'); and third, the concept of innovation (the second 'i'), which we have used as a vehicle for transparency rather than as a 'solution' per se. If our proposition in Chapter 1 of the book is to come true – that is, individual privacy and collective transparency are best embedded within a complementary privacy framework which offers a better fit than the current split of control between the roles of the NHS and the roles of the individual, then how might it be achieved? It is suggested that when facilitated by transparency, 'control' and 'privacy' form a continuum, driven by the desire for 'choice'. What this suggests is that the 'choice of control' could facilitate 'control' *and* 'choice'. Hence, pragmatically speaking, this is an indication that 'control and choice' together, could replace the concept of privacy by empowering 'informed patients' to 'put patients at the heart of everything the NHS does' and to be 'accountable to the public, communities and patients'.

In this final chapter, we argue that to address the problem of 'privacy' being imposed on society as an individualistic concept, we must apply technology as an impartial vehicle to deliver choice. Our proposal is based on the principle that 'collective transparency' and 'individual privacy' are complementary, and this proposal is characterised by the proposed implementation of proactive rather than reactive measures. The practical implementation part of the solution is through innovation, via portals named 'MIi Fit' for individuals to control and define their own concept of 'privacy,' and 'WIi Fit' for the NHS to transparently show how 'collective transparency' is complementary to individual privacy. Our proposed solution offers a flexible and robust model designed to empower patients to play a critical role in defining how their healthcare information is shared through a consent-based system.

The solution is based on the theoretical solution as discussed in Chapter 5, which provided the framework for options of varying levels of control over information for the patient to address the issues outlined in Chapter 3. The practical issues outlined in Chapter 4 are underpinned by a historical role reversal, where law and technology are used as vehicles, with the wrong drivers which we propose is a result of the role reversal. We discussed the irony inherent within the *Information Revolution* publications, which promise choice and control to patients but do not consider repositioning the control of information by individuals as an enabler. We have suggested that the privacy framework per se is fit for purpose, but that the manner in which information is governed renders it unfit for purpose. Therefore, the roles of the individual and the NHS must be reconsidered. The NHS assumes a paternal 'proxy' individual role, which means that the role of the individual is masked, so they cannot enforce autonomy-based laws.

Although 'confidentiality' is the ruling concept that governs the legal processing of health data, it is not currently always underpinned by the consent of the patient, and as a result, it is often illegitimate. As was highlighted earlier in Chapter 4, placing the theoretical limitations into a real life example outlined the technical information governance controls designed for individuals, which are being exercised by the NHS through technology in systems that contain patient information. We have also argued before[1] that the wording and intent of the laws and policy underpinning these technical controls are based on individuals exercising their rights.

Our proposed 'MIi Information Revolution'[2] invalidates the 'proxy-individual' role of the NHS to allow individuals to exercise autonomy-based law. The theoretical element, as analysed in Chapter 5 binds the first two issues – 'mindset' and 'information' – by creating a framework of choices of varying levels of control of information, which individuals may choose based on their individual definition of privacy. We argue that this will validate 'confidentiality' by patients consenting to the current 'proxy-individual' control or accepting varying levels of control.

Innovation – WIi and MIi Fit Portals

We argue that privacy in the context of 'indirect care' including research, public health, commissioning, and service planning is something that each individual should have the choice to conceptualise as a social or individualised concept.

1 See Chapter 4.

2 See Chapter 5.

In contrast when privacy is considered in the context of direct care it will most likely be viewed as 'individualised' when decisions only affect an individual's direct care, for example, when sharing information between clinicians, social workers, family, and care givers. We further argue that any solution to privacy concerns in healthcare must combine law and technology. However, by advancing what is technically feasible, we can influence and improve the overall quality of the solution.

How can the proper designation of the roles of the individual and the NHS empower real 'control'? In this respect, we have introduced the second 'i,' which stands for innovation, to realise the changes needed in terms of the 'mindset' surrounding information. We suggest that technology is an impartial governance layer for dispersal of intelligence gathered from collective transparency, and should be positioned as complementary to individual privacy through accessibility to the WIi Fit and MIi Fit portals. Further, by placing the theoretical elements in context, we have designed a social networking style portal (MIi Fit and Wii Fit), which, as illustrated through examples, demonstrates how the portal can empower people to make choices about their healthcare (meeting the aim of the *Information Revolution*), and also determining how their information is managed and shared (or not) to empower those choices.

The creation of such a transparency tool is subject to safeguards that only authorise the disclosure of information for the necessary 'medical purposes' of improving patient care, or when disclosure is in the public interest,[3] where there is no reasonably practicable alternative to consent,[4] including rare conditions.[5] Previously, the National Information Governance Board (NIGB)[6] as a patient

3 Section 60(1) of the Health and Social Care Act 2001: '(i) does the application concern a medical purpose necessary or expedient in the interests of improving patient care or in the public interest?' It can include identification of subject population, distortion of results and a temporary measure as a precursor to anonymisation.

4 Health Research Authority Confidentiality Advisory Group (HRA CAG) considers Section 60(3) of the Health and Social Care Act 2001: '(ii) is there no reasonably practicable alternative to bypassing consent?'.

5 Department of Health, 2001. Health and Social Care Act 2001: Sections 60 and 61, 'Background Information' gives an indication of situations that may give rise to this, including the number of patients in the sample as affecting practicability.

6 National Information Governance Board for Health and Social Care (replaced the PIAG – the Patient Information Advisory Group). NIGB was an independent statutory body established to promote, improve and monitor information governance in health and adult social care. It provided advice on the appropriate use, sharing and protection of patient and service user information and was responsible for advising on the use of powers under section 251 of the NHS Act 2006 to permit the duty of

advocate and the organisation responsible for advising the Secretary of State worked to inspire public confidence. From 1 April 2013, the NIGB's functions for monitoring and improving information governance practice have been transferred to the Care Quality Commission, which has established a National Information Governance Committee to oversee the work. Functions relating to Section 251 of the NHS Act 2006 (access to people's personal and confidential information for research purposes)[7] were transferred to the Health Research Authority's (HRA) Confidentiality Advisory Group (CAG). The CAG provides independent expert advice to the HRA (for research applications) and the Secretary of State for Health (for non-research applications) on whether applications to access patient information without consent should or should not be approved.

The role of CAG is to review applications and to provide advice as to whether there is sufficient justification to access the requested confidential patient information.[8] However, like its predecessor, the final decision still remains with the Secretary of State which may create a conflict of interest considering the Secretary of State's concern over efficiencies and the UK's research reputation. The NIGB did perform convincingly as a watchdog, advising against the acceptance of two-thirds of applications for bypass regulations addressed in 2002. However, the Secretary of State did reject NIGB advice on several occasions.[9] According to Section 7(1)(d) of the regulations,[10]

---

confidentiality to be set aside, where other legal routes are not available. The NIGB provided this advice to the Secretary of State for Health, but also advised on: patients, service users and carers; health and social care organisations and practitioners; researchers and others seeking to use patient and service user information.

7 In England and Wales, section 251 of the NHS Act 2006 (originally section 60 of the Health and Social Care Act 2001) provides the statutory power to ensure that NHS patient identifiable information needed to support essential NHS activity can be used without the consent of patients. The power can be used only to support medical purposes that are in the interests of patients or the wider public, where consent is not a practicable alternative and where anonymised information will not suffice. It should be noted that although section 251 approval can temporarily set aside the common law duty of confidentiality, compliance with the Data Protection Act (1998) must still be maintained and data must still be fairly collected – i.e., individuals have a right to know who holds information about them and why. See www.dt-toolkit.ac.uk/routemaps/station.cfm?current_station_id=383.

8 www.hra.nhs.uk/about-the-hra/our-committees/section-251/#sthash.wjw81OSh.dpuf.

9 *Hansard*, HL Deb 21 May 2002, vol. 635, col. 744.

10 Sec. 7(1)(d) DPA 1998 is enacted through The Data Protection (Subject Access) (Fees and Miscellaneous Provisions) Regulations 2000, SI 2000/191. These Regulations

persons processing Patient Identifiable Data (PID)[11] must annually review their need for the information and the practicability of reducing it, but have no duty to work towards alternative solutions such as anonymisation.[12] The NHS must monitor this and transparently communicate reviews to patients. Otherwise the 'transitional' nature of bypassing consent may never be realised.

Therefore, CAG could support the NHS in monitoring reviews. However, it can be argued that such delegation of responsibility is inappropriate, usurping the judicial function of the balancing of public interest considerations, as supported by Thorpe LJ in *A Health Authority v X*.[13] This reliance on the judiciary must be diminished when power is transferred to individuals, because they will have access to such applications, bypassing consent and acting as judge and jury, where necessary, through enforcement bodies or regulators such as the ICO.

However, some legislative provisions for exceptions do require re-examination before being implemented through technology. The Health Service (Control of Patient Information) Regulations Act 2002 authorises the procurement of Patient Identifiable Data for a broad set of purposes.[14] It is not only the breadth of information that is of concern, but also those with access – which includes anyone 'employed or engaged by a government department or other public authority in communicable disease surveillance',[15] permitting a re-run of the uncertainty of *Ackroyd*.[16] Moreover, a proposed amendment to insert a clause stating that patient confidentiality should remain paramount[17] was vigorously

---

make miscellaneous provisions in respect of the exercise of the right of access to personal data conferred in section 7 of the DPA 1998.

11 Patient Identifiable Data is defined as a patient that can be directly linked back to a living individual.

12 Except perhaps the broadly phrased section 7(1)(d) of the DPA 1998.

13 [2002] All ER 780, 788.

14 Some legislative provisions require tweaks to reconsider the breadth of information available and the spectrum of people with access. In cancer research for example, it allows: (1) 'patients referred for the diagnosis or treatment of neoplasia' and (2) any patient where processing is 'with a view to diagnosing communicable diseases and other risks to public health', recognising trends and risks in such diseases and the management and monitoring of such (the Public Health Service Laboratory (PHLS) provisions).

15 Regulation 3(3)(c) The Health Service (Control of Patient Information) Regulations 2002, SI 2002/1438. The supposed safeguard is that anyone in receipt of such information is bound by confidentiality.

16 *Ackroyd v Mersey Care NHS Trust (No.2)* [2006] EWHC 107.

17 Subject to the work of cancer registries and protection of the public from communicable diseases. See *Hansard*, HL Deb 21 May 2002, vol. 635, col. 730.

rejected. Where the regulations apply, the obligation of confidence is 'modified' so that no one found in compliance with the regulations breaches confidence.[18] Although Parliament has passed seemingly contradictory legislation – protecting individual rights with the HRA and DPA, and, removing substantial portions out of those protections in the next legislative breath, which might be regarded as damning evidence of untrustworthiness[19] – what that could be perceived as contradictory legislation should be highlighted as complementary in the WIi Fit? It actually empowers the true intentions of the DPA through the CAG without the need for judicial intervention. Successful implementation is seen in the Secondary Uses Service (SUS),[20] which employs security provisions to protect data while using the data for 'public good' services.[21]

Responsibility for consulting with patients before confidential patient information is disclosed for purposes that extend beyond immediate care ('secondary purposes') is established through the interaction between three areas of law: the Data Protection Act 1998, the common law duty of confidence, and the Health Service (Control of Patient Information) Regulations 2002 (stipulated by powers now contained in s. 251 of the NHS Act 2006).[22] The Health and Social Care Act 2012 has seemingly diluted that responsibility to consult, at least as it pertains to any information that the Health and Social Care Information Centre requires health professionals to disclose. This contradicts other moves to support an individual's involvement in healthcare decisions that directly affect them.[23]

The NHS, as the only entity with an overarching view of all data, must unite pockets of collective transparency through appropriate standards for

---

18 Regulation 4, The Health Service (Control of Patient Information) Regulations 2002, SI 2002/1438.

19 See Metlay, D., 'Institutional Trust and Confidence: A Journey into Conceptual Quagmire', in Cvetkovich, G. and Lofstedt, R. (eds), *Social Trust and the Management of Risk* (Earthscan 1999) 32, regarding inconsistency between words and actions as a major cause of public distrust.

20 The Secondary Uses Services. See NHS Connecting for Health, 'Secondary Uses Service' www.connectingforhealth.nhs.uk/systemsandservices/sus/background.

21 SUS comprises the development, implementation and management of a related set of systems and services, being implemented within a consistent IG model, which ensures the security and confidentiality of PID through RBAC, encrypted pseudonyms and statistical rules. These datasets contain patient information without any form of de-identification.

22 M.J. Taylor and J. Grace, 'Disclosure of Confidential Patient Information and the Duty to Consult: The Role of the Health and Social Care Information Centre' (2013) *Med. L. Rev.* 1–33.

23 Ibid.

comparability to enact its 'positive' duties surrounding the safeguarding of positive freedoms, whilst investing in publicity to address cultural barriers to uptake. The banking industry invested billions into education and marketing, whereas the NHS tends only to conduct leaflet drops about initiatives such as the SCR[24] – uptake of which could have been the vehicle for obtaining consent and establishing control, whilst creating choice by illustrating the value of collective transparency.

As information 'owners', individuals will dictate the required control over information access, usage and distribution by their own informed justifications, which are made real through a portal we suggest should be named the MIi Fit. This subjective view of privacy must be accompanied by a clear, objective view of information that is essential for the 'public good', with justifications for its use set by the NHS and transparently communicated through a portal named the WIi Fit. This establishes the individual as information owner and controller at one end of the spectrum and as provider of consent for confidentiality at the other end of the spectrum, empowered by choice. This section considers what individuals can do at various levels of the continuum of autonomy towards 'control', illustrating how control may become an alter-ego of privacy. It assesses how the transparency and innovation the NHS creates could facilitate choices moving from the individualised to the sociological view and all permutations in between. It outlines four key options along this cycle to illustrate how 'choice' would be achieved (see Figure 3.2).

Option 1: 'Individualistic Control'

The first option gives individuals the opportunity of ongoing access to their information rather than the one-time 'Subject Access Request' information currently available, moving all power to the individual and removing the NHS from its self-imposed role as 'proxy individual'. Acceptance of power for the individualistic viewpoint would set the default control with individuals, who would only reveal information that directly benefited them individually. All information would be theirs, but they could only view the MIi Fit portal, and some information would necessarily be within the 'primary' control of the NHS, required for 'pubic good', underpinned by a legal basis. This option provides individuals with total power but no autonomous control, as they would be uninformed and potentially vulnerable.[25] However, it validates the

24 See NHS. 'Summary Care Records', www.nhscarerecords.nhs.uk/optout.

25 Patients would not be able to unilaterally change their record. It would need checks and balances by professionals as part of their safeguarding duties in line with legislative safeguards.

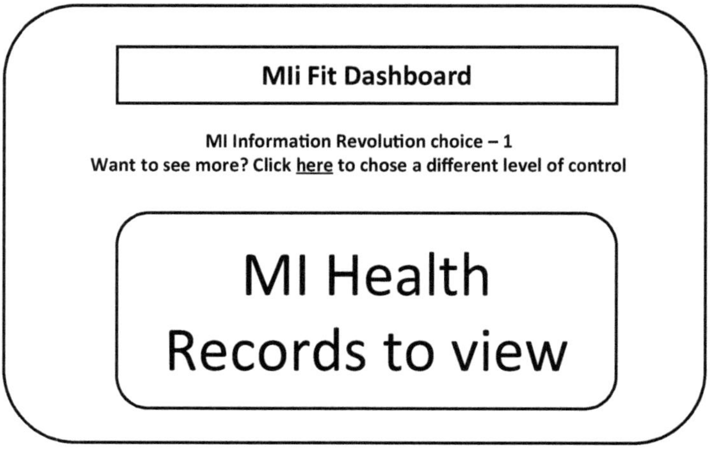

Figure 6.1 View of MIi Fit interface for Option 1

individualistic logic applied in *A v X*[26] and the informational self-determination concept of *Von Hannover v Germany*.[27] Nonetheless, it deprives both individuals with an interest,[28] and the individuals themselves from a broader societal view, thereby limiting their autonomy, which is in contradiction to the logic of traditional 'individualistic' approaches. Some individuals may decide to accept this (Figure 6.1, Option 1); those who do not want to accept even this limited amount of control can at this point give consent for the NHS to control all of their information through the legitimised duty of confidentiality.

Example scenario of an 'Option 1' decision

Mrs Jones has received her 'patient information leaflet' and decides she wants to take control of her information for her individual care. She logs on to her home computer and checks her online record on the MIi Fit to ensure that the information in her record is accurate. When she went to see the doctor near her daughter's house a few weeks ago, she was prescribed some antibiotics that she has had an allergic reaction to in the past. She was surprised that this information had not been accurately recorded

26 *A v X (Disclosure: Non-Party Medical Records)* [2004] EWHC 447, QBD.

27 *Von Hannover v Germany* (App no 59320/00) (2005) 40 EHRR 1 [50]–[53].

28 For example, the court in *A London Borough Council v Mr and Mrs N (foster carers of the Child) (1), P (A Child by her Guardian Pauline Bennett)* [2005] EWHC 1676 had to weigh the importance of disclosure and the right of a parent to know about any health risk to which their child was exposed. The local authority had no duty to inform the parent as it would impinge upon the foster parent's right to respect for his family life and breach the duty owed to him not to disclose confidential details relating to his health.

on her record, so logs on to check that it has been updated. She is worried that her safety could be compromised if she was not competent to explain her own allergies and condition. She is concerned that she could be prescribed medication that might kill her. Mrs Jones is relieved to see that the details of her allergy are now on the record. She uses the system to review alternative antibiotics, which do not contain the ingredient to which she is allergic. She finds two brands which could be offered as alternatives and emails them to her doctor to see if she can be tested for allergic reactions to them.

Mrs Jones will share this information on the file once it is confirmed, as it will directly benefit her treatment. However, she declines to share it with others who may also benefit from the alternative medication. She looks at other items in her record, including a record of the knife wound she received in 1997 when she was attacked at the airport. She sees that this has been shared with the police under the Crime and Disorder Act. She looks at the provision which covers this and learns that it is a legal requirement to share such information for reasons of public safety. Unbeknownst to Mrs Jones, by choosing to share information only for her individual care, she is limiting herself from benefiting from a broader societal view, thereby limiting her autonomy, which is in contradiction to the logic of traditional 'individualistic' approaches.

Technical controls

Mrs Jones also wants to determine that only those with a need to know can see her data, so that she can assure how the 'access control' technical IG controls are set. In the case of her choices, this means that only those who provide her direct care can see her data. She checks the technical controls and sees that it is set to only those with a clinical legitimate relationship. She is happy with this and makes sure that the 'care.data' option is marked as 'do not share'. It is ticked, which means her data is not passed on to the Health and Social Care Information Centre for purposes other than direct care. This is correct in accordance with Mrs Jones' wishes. She can change it online at any time.

Option 2: Restricted Access

We suggest that those who would choose Option 2 are not limited to accessing their data for this individualistic view, such as that offered by HealthSpace, but can also experience restricted access[29] without the 'liberty' of decisional privacy required for human dignity.[30] They can access the MIi Fit and WIi Fit,

---

29 A. Allen, *Uneasy Access: Privacy for Women in a Free Society* (Rowman and Littlefield 1988).

30 E. Bloustein, 'Privacy as an Aspect of Human Dignity: An Answer to Dean Prosser' (1964) 39 *NYU L. Rev.* 962.

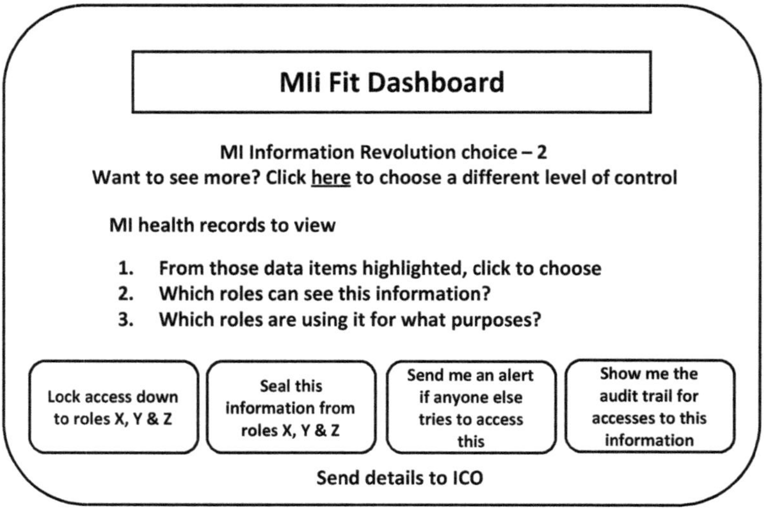

Figure 6.2 View of MIi Fit for Option 2

as this affords two-way access control empowered via acceptance of power and individual operation of the 'patient choice' IG controls via technology to control the information the NHS suggested was in its 'sphere'. This supports Mill's[31] public/private distinction of governmental control and self-regulation. Posner[32] legitimises this in his argument that organisational privacy takes precedence for economic reasons. Although this may reinforce misconceptions about privacy, it is particularly apt for the collective transparency agenda. It is this access that the *Information Revolution* aspires to, but labels 'control'.[33] This would allow individuals a clear view of all roles within the care system that are allowed access through 'patient choice' IG controls, which would help to inform individuals' decisions accordingly (Figure 6.2, Option 2; Figure 6.3, Options 2–4).

31 J.S. Mill, *On Liberty* (Longman, Roberts and Green 1869).

32 R.A. Posner, *The Economics of Justice* (Harvard University Press 1981).

33 Department of Health, 'Equality and Excellence, Liberating the NHS' (White Paper, Cm 7881, 2010); Department of Health, 'An Information Revolution: A Consultation on Proposals' (2010). www.dh.gov.uk/prod_consum_dh/groups/dh_digitalassets/@dh/@en/documents/digital asset/dh_120664.pdf Para. 2.7. The options here provide a stark contrast to the definition the Department of Health assume of 'control' as 'access'.

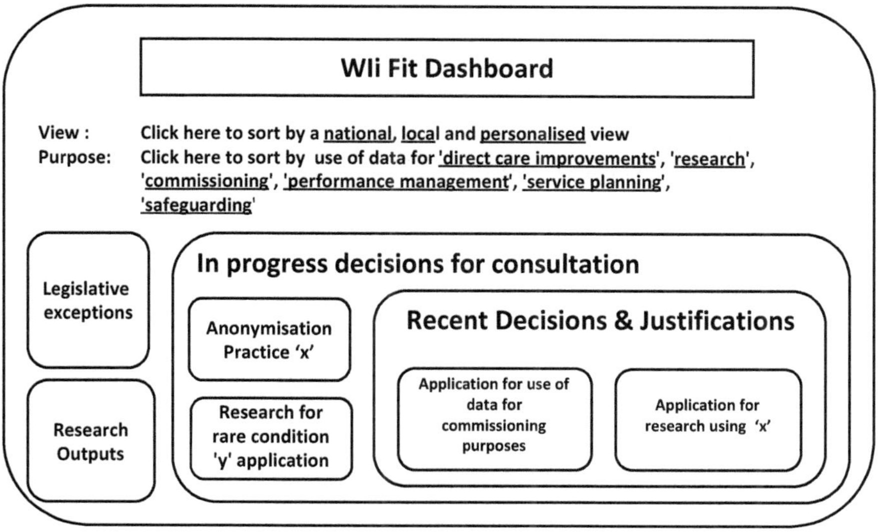

Figure 6.3 View of WIi Fit interface for Options 2–4 (showing both 'why' (WI) information has been shared and how 'we' (WIi) can benefit)

> **Example scenario of an 'Option 2' decision**
>
> Ms Miller has received her 'patient information leaflet' and decides she wants to take control of her information within the limits imposed by the NHS so that she can see both the MIi Fit and the WIi Fit interfaces. However, she accepts without question the restrictions to access/control imposed by the NHS. She logs on to her home computer and checks her online record on the MIi Fit, and she checks the WIi Fit to see the benefits to society afforded by the use of her data. She can see that the NHS has used her data for a research study on cancer granted under regulations of s. 251 of the NHS Act 2006 and is pleased.

Option 3: Boundaries

As for 'others', those who wish to accept more control and to assess the NHS's 'information guardian' choices surrounding imputed/implied consent, can choose Option 3 (Figure 6.4). This would give access to the 'access control' and 'access monitoring' IG controls. This would suggest a move from Allen's[34] 'restricted access' towards Altman's[35] boundaries theory of informational privacy. Under

---

34 See note 29.

35 Altman, I., 'Privacy Regulation: Culturally Universal or Culturally Specific?' (1977) 33(3) *J. Social Issues* 66.

such conditions, in our view, this would solve the issue in *I v Finland*[36] because individuals would be able to exercise decisional privacy[37] by reviewing and accepting the rationale of 'public good' exceptions set through provisions such as s. 251. The application and review process through the NIGB and ECC would be accessible, so that individuals could view the access logs to ensure that the correct entities have been granted access to view the correct portions of their records and check the monitoring logs to ensure that only groups/people with 'legitimate relationships' have accessed it. This ensures the 'secondary' control articulated by Johnson.[38] Control could be more easily conceptualised by representing 'privacy' (Figure 6.1) more tangibly, such as property,[39] so that 'divisions' can be built through application, following Warren and Brandeis' conceptualisation of privacy as both a property right and a personal right.[40] Much like property, maintenance is required, which is the individual's 'responsibility'. Additionally, much like the situation with easements, rules must be established regarding what will typically be accepted if clearly communicated, and if the benefits are transparent. However, unlike trespass on property, access to information cannot be reversed, but as no new information is acquired, the unapproved suggestions for access are only 'trespasses' until approved.[41]

It is interesting to note that in healthcare the property concept moves towards the control end of the spectrum, but it was originally conceived as an individualistic expression[42]; applying the same approach it highlights how 'privacy in public'[43] as a concept can be achieved. This realises the subtle difference between individual starting points for privacy and individualistic conceptions of privacy, thereby underpinned by legislation shown in Figure 6.3. Warren and Brandeis'[44] individualistic conception of privacy is validated by

36 *I v Finland* Application no. 20511/03, 17 October 2008.

37 S. Margulis, 'Perceptions of Privacy: Current Status and Next Steps' (1977) 33(3) *J. Social Issues* 5, 10.

38 C. Johnson, 'Privacy as Personal Control' in Carson, D. (ed.), *Man–Environment Interactions: Evaluations and Applications: part 2* (Washington, DC: Environmental Design Research Association 1974).

39 J. Thomson, 'The right to Privacy' (1975) 4(4) *Philosophy and Public Affairs* 295.

40 S. Warren. and L. Brandeis, 'The Right to Privacy' (1890) 4 *Harv. L. Rev.* 193.

41 W. Parent, 'Privacy, Morality and the Law' (1983) 12(4) *Philosophy and Public Affairs* 269; for example, there is no consensus as to whether privacy is a property right or a personal one, which we have discussed in Chapter 2.

42 See note 40.

43 J. Moor, 'Towards a Theory of Privacy in the Information Age' (1997) 27 *Computers and Society* 3, 27.

44 See note 40.

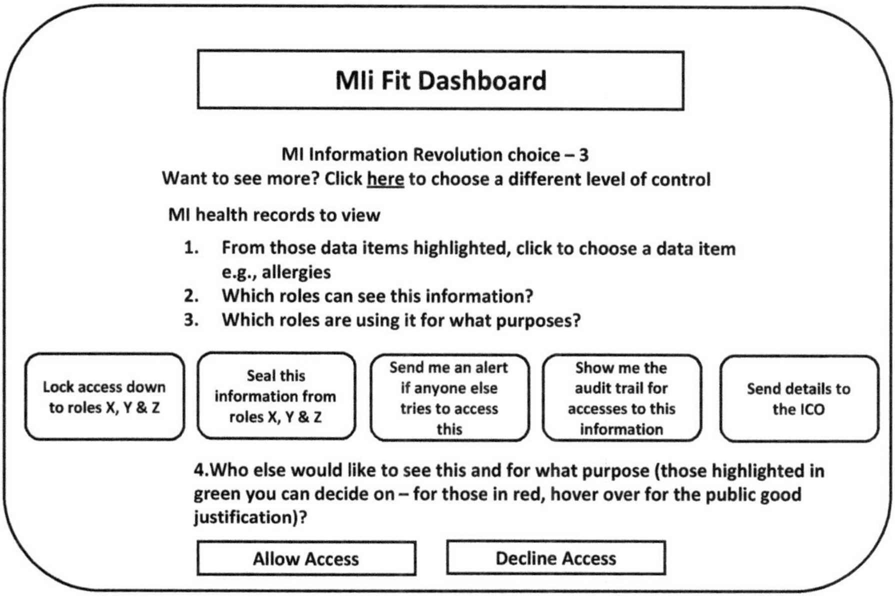

Figure 6.4 View of MIi Fit for Option 3

control, which rejuvenates individualistic laws through the use of technology to facilitate individual starting points for control, along with acknowledgement of the sociological view through control.

Example scenario of an 'Option 3' decision

Ms Dendle has received her 'patient information leaflet' and decides she wants to take control of her information and check that the limits imposed by the NHS are appropriate, by checking on both the MIi Fit and WIi Fit interfaces.

Ms Dendle wants to exercise control over the 'patient choice' controls so that her preferences can set the access controls for those who can see her data. Ms Dendle decides that she will seal and lock part of her record relating to a set of tests she had from all support staff and those not involved in administering her direct care.

Option 4: Sociological Control

Our proposal, for those who are willing to accept complete control in its most robust form, extends the mutual benefit from 'owned' (or perhaps 'sub-let') property to the individual and society to its full potential through the fourth option (Figure 6.5: Option 4), thus completing the full information revolution. So, for instance, individuals who choose to accept control and not just access,

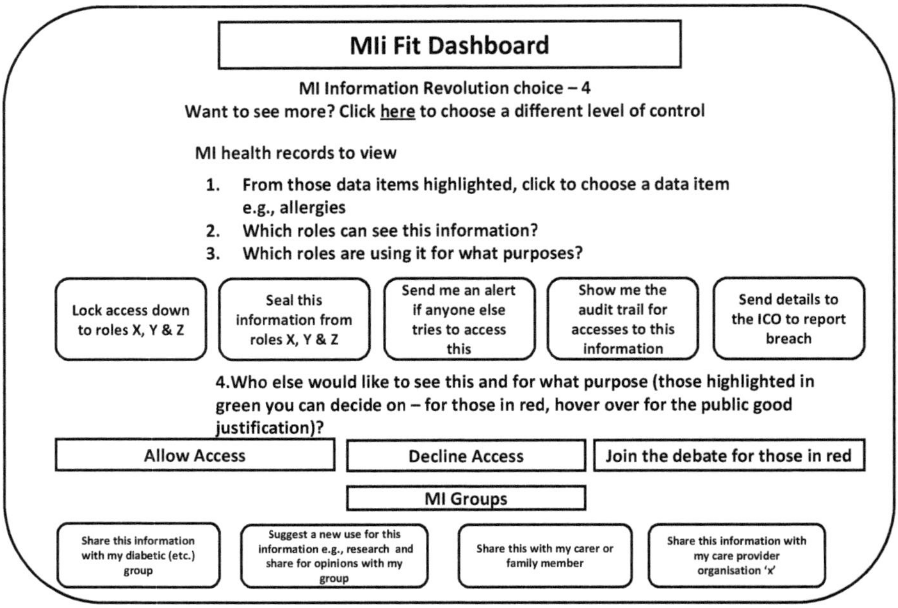

Figure 6.5 View of the MIi Fit for Option 4

following the spirit of Parent's[45] conception of privacy, control of all 'IG' controls moves individuals from the 'boundaries' conception of informational privacy to what is termed as 'sociological' control. In this optimal manifestation of 'privacy', individuals can proactively make appropriate use of regulations and legislations, such as appealing to the Information Commissioner Office (ICO) when Data Protection principles are alleged to be breached by the boundaries set by the NHS. We argue that seeking to realign boundaries in this way breathes new life into the social phenomenon of privacy[46] while allowing the NHS to fulfil its safeguarding duties.

Furthermore, by extending the 'restricted-access/control' theory,[47] individuals may also choose to proactively provide additional information they think may help the 'public good' or health communities they wish to join,[48] which we argue

45 See note 41.

46 See I. Altman, *The Environment and Social Behavior: Privacy, Personal Space, Territory, Crowding* (Brooks/Cole 1975).

47 See J. Moor, 'Towards a Theory of Privacy in the Information Age' (1997) 27 *Computers and Society* 3, 27.

48 See N. Zakaria and J.M. Stanton, 'The Social Dynamic of Health Disclosure: Who Do Patients Tell and When?' (2008) 1(1) *Computer and Information Sci.* 72.

would support the concept of privacy as a set of norms[49] necessary not only to control access but also to enhance personal expression and choice.[50] The active contribution of personal information moves the boundaries of 'control' beyond Moor's theory, extending informational privacy into privacy of the self. There is evidence from Greenhalgh's[51] review of 'HealthSpace' and Zakaria's[52] research into patient disclosure patterns which has showed desire amongst patients for such choice.

This also echoes the foundations of privacy as control over information about oneself,[53] alongside each individual's realisation of 'definite' privacy rights.[54] It gives power to the conceptualisation of privacy as protection from unwanted access[55] by others, alongside the perception of 'value'[56] that accords us the ability to control the access others have to us.[57] It is further argued that 'informed consent'[58] and the 'publicity principle' make this social power more democratic,[59] even replacing or joining a new incarnation of the now defunct Ethics and Confidentiality Committee in debates, following the sentiments of GMC[60] and MRC[61] guidance, but also defying[62] the fear of losing judicial

49 See F. Schoeman, (ed.), *Privacy and Social Freedom* (CUP 1992).

50 Personal Health Records could facilitate this. Some Trusts have already implemented Personal Health Records, for example South London and Maudsley, which allow patients to input to and share records as they feel appropriate. See South London and Maudsley Primary Care Trust, 'SLaM Electronic Personal Health Records' www.slam.nhs.uk/media/254920/microsoftmaudsley%20faqs.pdf.

51 T. Greenhalgh, K. Stramer, T. Bratan, E. Byrne, J. Russell, S. Hinder, H. Potts, The Devil's in the Detail: Final Report of the Independent Evaluation of the Summary Care Record and HealthSpace Programmes' (University College London 2010) 6, www.ucl.ac.uk/news/scriesummary.pdf.

52 See note 48.

53 See note 40.

54 See W. Prosser, 'Privacy' (1960) 48 *Calif. L. Rev.* 383, 389.

55 See S. Bok, *Secrets: On the Ethics of Concealment and Revelation* (Pantheon 1982).

56 See R. Gavison, 'Privacy and the Limits of Law' (1980) 89 *Yale L. J.* 421–471; Anita Allen, *Uneasy Access: Privacy for Women in a Free Society* (Rowman and Littlefield 1988); A. Moore, 'Privacy: Its Meaning and Value' (2003) 40(3) *Am Philos. Q.* 215–217.

57 See J. DeCew, *In Pursuit of Privacy: Law, Ethics, and the Rise of Technology* (Cornell University Press 1997).

58 See note 47.

59 See A.D. Moore, 'Privacy: Its Meaning and Value' (2003) 40(3) *Am Philos. Q.* 215–227; see also note 47.

60 GMC, 'Patient Information in Medical Research' (September 2000) para. 34.

61 MRC, 'Patient Information in Medical Research' (2000) para. 2.2.2.

62 The Medical Research Council also involves research ethics committees in the procedure stating that the 'judgement that consent is impracticable is never that of the

scrutiny.[63] Individuals can challenge the NHS's interpretation of the legislative/regulatory process rather than just the rationale and, in so doing it would move the starting point to a new concept unique to knowledge-based services/organisations, being termed 'proxy-sociological'. This action can be taken by the NHS or by individuals when pushing beyond a full revolution of the theories, because transparency changes the dynamic that made the NHS the only 'primary' decision maker. Only then can normatively private situations[64] be legitimate, as regulations are defined by the people that they affect, thereby avoiding the necessity of 'overzealous'[65] reliance on Human Rights Act 'fundamental' privacy right[66] claims such as *Finland*.[67] Likewise, it avoids the vulnerabilities of society due to the precedence of other groups' privacy,[68] alongside the state's conflict of interest, as has been highlighted in *Interbrew*.[69] Such individualistic interpretations by the courts are acceptable if there is individual control and visibility.

At the other end of the spectrum, this sociological perspective is also legitimately achieved where these options are presented but declined, and therefore consent is given to the NHS to control an individual's health record in a way that ensures the sociological aspects of 'privacy' are respected. This validation of the NHS's 'information guardian' role means that the extension of the state's ability to safeguard society's rights must be respected,[70] which provides further justification to societal considerations.[71] The quasi-vicarious ability of the NHS to litigate in order to safeguard society's rights would no longer be exercisable only against the NHS itself, as responsibility and accountability would be visible and evidenced through audit trails. We argue that legislation would consequently no longer 'miss the mark'[72] as responsibility and accountability would be allocated so that legislation could be used by the information controller (the NHS or the individual) to target the wrongdoers. Therefore, this progression is not linear but circular, both eventually

researcher alone: unless an ethics committee concurs, and health professionals agree to participate in the study on this basis, the research cannot take place'.

63 C. Foster and N. Peacock, *Clinical Confidentiality* (Monitor Press 2000) 16.

64 See note 47.

65 See Lord Woolf's warnings in *Daniels v Walker* [2000] 1 WLR 1382.

66 *R v Department of Health ex parte Source Informatics* [2001] QB 424.

67 *I v Finland Application no. 20511/03*, 17 October 2008.

68 *Ackroyd v Mersey Care NHS Trust (No.2)* [2006] EWHC 107 and *Ashworth Security Hospital v MGN Ltd* [2001] 1 WLR 515.

69 [2002] EWCA Civ 274, [2002] 2 Lloyd's Rep 229.

70 See *Ackroyd v Mersey Care NHS Trust (No.2)* [2006] EWHC 107.

71 *Ashworth Security Hospital v MGN Ltd* [2001] 1 WLR 515 35.

72 P. Leith, 'The socio-legal context of privacy' (2006) 2 *IJLC* 2, 105.

disintermediating the 'proxy-individualistic' role through consent and making the 'sociological control' stage the optimal stage, where individual control replaces 'privacy'. This 'proxy-sociological'[73] perspective assumed by the NHS would be facilitated by technology, as 'public good' data could still be 'private' through anonymisation. However, it can also be argued that data cannot truly be anonymised in health.[74] Regardless, the NHS would also need to consider privacy from society's viewpoint.

The NHS has a dual role to play in innovation – both developing the WIi Fit and MIi Fit interfaces and promoting a secure infrastructure to store and communicate information reported in a standardised way through both portals.[75] This should be facilitated by technical standards designed to implement IG controls (which could be exercised by individuals by choosing Options 2–4 (Figure 6.3)) into IT systems. The NHS must continue to drive uptake of Electronic Health Records (EHRs) to enable individuals' access. This has been a blocker to the uptake of HealthSpace, as implementation of the Summary Care Record[76] has been on a regional basis. One method to instil confidence in EHR uptake is to improve its security provisions in order to minimise publicised incidents[77] and instil confidence in an NHS that is capable of protecting complex, interoperable EHRs.[78]

The lesson is clear: following the lead of other industries such as the banking industry, the NHS should produce identity cards, rolling out unique NHS numbers[79] and card readers whilst continually updating security patches and

---

73 The 'proxy-sociological' perspective is a term created to explain a viewpoint taken that starts from the perspective of society as a whole, facilitated by the 'WIi Fit' view of collective transparency.

74 See J. Miola, 'Owning Information – Anonymity, Confidentiality and Human Rights' (2008) 3(3) *CE* 116.

75 Intellect, 'NHS Chief Executive innovation review – the ICT industry's response' (August 2011).

76 For a continual update and further information, see NHS, 'Summary Care Record: Your Emergency Care Record' www.nhscarerecords.nhs.uk/faqs.

77 Kablenet, 'Lib Dems Call for New NHS Data Security Rules', *The Register* (28 November2008), www.theregister.co.uk/2008/11/28/lib_dem_nhs.

78 See A. Sheikh, 'Confidentiality and Privacy of Patient Information and Records: A Need for Vigilance in Accessing, Storing and Discussing Patient Information' (2010) 16(1) *MLJI* 2, 5: 'If custodians cannot be trusted to protect the personal health information stored on a simple portable device such as a USB key, how will they ever manage to protect the massive amounts of personal health information that will eventually reside within complex systems of interoperable electronic health records?'

79 Everyone registered with the NHS in England has their own unique NHS number – this could be used as a unique identifier. For further details see NHS

creating security alerts to facilitate innovation uptake. The NHS should create a user interface based on familiar social networking technology, where individuals are empowered through technology to view and control their information as stringently as they choose. By having access to the two views through these portals – the WIi Fit and MIi Fit – individuals would realise the mutual benefit of balancing individual privacy (MIi Fit) and collective transparency (WIi Fit). The controls on the MIi Fit interface should incorporate IG controls exercisable with this balance in mind while promoting increased awareness of individuals' currently underused redress channel through the ICO.[80] The intentions of the HRA and DPA, regarded as effecting change in legal ownership of personal data and vesting it almost exclusively in the data subject, could feasibly be implemented through technology with the advantage of a secure infrastructure run by the NHS. Through technology, the NHS would be providing an impartial governance layer – a technical vehicle for proper implementation of the law – overseen by individuals.

Example scenario of an 'Option 4' decision

Mr Miller has received his 'patient information leaflet' and decides he wants to take control of his information and check that the limits imposed by the NHS are appropriate, by controlling both the MIi Fit and WIi Fit interfaces from a sociological perspective. He logs on to his home computer and checks his online record on the MIi fit before releasing the contents to be used for the benefit of the community, after reviewing the benefits of collective transparency which he can see on the WIi Fit.

Mr Miller wants to exercise control over the 'patient choice' controls so that his preferences can set the 'access controls'. Mr Miller decides that he will allow all direct care clinicians the right to see all of his record.

He wants to check the 'access control' technical controls, to ensure that the correct technical settings are assigned to the correct workgroups. He checks the audit trail and all alerts to ensure he is fully aware of any accesses which have needed to be drawn to the attention of an IG Officer.

He looks on the WIi Fit to see what applications are underway to use data about Mr Miller for research purposes. He can see that the NHS are applying to the Confidentiality Advisory Group to use his data for a research study on arthritis in the under-65s under regulations of s. 251 of the NHS Act 2006. He reads the full application but is left wondering why they cannot use anonymous data for this. He would not mind them using his data but cannot see why the people using it have

---

Choices, 'The NHS Number', www.nhs.uk/NHSEngland/thenhs/records/Pages/thenhsnumber.aspx.

80 This is currently underused by patients; see the ICO website at www.ico.gov.uk/for_the_public.aspx.

to know it is him. He sends an email to the address on the WIi Fit asking why confidential information is required for this. He also queries who identified him as eligible for such a study as he wonders whether this was a breach of confidentiality. He checks the audit trail but sees no mention of this. He includes this query on the email and wonders whether this is a data protection breach that he should be notifying the ICO of. He knows he can do this through the MIi Fit so is happy to wait for an explanation.

Thinking about the arthritis study he wonders whether it would be useful to share his experience of the physiotherapy he recently underwent. As a result of the physiotherapy he felt much better and was able to return to work in less than one month although the estimated recovery time was three months. He wanted others to benefit from this so went onto the WIi Fit to suggest that this should be included in the data base so that people like him could log on and have an informed choice of which treatment path to choose. He adds the information to his MIi Fit portal in the section allocated to his notes so that any clinicians know the patient has voluntarily offered this information and that it does not alter the 'master' copy of his record.

Thinking about future treatment, Mr Miller decided he would like to be able to benefit directly from the experiences and treatment choices of others who have characteristics like him. He would like to log on to the Wii Fit and select from some drop down options his gender, age, local area, existing conditions, allergies and factors in treatments that are important to him. To narrow down the search results he would choose to receive data on those who have logged that the treatment they received resulted in 'recovery within three months' and was 'painless'. He would like to benefit from the tacit knowledge of other people like him so that he knows first-hand how others experienced the treatment options, rather than him being told what is best for him by a GP. He sends this idea out to his network on the MIi Fit, which comprises other arthritis sufferers who have signed up to join the group on the WIi Fit. He thinks that even if 100 of the 3,500 people in that group volunteer their information then that is enough to get a reliable opinion on the best options for him. His alternative would be to ask only the one or two people he knew with similar conditions so he did not feel he could lose from suggesting this.

Example scenario of 'Option 4' decisions: The concept of confidentiality legitimised by consent

Mrs Walker is a busy single parent who has an unspectacular medical history. She has had a look at the 4 options of control and does not want to take any of them – she does not have the time and trusts that the NHS will use her information appropriately. She is fully informed through the MIi and WIi Fit of what the NHS is doing with her information but says that she is happy with the way they are balancing her 'individual privacy' and 'collective transparency' and does not require more control. By doing this she is providing the 'informed consent' to the NHS which is required to validate the ruling concept of 'confidentiality'. This has the same outcome as stage 4 decisions, only the NHS are making the decision on behalf of the individual for the benefit of society.

Sharing information with other Agencies

Although we recognise that there are areas in which the individual cannot use the MIi and WIi fit to make decisions, this must be communicated in a general, uniform manner through a notice on the MIi and WIi fit portal, explaining that information can be shared when it is in the best interests of the patient, and also when there is a legal basis governing the handling of certain health information. The sharing of data among certain agencies may be deemed in the interest of the individual or society at large. The NHS would need to transparently demonstrate that whether it is to society or the individual, the benefit of breaching confidentiality outweighs the duty of confidentiality. We have identified some scenarios where the sharing of data will yield substantial benefit to society, such as in the areas of public health, police matters, the justice system, children's services, and, finally, in determining the competence of an individual under the provisions of the Mental Capacity Act.

Where there is an identifiable public health risk, such as in the case of tuberculosis or another infectious disease, there are legal provisions, including Control of Infectious Diseases Regulations (Statutory Order 2002), which designate that a 'proper officer' with the local authority must be notified of the situation. Although the individual would not have a choice in the sharing of this health information because of the Statutory Order establishing the legal basis for such action, the individual should nonetheless be informed of the need to share health information to prevent the spread of disease. In the case of police matters, one example is a patient with a knife wound or gunshot wound that must be reported to the police. The Police and Criminal Evidence Act and the Crime and Disorder Act form the legal basis for such disclosure.

The justice system may compel the sharing of health information when, for example, a court order is obtained compelling the NHS to disclose confidential information to the court to aid in criminal proceedings. This could be related to issues such as the prevention of fraud. For example, details of prescription activity could be released to the court in an attempt to track down a specific individual suspected of fraud. Additionally, there are special legal provisions for children pursuant to the Children Act 2004. This means that information must be shared to safeguard a child who could be at risk of neglect, violence, abuse, or other harm.

There are other occasions when the sharing of information is not for safeguarding of the public but, rather, is required to ensure that direct care provided to an individual is safe and effective in the context of providing better and more efficient 'integrated care'. For example, social services and educational systems must be made aware of a diagnosis of Attention Deficiency Hyperactivity Disorder (ADHD) in a child to ensure the child receives proper ongoing care and treatment. The same applies to vulnerable adults who, for example, are transferred from a hospital setting into a care home setting. The care home staff who need to look after the patient may need access to some confidential information in order to provide safe and effective care. This could include information on patient allergies, eating and sleeping habits, and mental health issues, some of which may pose a danger to fellow service users.

We argue that other choices can be made via the WIi and MIi Fit as part of a broader discussion. There are three broad areas in law in which patient autonomy is limited: the Mental Capacity Act; the Mental Health Act; and statutes related to the autonomy of young people to keep certain information from their parents. Any reviews of principles and practices in these areas must consider whether patient control of health records and access to the WIi and MIi Fit portals may be affected. An example follows.

> Mr Jones is a 97-year-old man in a full-time care home. He is visited by his son regularly, who is one of his caregivers and stays in regular contact with caregivers in the home. Mr Jones sees his GP every six weeks for a check-up. He has never used a computer. He has received a leaflet about taking control of his medical information. When Mr Jones and his son next visit the GP, they decide together that his son will control his information, taking the stage 4 option. His son plans to discuss the choices with his father as he makes them to ensure they are in his father's best interest. This means they are able to discuss options at times when his father, who suffers from dementia, is more lucid.

Additionally, children, by virtue of their age, lack the necessary competence to make information sharing decisions. However, as we have discussed before in Chapter 4, Gillick[81] competency and Fraser guidelines have been used to help assess whether a child has the maturity to make his or her own decisions and to understand the implications of those decisions.[82] Of course, Gillick

81 Oxford Radcliffe Confidentiality guidelines; http://confidential.oxfordradcliffe.net/Gillick; Gillick v West Norfolk and Wisbech AHA (1986) AC112 HL.

82 A further incongruity is also provided by Access to Health Records Act 1990, which allows a child under 16, deemed 'Gillick competent' by a doctor, to veto a parent's access to medical information held by that doctor, even though the parent can consent to treatment which the child cannot veto. The result is that a doctor, if he judges the

competency cannot be assessed online but, rather, only when a child presents at the physician's office. Under normal circumstances, Gillick competency can be assessed, and the decision can also take into account choice of control over the MIi Fit. Individuals can choose read-only access to the WIi Fit at any age, which demonstrates the value of collective transparency but does not identify individuals.

Implementation: How Can This Be Delivered?

There is an argument that the proliferation of information technology has had the paradoxical effect of actually creating more barriers to communication. Although it seems easy and convenient to suggest the internet as the mechanism through which the public can control their data, one of the distinctive challenges would be, quite simply, what to do about those who are not IT literate or do not have a computer. The proposed portal access will be over and above existing channels such as leaflet drops and conversations with GPs. GP surgeries, health centres, hospitals, community centres and libraries should have free access to such services, which would support ministerial commitments for 'online access for all'.

Patients' access to their own medical records is an important element of patient-centred healthcare.[83] We argue that our proposed 'portal' access to personal healthcare records has the potential to profoundly influence the delivery of healthcare by changing the loci and control/'ownership' of the record from one that is distributed amongst the various healthcare providers to one with a single source that is accessible from anywhere in the world and under the shared ownership and control of the patient and NHS. As we have discussed in the previous chapter, a recent report by a coalition of six health-based All-Party Parliamentary Groups proposes that patients should be allowed to 'own' and interact with their medical records if they are to be fully involved in their own care.[84] EHRs provide patients with a means to a

---

child to be 'Gillick competent', can only disclose information to the parent with the child's consent regardless of parental responsibilities.

83 S. G. S. Shah, R. Fitton, A. Hannan, B. Fisher, T. Young, and J. Barnett, 'Accessing Personal Medical Records Online: A Means to What Ends?' (2015) 84(2) *Int. J. Med. Informatics* 111–118.

84 The report cites Denmark's electronic health record system, which since 2003 has allowed patients to access and partially edit their individual health records (as discussed in Chapter 2). A report by the All Party Parliamentary Groups on Global Health; HIV/AIDs; Population, Development and Reproductive Health; Global Tuberculosis; and Patient and Public Involvement in Health and Social Care, Patient empowerment: for better quality, more sustainable health services globally, May 2014.

range of ends, which extend above and beyond savings. Most notably, access and utilisation of EHRs enabled people to have an enhanced role in managing their personal health.[85] The report provided compelling arguments which recommended that the underlying aim should be to prioritise and invest in access to patient decision aids to involve patients in making shared decisions about their care. It highlighted the successfully implemented example of the Health Decision Sciences Centre at Massachusetts General Hospital, which allows doctors in primary and secondary care to 'prescribe' an aid through a patient's electronic medical record which they can then access outside of their consultation. However, 'the experiences of other countries suggest that access alone is unlikely to drive significant use of records by patients, but that some degree of co-ownership or interactivity with their health information can'.[86]

We further argue that the opportunities that this technical solution might offer cannot be underestimated. Although our proposal for a technical solution is unique in its context, there are a few examples of similar unencumbered uses of technology under comparable circumstances, one of which is 'online banking'. These examples include highly sensitive or valuable information, and we are only prepared to share it with a system or person that we control or trust. Similar to the online banking model, to make this operate securely would also require a significant level of investment from the NHS in terms of technological security measures. It is acknowledged that not all households have access to the internet, nor do all patients have the competency to make information sharing decisions. The portals are designed to be used with others if required, for example in a doctor's office with a clinician or support staff where assessments of competence would be made in the same way they currently are regarding information sharing decisions. There would also be the functionality to allow decisions to be made jointly with family members and/or carers. No member of the public would be disadvantaged should they choose not to use this mode of communication. How likely are people to use technology for engagement of such information?

Individuals cannot answer the question of whether they would value control of their records through the portal, without knowing what it will mean for them. Research from the Institute for Insight into the Public Services (IIPS)

---

85 See note 83; Lemai Nguyen et al., 'Electronic Health Records Implementation: An Evaluation of Information System Impact and Contingency Factors' (2014) 83(11) *Int. J. Med. Informatics* 779–796.

86 A report by the All Party Parliamentary Groups on Global Health; HIV/AIDs; Population, Development and Reproductive Health; Global Tuberculosis; and Patient and Public Involvement in Health and Social Care, Patient empowerment: for better quality, more sustainable health services globally, May 2014.

shows that consumers are generally willing for their data to be shared across public services as long as there are demonstrable benefits.[87] This willingness to share data relies heavily on the confidence and trust of people that their data is being properly protected. While it is difficult to envisage how patient control of health records might be used, local and international examples demonstrate a wide range of possibilities, for example:

- secure messaging between clinician and patient that reduces the need for face-to-face appointments;
- making an appointment;
- reviewing and correcting records, including medication errors;
- seeking a repeat prescription;
- detailing who health service providers should contact in case of emergency, for example, if the patient arrives unconscious in A&E; and
- updating advanced directives, including whether the circumstances in which the person would or would not wish to be resuscitated.

Significantly, the Health Foundation's research[88] has also found that patient access to, and control over, their health records supports a new paradigm of health relationships:

- It improves relationships with clinicians by creating transparency, promoting informed discussions and engendering a sense of involvement.
- It means patients are better informed about care and medication, and enabled to correct errors and omissions.
- It provides flexibility for patients – who don't have to go to the GP practice or hospital.
- It increases patients' ability to contribute to decision making.
- It increases people's ability to manage their own healthcare and their confidence to do so.
- It improves compliance in heart disease, hyperlipidemia and depression.[89]

---

87 IIPS, 'Data and Privacy: How Concerned Are Citizens about Data Sharing in the Public Services? (May 2008).

88 Health Foundation response to Conservative Party consultation on the personal ownership of health records www.health.org.uk/areas-of-work/influencing-policy/consultation-responses/the-personal-ownership-of-health-records/.

89 www.health.org.uk/areas-of-work/influencing-policy/consultation-responses/the-personal-ownership-of-health-records/.

In theory, the principle of greater personal ownership of information could have a potentially positive impact for consumers. We would expect that personal ownership of records might encourage people to take greater responsibility for their health as they would be much closer to their information. Greater familiarity with their records could make it easier to communicate effectively with a mix of providers and allow for patients to be on a more even footing with professionals or advocates.

Conclusion. Control as an Alter Ego of Privacy – Empowering 'Choice' *and* 'Control'

This book is about promoting informed decision making, and facilitating actions designed to improve an individual's personal capacity to make informed choices about sharing their health data. The proposal we offer here aims to provide a direction to build on rather than equivocation with existing postulates. The *Information Revolution* promises choice and control to patients but doesn't consider repositioning the control of information by individuals as an enabler. The NHS assumes a paternal 'proxy' individual role which means the role of the individual is masked so they cannot enforce autonomy-based laws. Although 'confidentiality' is the ruling concept which governs the legal processing of data, in health it is not currently always underpinned by the consent of the patient, so it is often illegitimate. We argue that the roles of the individual and the NHS need to be reconsidered and that the required mindset and informational changes can be implemented through the technology of the MIi Fit and WIi Fit.

Currently there is limited transparency for the public as to whether the NHS is balancing this critically important informational relationship (collective transparency and individual privacy) or whether its approach is fit for purpose. We understand the value of both individual privacy and 'collective transparency' in healthcare information as complementary and there must be a change of mindset around 'privacy', moving privacy from an individualistic concept to a concern for society. The balance required between 'individual privacy' and 'collective' transparency' reflects this which can be achieved through MIi Fit and WIi Fit.

However, the question remains whether this practical solution can be applied to different jurisdictions. Does this provide a new vision for sharing of personal medical data which could applied to any country as it is administered through the internet? Of course it does. Our model is an exploration of 'the art of the possible'. We are – after all – living in a globalised society where there are no geographical boundaries; best practices from one part of the world can be replicated in other parts of the world.

It is further argued that an internet based portal could allow people to access and control their own data, or allow others to, wherever in the world they may need treatment. In Chapter 2, while analysing how healthcare data is handled in Europe and the USA[90] in an attempt to find the best practice that could be applied within the UK framework, we found that there is no clear common practice in healthcare across Europe. This is something which needs to change to make the current financial regime sustainable – could passing control of information over to the patient contribute to this? The principle that individuals are the controllers of their own health data, with the right to make decisions over access to the data and to be informed about how it will be used is outlined in EU law and European jurisprudence but is rarely fully implemented in health systems. Our conclusion is that even in those countries that have substantially invested in eHealth applications in Europe such as Denmark, Sweden, Estonia, and Spain are yet to develop a population that can fully control their own health data.

In England, the challenges of fully implementing online proposals such as the Summary Care Record and HealthSpace alongside the delay in the care. data roll out highlight the inherent problems with sharing of healthcare data. We argue that this perception can be changed by our solution as it can ensure the shift from patient 'access to' their healthcare information to 'control of' that information to facilitate and support patients playing a greater role in managing their health and their treatment. We also argue that the solution helps with this because the portal will provide the means to support patients' active contribution to improved healthcare outcomes rather than the rationale that drives the change. The clinician and/or individual can 'own' the information through the appropriate transparency and control and the individual would never directly alter the master copy of the record. Any additions would be made to a 'patient' copy of the record. Legal liability would be addressed by the individual being made aware of the repercussions of sharing decisions, perhaps face to face or as deemed appropriate. This would mean patients would control their own health records, granting access to their carers as required.

As of January 2014, the use of an 'EMR' in the USA has become mandatory under the American Recovery and Reinvestment Act of 2009, which also allows the sharing of the whole medical record between different providers.[91] In the

90 M. Pine, M. et al., 'Harnessing the Power of Enhanced Data for Healthcare Quality Improvement: Lessons from a Minnesota Hospital Association Pilot Project' (2012) 57(6) *J. Healthcare Management* 406–418, 419–420.

91 T. Ferguson, 'Online Patient-Helpers and Physicians Working Together: A New Partnership for High Quality Health Care' (2000) 321 *BMJ* 1129–1132.

USA, the law provides incomplete, unclear, and somewhat inconsistent answers to the question of who owns medical information. This can be changed by our solution as it gives patients the right to control access to their medical information, and to inspect and to provide the opportunity for the patient to contribute new information to their medical record. However, it does not entail the right to destroy or exclusively possess medical information. The solution helps with this because healthcare providers can own a patient's medical information per se in the same way that owning a book does not equate with owning its intellectual content. Likewise, a doctor's or hospital's ownership of medical records does not foreclose or interfere with others' ownership of different embodiments of the same information. Multiple ownership of different pieces of a patient's medical history, however, makes it difficult for anyone to assemble a complete record.[92] Therefore the concept of 'control' should replace the unhelpful concept of ownership per se.

The information is not necessarily currently fit for sharing with the individual or for collective transparency. Information within health records must be standardised and understandable to enable information to be controlled by the patient to the extent they choose to do this. We argue that online records are required to facilitate this. Timescales are required to address the information issues – it is accepted that the information is not always in a fit state to share (e.g., a mix of paper and electronic records, the coding is too complex to share, etc.). It is suggested that metadata be used, not actual medical notes, so that summary data is stored. In time the same portal could evolve to show the actual data recorded but this is acknowledged to be an aspiration.

At present, technical controls within medical information systems are laudably designed for control by patients but are controlled by clinicians. Innovation needs to be used by the patient as an impartial vehicle to deliver control – allowing the individual to control their own information and to use the autonomous laws as intended. The problem of control cannot be solved without applying relevant technology. The practical implementation part of the solution is through innovation – portals named the MIi Fit for individuals to control (and define) their own privacy and the WIi Fit for the NHS to transparently show how 'collective transparency' is complementary to individual privacy. The records are stored in fragmented systems so it may be difficult to get the systems to talk to each other so that a full audit trail can be implemented across all records. Again, the WIi Fit and MIi Fit looks are suggested to implement what is possible in the short term in line with government pledges to allow public access to GP records. However the concept is scalable so when the technology

92 Mark A. Hall, 'Property, Privacy, and the Pursuit of Interconnected Electronic Medical Records' (2010) 95 *Iowa L. Rev.* 647.

becomes more interoperable, the portal is made available. However, questions remain around the technical security of the portal. It is absolutely necessary to design an enhanced security concept in this context. It is expected that standards, education and awareness would all have a part to play in the technical security of the portal.

The portal will also empower individuals to control their legal rights and ensure sharing choices are legal in line with EU law. The legal ownership of records will be clarified. The clinician and/or individual can own the information through the appropriate transparency and control and the individual would never directly alter the master copy of the record. Any additions would be made to a 'patient' copy of the record. Legal liability would be addressed by the individual being made aware of the repercussions of sharing decisions (i.e., obtaining informed consent), perhaps face to face or as deemed appropriate.

We argue that the 'choice of control' over personal health information should be moved to individuals which will render 'privacy' as it is currently viewed as a largely negative concept, redundant, while validating 'confidentiality' as a positive concept, activated legitimately through consent from empowered individuals. However, the opportunity to eradicate negative and redundant privacy connotations and replace them with 'control' as a positive enabler will also provide background discussion on the current government framework which contextualises this. It is proposed that combining theory and practice in this way means that 'control' can replace the 'privacy' myth and that control of information is a vital step towards empowering choice of care. 'MI Information Revolution' should be considered as the 'Real Information Revolution' empowering the choice of a full (or partial) revolution from choice *of* control to choice *and* control.

The theoretical element binds the first two issues outlined as problematic – mindset and information – by creating a framework of varying levels of control of information individuals may choose based on their own definition of privacy. This will validate 'confidentiality' by patients consenting to the current 'proxy-individual' control or to accept varying levels of control. This is phrased the 'MI Information Revolution'. The practical implementation part of the solution is through the third issue outlined – innovation: portals named the MIi Fit for individuals to control (and define) their own privacy and the WIi Fit for the NHS to transparently show how 'collective transparency' is complementary to individual privacy. Combining theory and practice in this way means that 'control' can replace the 'privacy' myth and also that control of information is a vital step towards empowering choice of care. As a result, 'MI Information revolution' should be considered the real information revolution. Because this is about individual behaviour, we must consider behavioural aspects and patterns. On a behavioural level, the power aspect of control that this vehicle introduces is based on the 'the expectation of having the power to participate in making decisions to obtain desirable consequences but also related to personal competence'.[93]

Could real 'control' replace privacy issues? We argue that when placing the theory and application together, control can be conceptualised as privacy in real life – matching the problems in the first part with the solutions suggested in the second part in a practical way and drawing conclusions to address whether control can, in reality, replace the privacy myth. The key difference is that the risk–benefit decision previously made by the NHS can now be made by the individual; if individuals decide to accept this control, they decide what privacy is – through control. The application of the 'MI Information Revolution' model through the MIi Fit and WIi Fit shows how technology can provide an impartial vehicle to distribute control and redefine 'privacy'. The *Information Revolution* promises choice and control to patients but does not consider the repositioning of Information Governance as an enabler. The privacy framework per se is fit for purpose – the way it is governed renders it unfit for purpose, and the roles of individuals and the NHS need to be reconsidered and are presented as the problem. The NHS assumes a paternal 'proxy' individual role, which means that the role of the individual is masked so that autonomy based laws cannot be enforced. Confidentiality is the ruling concept that governs the legal processing of data, but it is often not underpinned by consent of the patient and is therefore illegitimate.

We encounter technology as a source of opportunities and when individuals feel empowered they are motivated to use technology more rigorously.[94] We further argue that this technological orientation provides us with the opportunity to use technology to control 'privacy'. Although we agree that this is 'more about perceived control,[95] it also highlights the mutual dependencies between 'control' and 'privacy'. As has been emphasised before the ultimate aim of privacy is to 'enhance autonomy and/or minimise vulnerability'.[96] This epitomises the control that the MIi Fit and WIi Fit offer. This encapsulates the Information Revolution's aims; therefore, it empowers the traditional notion of privacy through control.

---

93 J. Rodin, 'Control by Any Other Name: Definitions, Concepts and Processes' in J. Rodin, C. Schooler and K. Schaie (eds), *Self Directedness: Cause and Effects Throughout the Life Course* (Erlbaum 1990).

94 Spiekermann, S. 'Perceived Control: Scales for Privacy in Ubiquitous Computing' (10th International Conference on User Modelling, July 2005), www.isr.uci.edu/pep05/papers/UM05_Spiekermann_final2.pdf.

95 Ibid.

96 See S. Margulis, 'Privacy as a Social Issue and Behavioral Concept' (2003) 59(2) *J. Social Issues* 243, 259.

This individual control involves the elements of choice that technology enables, providing a method of communicating where the two *Liberating the NHS* consultations' aims – choice and control – meet seamlessly. The control that technology offers promotes 'the active belief that one has a choice among responses that are differentially effective'.[97] This resolves one of 'man's perpetual battles',[98] providing 'the resolution of the discontinuity between advancing technology and man's ability to control it',[99] which in turn extends the logic that 'privacy' is fundamental, but only if perceived as control. Technology has continually forced the re-evaluation of the premises under which society operates and the assumptions upon which society balances new technology with perceptions of basic needs. Law generally develops in order to enforce those assumptions, but in the case of privacy, it encountered the essence of two basic needs – the NHS's control is the blocker of 'privacy', whilst individual control of technology is the enabler.

Similarly, although there is an argument that technology can be 'privacy-destroying',[100] this is only applicable when the information owner is not in 'control' and does not understand the security measures that technology offers. The technology has the ability to provide an impartial governance layer to replace the NHS, a vehicle for power dispersal without usurping any power and provides instrumental leverage over information. Hence, individuals must embrace technology and its security – attempts have already been made to develop legal responses to the assault on informational privacy by 'privacy-destroying' technologies through self-regulation, privacy-enhancing technologies, legislation, and property rights-based solutions.[101] In the proposed solution they already exist and can be built upon to guide 'divisions' relating to responsibility. Notwithstanding this, information and communication technology offers a solution to interpret and implement laws such as the Data Protection Act. The user model would implement familiar social media networking-style IG controls, such as those used on Facebook. The MIi Fit providing the interface for individual control and shared records for 'public good' would be facilitated through the WIi Fit interface, facilitating intelligence-based decision making through user control. Juxtaposed against the current agency model, where users trust that their agent (the NHS) and the network adhere to privacy preferences (IG controls), the electronic persona can flourish through

97 E. Langer, *The Psychology of Control* (Sage Publications 1983).

98 Ibid.

99 B. Mazlish, 'The Fourth Discontinuity' (1976) 8 *TC* 1.

100 See S. Garfinkel, *Database Nation: The Death of Privacy in the 21st Century* (O'Reilly Media 2000).

101 A. Froomkin, 'The Death of Privacy?' (2000) 52 *SLR* 1461, 1461.

the control, which is comparable to property rights[102] that increase in value through information sharing, benefiting individuals and society.

Although the 'user model' uses technology to interpret data protection rights as the NHS previously did, the Data Protection Act has served its purpose for the NHS, providing the basis for organically grown statutory provisions and behaviours.[103] However, it has not served its purpose for individuals. The DPA is required as guidance for individuals so that they know when they have a right to bring their grievances to the ICO. This would be facilitated by the technological interface, as individuals would be able to view audit trails of who has accessed what and for what purpose, which would serve as evidence for the ICO.

The *Information Revolution* can therefore facilitate real choice and control by providing the *choice of control* to individuals over their health records. This requires a focus on the value of information – what privacy is and what it means to individuals. The authors' own view is that the NHS's role is only the 'facilitating' part of the solution; the NHS must establish the information and innovation foundations to arrive at the solution to the problem of dispelling the 'privacy myth'. Most importantly, it must influence the mindset of society by transparently communicating the rationale for the various conceptions of 'privacy' to empower society to replace 'privacy' with control – empowering 'MI information revolution'. Individuals must then provide the missing part of the solution for themselves – choosing whether they want to alter their mindset to use information and innovation in a way to facilitate the MIi and/or WIi Fit, and ultimately, how they choose to conceptualise 'privacy'. The roles that individuals could undertake – if they choose to take advantage of the foundations laid by the NHS to allow them to control their information – are segmented into four options – each representing a 90-degree turn of the information revolution. As this is a choice and not an obligation (unlike the NHS's obligations), we position 'informed responsibility/control' as an alter ego of privacy, asserting that this would be underpinned by transparency and consideration of the value of primary and secondary information markets when viewing information as both intermediate and final goods. Examining the 'information' aspect for individuals, it plots the stages of mindset change that society may choose alongside the information available at each stage.

The thrust of the book has been that control could replace privacy at one end of the spectrum and confidentiality would be underpinned by consent

---

102 J. Litman, 'Information Privacy/Information Property' (2000) 52 *SLR* 1283; R. Murphy, 'Property Rights in Personal Information: An Economic Defence of Privacy' (1996) 84 *Geo. L. J.* 2381.

103 For example s. 251 of the NHS Act 2006.

at the other, while both would be accompanied by acknowledgement of varying levels of responsibility for the self through the MIi Fit and for society through the WIi Fit. Our proposed solution exploits the radical nature of the innovative technology for determining when an individual's control over information could start and end – a vehicle to communicate the suggested boundaries. Technology is presented as an impartial governance layer to replace the NHS's paternalism – a mechanism for power dispersal to define individual privacy without usurping any power. Individuals are empowered to control the boundaries of their responsibility through direct control of IG controls. Control could therefore reduce reliance on the HRA and rejuvenate the DPA as guidance for individuals, accompanied by direct redress through the ICO. Information would be recognisable as a property right that is 'leased' by society; therefore, enablers such as s. 251 NHS Act applications and their justifications must be transparent, accessible to and understandable by the public. This will empower individuals to act as juries for use of their own information for societal good.

It appears to the authors that this process, through increased transparency and awareness, will empower individuals to see for themselves the complementary nature of 'individual privacy' and 'collective transparency'. On the other hand, trying to implement the Information Revolution's aims of choice and control without first empowering individuals to reconceptualise privacy through the *choice of control* will continue to prove ineffective. This leads us to the conclusion that those who choose any degree of control (even those who defer control to the NHS) will reap the benefits of the 'real' information revolution, which, incidentally, will facilitate the *Information Revolution's* mantra of 'no decision about me, without me'.

Bibliography

Acquisti, A. and Grossklags, J., 'Privacy Attitudes and Privacy Behavior: Losses, Gains, and Hyperbolic Discounting' in Camp, J. and Lewis, S. (eds), *The Economics of Information Security* (2004).

Allen, A.L., *Uneasy Access: Privacy for Women in a Free Society* (Rowman and Littlefield 1988).

——*Unpopular Privacy: What Must We Hide?* (OUP 2011).

——'Natural Law, Slavery, and the Right to Privacy Tort' (2012) 81 *Fordham L. Rev.* 1187.

——'Privacy Law: Positive Theory and Normative Practice' (2013) 126 *Harv. L. Rev.* F. 241.

Altman, I., *The Environment and Social Behaviour: Privacy, Personal Space, Territory, Crowding* (Brooks/Cole 1975).

——'Privacy Regulation: Culturally Universal or Culturally Specific?' (1977) 33(3) *J. Social Issues* 66.

Anderson, J.G., 'Social, Ethical and Legal Barriers to E-health' (2007) 76 *Int. J. Med. Informatics* 481, 480–483.

Aplin, T., 'The Development of the Action for Breach of Confidence in a Post-HRA Era' (2007) IPQ 19.

Aplin, T., Bently, L., Johnson, P. and Malynicx, S., *Gurry on Breach of Confidence* (2012).

Appari, A. and Johnson, M., 'Information Security and Privacy in Healthcare: Current State of Research' (2010) 6(4) *Int. J. Internet and Enterprise Management*, 279–314.

Aronson, J. (2001) 'The Communication and Internet Revolution', in Baylis, J. and Smith, S. (eds), *The Globalisation of World Politics* (OUP 2001).

Awad, N.F. and Krishnan, M.S., 'The Personalization Privacy Paradox: An Empirical Evaluation of Information Transparency and the Willingness to be Profiled Online for Personalization' (2006) 30(1) *MIS Quarterly* 13–28.

Bamberger, K.A. and Mulligan, D.K., 'Privacy in Europe: Initial Data on Governance Choices and Corporate Practices' (2013) 81(5) *Geo. Wash. L. Rev.* 1529, 1529–1663.

Bansal, G., Zaheid, F.M. and Gefen, D., 'The Impact of Personal Dispositions on Privacy and Trust in Disclosing Health Information Online', Americas Conference on Information Systems, Keystone, CO, USA. http://aisel.aisnet.org/amcis2007/57.

Barney, D. *The Network Society* (Polity Press 2003).

Basu, S., 'Privacy Protection: A Tale of Two Cultures' (2012) 6(1) *Masaryk University Journal of Law and Technology*, 1–34.

Beardsley, E.L. 'Privacy: Autonomy and Selective Disclosure' in Pennock and Chapman (eds), *Privacy* (Nomos XIII) (New York: Atherton 1971).

Beniger, J.R., *The Control Revolution: Technological and Economic Origins of the Information Society* (Harvard University Press 1986).

Benn, S.I., *A Theory of Freedom* (CUP 1988).

Bergkamp, L., 'The Privacy Fallacy: Adverse Effects of Europe's Data Protection Policy in an Information-Driven Economy' (2002) 18 *Computer Law and Security Review* 1.

Bernstein, E.B., 'Health Privacy in Public Spaces' (2015) 66(5) *Alabama L. Rev.* 989.

Bessant, C., 'The Duty of Confidence' in C. Bessant (ed.), *Information Sharing Handbook* (Law Society, London 2009) 128.

Beurden, A., 'The European Perspective on E-health' in Callens, S., (ed.), *E-health and the Law* (Kluwer 2003).

Big Brother Watch UK, 'Broken Records: the Worrying Lack of Security Around Your Medical History, and How It Could Be Changing for the Worse' (2010) www.bigbrotherwatch.org.uk/brokenrecords/pdf.

Black, A., Car, J., Pagliari, C., 'The impact of eHealth on the Quality and Safety of Healthcare: A Systematic Overview' (2011) *PLoS Medicine* 8.

Bloustein, E., 'Privacy as an Aspect of Human Dignity: An Answer to Dean Prosser' (1964) 39 *NYU L. Rev.* 962.

Blumenthal, D. and Tavenner, M., 'The "Meaningful Use" Regulation for Electronic Health Records' (2010) 363(6) *N. Engl. J. Med.* 501, 504.

Bok, S., *Secrets: On the Ethics of Concealment and Revelation* (Pantheon 1982).

Bomash, K., 'Privacy and Public Health in the Information Age: Electronic Health Records and the Minnesota Health Records Act' (2009) 10(1) MINN. J.L. SCI. & TECH. 117–141.

Bork, R., *The Tempting of America: The Political Seduction of the Law* (Simon and Schuster 1990).

Brillon, S., 'The European Data Protection Legislation and the Medical Records' in Callens, S. (ed.), *E-Health and the Law* (Kluwer 2003).

Brinn, L. 'Ownership of Electronic Health Information Must Be Addressed' (2009) www.fuqua.duke.edu/news_events/releases/schulman_jama_health_info.

British Medical Association Guidance, Confidentiality and Disclosure of Health Information (BMA 1999).

Brown, B., 'New Technologies Have Created New Threats to Electronic Protected Health Information' (2009) 11 *J. Health Care Compliance* 35.

Buchanan, T., Paine, C.B., Joinson, A.N. and Reips, U.-D., 'Development of Measures of Online Privacy Concern and Protection for Use on the Internet' (2006) 58(2) *J. Am. Soc. Information Science and Technology* 57–165.

Burgoon, P.R., Burgoon, J.K.M, et al., 'Privacy Between Physicians and Patients: More Than a Matter of Confidentiality' (1989) 29 *Social Science and Medicine* 1381–1385.

Castells, M., *The Rise of the Network Society. The Information Age: Economy, Society and Culture* (2nd edn, Vol. 1, Blackwell 2000).

Cate, H., 'Protecting Privacy in Health Research: The Limits of Individual Choice' (2010) *Faculty Publications,* Paper 235.

Children's Legal Centre, 'Landmark Decision for Children's Rights' (1985) 22 *Childright* 11–18.

Chopra, A., Parl, T. and Levin, P., '"Blue Button" Provides Access to Downloadable Personal Health Data' *White House Blog* (7 October 2010).

Chretien, K.C., 'Online Posting of Unprofessional Content by Medical Students' (2009) 302(12) *JAMA* 1309–1315.

Christiansen, John R., 'Why Healthcare Information Isn't Property – And Why That Is To Everyone's Benefit' (2009) 27 *Health L. Dig.* 3, 5–6.

Clark, J., 'HIPAA as an Evidentiary Rule? An Analysis of Miguel M. and Its Impact' (2013) 26 *J. L. & Health* 1, 9.

Cohen, J., 'What is Privacy for?' (2012) 126 *Harv, L. Rev.* 1904.

Craig, J., 'Invasion of Privacy and Charter Values: The Common-Law Tort Awakens' (1997) 42 *McGill L. J.* 355, 360.

Cresswell, K.M. et al., 'Comparative Case Study Investigating Sociotechnical Processes of Change in the Context of a National Electronic Health Record Implementation' (2012) 18(4) *Health Informatics J.* 251–270.

Cruickshank, J., Packman, C. and Paxman, J., 'Personal Health Records: Putting Patients in Control' (2020health.org, September 2012).

Database State. A Report Commissioned by the Joseph Rowntree Reform Trust Ltd (Joseph Rowntree Reform Trust Ltd 2009).

Davis, K.B., 'Privacy Rights in Personal Information: HIPPA and the Privacy Gap Between Fundamental Privacy Rights and Medical Information' (2001) 19 *J. Marshall J. Computer & Info. L.* 535–556.

DeCew, J., *In Pursuit of Privacy: Law, Ethics, and the Rise of Technology* (Cornell University Press 1997).

DeCruz, S.P., 'Parents, Doctors and Children: the Gillick Case and Beyond' (1987) *J. Soc. Welfare L.* 93–108.

De Hert, P. and Papakonstantinou, V., 'The Proposed Data Protection Regulation Replacing Directive 95/46/EC: A Sound System for the Protection of Individuals' (2012) 28(2) *C.L.S. Rev.* 130–142.

Department of Health, 'Building a Safer NHS for Patients: Implementing an Organisation with a Memory' (2007).

——'NHS Information Governance, Guidance on Legal and Professional Obligations' (September 2007).

——'Equality and Excellence, Liberating the NHS' (White Paper, Cm 7881, 2010).

——'Liberating the NHS: An Information Revolution' (2010).

——'An Information Revolution: A Consultation on Proposals' (2010).

——'Liberating the NHS: Greater Choice and Control. A Consultation on Proposals' (2010).

——'Summary of Responses to the Consultation on the Additional Uses of Patient Data' (2010).

——'The Power of Information: Putting all of us in control of the health and social care information we need' (May 2012).

——'Information: To Share or Not to Share? The Information Governance Review' (March 2013).

——'Information: To Share or Not to Share? Government Response to the Caldicott Review' (September 2013).

——'Protecting Health and Care Information: A Consultation on Proposals to Introduce New Regulations' (June 2014).

Deutsch, K., 'Soziale und politische Aspekte der Informationsgesellschaft' in: Philipp Sonntag (ed.), *Die Zukunft der Informationsgesellschaft* (Haag & Herchen 1983) 68–88.

Dickens, B., 'Medical Records – Patient's Right to Receive Copies – Physician's Fiduciary Duty of Disclosure: *McInerney v. McDonald*' (1994) 73 *Can Bar Rev.* 234.

Di Iorio, C.T. and Carinci, F., 'Privacy and Health Care Information Systems: Where is the Balance?' in George, C, Whitehouse, D., Duquenoy, P. (eds), *e-Health: Legal, Ethical and Governance Challenges* (Springer-Verlag 2012).

Donelan, K. and Miralles, P.D., 'Consumers, EHRS and PHRs: Measures and Measurement' in Blumenthal, D. et al. (eds), *Health Information Technology in the United States: Where We Stand* (Robert Wood Johnson Foundation 2008) 56–72.

Donnelly, L., 'Hospital Records of All NHS Patients Sold to Insurers' *The Daily Telegraph* (London, 24 February 2014).

Doran, K., 'Medical Confidentiality: The Role of the Doctrine of Confidentiality in the Doctor–Patient Relationship' (1997) 3 *MLJI* 21.

Drucker, P. *The Age of Discontinuity* (Harper & Row 1969).

Dumortier, J. and Verhenneman, G., 'Legal Regulation of Electronic Health Records: A Comparative Analysis of Europe and the US' in George, C., Whitehouse, D., Duquenoy, P. (eds), *e-Health: Legal, Ethical and Governance Challenges* (Springer 2013).

European Commission, 'e-Health Task Force Report – Redesigning Health in Europe for 2020' (Publications Office of the European Union 2012).

——2004, 'e-Health – Making Healthcare Better for European Citizens: An Action Plan or European e-Health Area', SEC (2004) 539 COM (2004) 356 final, Brussels.

——2006, 'ICT for Health and i2010, Transforming the European Healthcare Landscape' (Publications Office of the European Union 2006).

——2008, 'Legally e-Health: Putting e-Health in its European Legal Context, Study Report' (European Communities, Luxembourg March 2008).

——2012, 'European Union e-Health Action Plan 2012–2020: Innovative Healthcare for the 21st Century: EC 2012', COM(2012) 736.

Evans, B.J., 'Congress' New Infrastructural Model of Medical Privacy' (2009) 84 *Notre Dame L. Rev.* 585, 596–597.

——'Would Patient Ownership of Health Data Improve Confidentiality?' (2012) 14(9) *Am. Med. Assoc. J. Ethics* 724–732.

Faccenda, M. and Parkin, L., 'Meaningful Use—What Does It Mean To You?' (2011) 23 *Health Law* 10.

Feenan, D., 'Common Law Access to Medical Records' (1996) 59 *MLR* 101.

Feinberg, J., *Harm to Self* (OUP 1986).

Feldman, D., 'Secrecy, Dignity or Autonomy? Views of Privacy as a Civil Liberty' (1994) 47 *CLP* 41.

——'Human Dignity as a Legal Value: Part 1' (1999) *PL* 682.

Ferguson, T., 'Online Patient-Helpers and Physicians Working Together: A New Partnership for High Quality Health Care' (2000) 321 *BMJ* 1129–1132.

Fortin, S. and Knoppers, B., 'Secondary Uses of Personal Data for Population Research' 5 (2009) *Genomics, Society and Policy* 80.

Foster, C. and Peacock, N., *Clinical Confidentiality* (Monitor Press 2000).

Fredman, S., *Human Rights Transformed* (OUP 2008).

Fried, C., 'Privacy' (1968) 77 *Yale L. J.* 475.

——*An Anatomy of Values: Problems of Personal and Social Choice* (Harvard University Press 1971).

——'Privacy' in Schoeman, F.D. (ed.) *Philosophical Dimensions of Privacy* (CUP 1984).

Friedman, C.P. Lakovidis, I., Debenedetti, L., Lorenzi, N.M., 'Across the Atlantic Cooperation to Address International Challenges in e-Health and Health IT: Managing Toward a Common Goal' (2009) 78 *Int. J. Med. Informatics* 778–784.

Froomkin, A., 'Regulation of Computing and Information Technology. flood Control on the Information Ocean: Living with Anonymity, Digital Cash and Distributed Databases' (1996) 15(2) *J. L. & Com.* 395.

——'The Death of Privacy?' (2000) 52 *Stanford Law Review* 1461.

Gavison, R., 'Privacy and the Limits of Law' (1980) 89 *Yale L. J.* 421–471.

General Medical Council, Confidentiality: Protecting and Providing Information (GMC 2000).

——*Confidentiality* (GMC 2009).

George, C., 'Internet Pharmacies: Global Threat Requires Global Approach to Regulation' (2009) 9(3) *Telehealth Law* 37–52.

Gerstein, R. 'Intimacy and Privacy' in Schoeman, F. (ed.) *Philosophical Dimensions of Privacy: an Anthology* (CUP 1984).

Gindin, S.E., 'Lost and Found in Cyberspace: Informational Privacy in the Age of the Internet' (1997) 34 *San Diego L. Rev.* 1153, 1195.

Goldstein, M., Repasch, L. and Rosenbaum, S., 'Emerging Privacy Issues in Health Information Technology' in Blumenthal et al. (eds), *Health Information Technology in the United States: Where We Stand* (Robert Wood Johnson Foundation 2008).

Gostin, L.O., *Public Health Law: Power, Duty, Restraint* (2nd edn, University of California Press 2009).

Grace, J. and Taylor, M., 'Disclosure of Confidential Patient Information and the Duty to Consult: the Role of the Health and Social Care Information Centre' (2013) 21(3) *Med. L. Rev.* 415–447.

Gray, B.H., Bowden, T., Johansen, I. and Koch, S., 'Electronic Health Records: An International Perspective on "Meaningful Use"' (2011) 1565 (28) *Issues in International Health Policy*, (Commonwealth Fund publication).

Gray, J.L., 'A Right to be forgotten: The Far-reaching Implications' (2011) 8(5) *Data Protection Law and Policy* 14.

Gray, K., 'The Privacy Rule: Are We Being Deceived?' (2008) 11 *DePaul J. Health Care L.* 89–94.

Greenhalgh, T., Stramer, K., Bratan, T., Byrne, E., Russell, J., Hinder, S., Potts, H., 'The Devil's in the Detail: Final Report of the Independent Evaluation of the Summary Care Record and HealthSpace Programmes' (University College London 2010) available at www.ucl.ac.uk/news/sciesummary.pdf.

Gross, H., 'The Concept of Privacy' (1967) 42 *NYU L. Rev.* 34.

Hall, M.A., 'Property, Privacy, and the Pursuit of Interconnected Electronic Medical Records' (2010) 95 *Iowa L. Rev.* 642, 647.

——and Schulman, K.A., 'Ownership of Medical Information' (2009) 301 *JAMA* 1282.

Halperin, R. and Backhouse, J., 'A Roadmap for Research on Identity in the Information Society' (2008) 1(1) *Identity in the Information Society* 71–87.

Hartlev, M. *Study of Legal Framework of Interoperable e-Health in Europe – Nation Profile Denmark.* (Copenhagen, Denmark: European Commission Directorate General Information Society 2008).

Hatzopoulos, V., 'Is It Healthy to Have an EU Health Law?' (2005) 30(5) *E. L. Rev.* 705, 697–711.

Hervey, T. and McHale, J., *Health and the European Union* (CUP 2004).

Heywood, R., Macaskill, A. and Williams, K., 'Patient Perceptions of the Consent Process: Qualitative Inquiry and Legal Reflection' (2008) *J. Professional Negligence* 106.

Hill, E.M., Turner, E.L., Martin, R.M. and Donovan, J.L., '"Let's Get the Best Quality Research We Can": Public Awareness and Acceptance of Consent to use Existing Data in Health Research: A Systematic Review and Qualitative Study' (2013) 13 *BMC Medical Research Methodology* 72.

Hiller, J., McMullen, M., Chumney, W. and Baumer, D., 'Privacy and Security in the Implementation of Health Information Technology (Electronic Health Records): US and EU Compared' (2011) 17(1) *Boston U. J. Sci. Technol. L.* 1.

Hirschleifer, J., 'Privacy: its Origin, Function and Future' (1980) 9 *JLS* 649.

Hodge, J.G., 'Health Information Privacy and Public Health' (2003) 31(4) *J. Law, Medicine and Ethics* 663–671.

Hoerbst, A., Kohl, C., Knaup, P., Ammenwerth, E., 'Attitudes and Behaviors Related to the Introduction of Electronic Health Records among Austrian and German Citizens' (2010) 79(2) *Int. J. Med. Informatics* 81–89.

Hooghiemstra, T., 'Introduction to the Special Privacy Issue' (2002) 9 *EJHL* 181.

House of Lords Constitution Committee, 'Surveillance: Citizens and the State' (2008–2009).

Hustinx, P., 'Ensuring Trust in e-Health through Strong Health Data Protection' (European Policy Summit 'Planning Europe's Healthcare Revolution' Friends of Europe, Brussels, 2 December 2009).

Information Commissioner's Office, 'Who Cares About Data Protection? Data Protection Act: Segmentation Research' (2003) 12.

——Anonymisation: Managing Data Protection Risk Code of Practice (November 2012).

——Determining What is Personal Data (2012).

——Proposed New General Data Protection Resolution: Article-by-Article Analysis Paper (2013).

Jellinek, D., 'Why Sharing Data Can Save Services' *The Guardian* (London, 23 January 2013).

Jenkins, G., Merz, J.F. and Sankar, P., 'A Qualitative Study of Women's Views on Medical Confidentiality' (2005) 31 (9) *J. Med. Ethics*. 499–504

Johnson, C., 'Privacy as Personal Control' in Carson, D. (ed.), *Man–Environment Interactions: Evaluations and Applications* (Washington, DC: Environmental Design Research Association 1974).

Johnson, J.L., 'Privacy, Liberty and Integrity' (1989) 3 *Public Affairs Q.* 15–34.

Joint Committee on Human Rights, 'Data Protection and Human Rights' (House of Lords, 2007–2008).

——'Legislative Scrutiny: Coroners and Justices Bill' (2008–2009).

Jones, M., 'Medical Confidentiality and the Public Interest' (1990) 6(1) *PN* 16.

Journard, S.M., 'Some Psychological Aspects of Privacy' (1966) 31 *LCP* 307.

Kaiser, J., 'Patient Privacy: Rule To Protect Records May Doom Long-term Heart Study' (2006) 311(5767) *Science* 1547–1548.

Kappel, K., 'Epistemological Dimensions of Informational Privacy' (2013) 10 *Episteme* 179–192.

Kaye, R., Kokia, E., Shalev, V., Idar, D. and Chinitz, D., 'Barriers and Success Factors in Health Information Technology: A practitioner's perspective' (2010) 3(2) *J Management & Marketing in Healthcare* 165, 163–175.

Kelvin, P., 'A Social-psychological Examination of Privacy' (1973) 12(3) *Br. J. Social and Clinical Psychology* 248–261.

Keshavjee, K., Bosomworth, J., Copen, J., Lai, J., Kucukyazici, B., Liani, R., Holbrook, A.M., 'Best Practices in EMR Implementation: A Systematic Review' (Proceedings of the 11th International Symposium on Health Information Management Research) 2006, 1–15.

Khan, A. and McKillop, I., 'Privacy-centric Access Control for Distributed Heterogeneous Medical Information Systems' *ICHI 2013* (Proceedings of the 2013 IEEE International Conference on Healthcare Informatics, Philadelphia, PA, 9–11 September, 2013) 297–306.

Kirby, M.D., 'Informed Consent: What Does It Mean?' (1983) 9 *J. Med. Ethics* 69–75.

——'A Patient's Right of Access to Medical Records' (1996) 12 *J. Contemp. Health Law and Policy* 93, 98.

Kluge, E.H.W., 'Patients, Patient Records, and Ethical Principles' in Greenes, R.A. et al. (eds), (*Medinfo* 8, Pt 2 1995) 1596–1600.

——'Informed Consent and the Security of the Electronic Health Record (EHR): Some Policy Considerations' (2004) 73(3) *In. J. Med. Informatics* 229–234.

Knoppers, B., 'Confidentiality and Accessibility of Medical Information: A Comparative Analysis' (1982) 12 *RDUS* 431.

Koocher, G.P. and Keith-Spiegel, P.C., *Children, Ethics, and the Law: Professional Issues and Cases* (University of Nebraska Press 1990).

Kottow, M., 'The Battering of Informed Consent' (2004) 30 *J. Med. Ethics* 565–569.

Kristensen, M., *Addressing the Challenges of an Ageing Population through e-Health* (Danish Health and Medicines Authority 2012).

Kuan Hon, W., Millard, C. and Walden, I., 'The Problem of "Personal Data" in Cloud Computing—What Information is regulated? The Cloud of Unknowing' (2011) 1(4) *IDPL* 211–228.

Kumm, M. and Ferrerez Cornelia, V., 'What's So Special about Constitutional Rights in Private Litigation? A Comparative Analysis of the Function of State Action Requirements and Indirect Horizontal Effect' in Sajo, A. and Uitz, R. (eds), *The Constitution in Private Relations* (Eleven International Publishing 2005).

Laurie, G. and Postan, E., 'Rhetoric or Reality: What is the Legal Status of the Consent Form in Health-related Research' (2013) 21 *Med. L. Rev.* 371–414.

Laurie, G. and Sethi, N., 'Towards Principles-Based Approaches to Governance of Health-Related Research Using Personal Data' (2013) *EJRR* 43–57.

Law Commission, 'Data Sharing between Public Bodies', Law Commission Consultation Paper No 214, (2013) available at www.lawcom.gov.uk/wp-content/uploads/2015/03/cp214_data-sharing.pdf.

Leith, P., 'The Socio-Legal Context of Privacy' (2006) 2 *Int. J. Law in Context* 105.

Letsas, G., 'Two Concepts of the Margin of Appreciation' (2006) 26 *OJLS* 705, 717.

Lever, A., 'Privacy: Restrictions and Decisions' (2013) 12(1) *Philosophy and Law* 1–7.

Liginlal, D., Sim, I., Khansa, L., Fearn, P., 'HIPAA Privacy Rule Compliance: An Interpretive Study Using Norman's Action Theory' (2012) 31 *Computers & Security* 206–220.

Litman, J., 'Information Privacy/Information Property' (2000) 52 *Stanford Law Review* 1283.

Lwin, M.O. and Williams, J.D., 'A Model Integrating the Multidimensional Developmental Theory of Privacy and Theory of Planned Behaviour to Examine Fabrication of Information Online' (2003) 14(4) *Marketing Letters* 257–272.

Lyon, D., *Surveillance Society: Monitoring Everyday Life* (Open University Press 2001).

McCartney, M., 'Care.data Doesn't Care Enough about Consent' (2004) 348 *BMJ* g2831.

Maclean, A., 'Giving the Reasonable Patient a Voice: Information Disclosure and the Relevance of Empirical Evidence' (2005) 7 *Med. L. Int.* 1,12.

Macleod, U. and Watt, G.C.M., 'The impact of consent on observational research: a comparison of outcomes from consenters and non-consenters to an observational study' (2008) 8(15) *BMC Medical Research Methodology* 1–6.

McConnell, H., 'International Efforts in Implementing National Health Information Infrastructure and Electronic Health Records' (2004) 40(1) *World Hospitals and Health Services* 33–37, 39–40, 50–52.

McHale, J., *Medical Confidentiality and Legal Privilege* (Routledge 1993).

McKee, M., Mossialos, E. and Baeten, R. (eds), *The Impact of EU Law on Healthcare Systems* (P.I.E.-Peter Lang 2002).

McKinsey Global Institute, 'Big Data: The Next Frontier for Innovation, Competition and Productivity' (McKinsey and Company 2011).

Manos, D., 'Privacy Experts Debate Patient Consent' (2009) *Healthcare IT News* (21 September 2009), available at www.healthcarenews.com/news/privacy-experte-debatepatient-consent.

Mantovani, E. and Quinn, P., 'e-Health and Data Protection – The Letter and the Spirit of Consent Legal Requirements' (2013) *Int. Rev. L. Computers & Tech.* 222–236.

Margulis, S., 'Perceptions of Privacy: Current Status and Next Steps' (1977) 33(3) *J. Social Issues* 5.

——'Privacy as a Social Issue and Behavioral Concept' (2003) 59(2) *J. Social Issues* 243, 259.

Marsh, Jr, R., 'Legislation for effective self-regulation: a new approach to protecting personal privacy on the Internet' (2009) 15 *Michigan Telecommun. Technol. L. Rev.* 543.

Mazlish, B., 'The Fourth Discontinuity' (1976) 8 *TC* 1.

Medical Research Council, *Personal Information in Medical Research* (MRC 2000).

Metlay, D., 'Institutional Trust and Confidence: A Journey into Conceptual Quagmire', in Cvetkovich, G. and Lofstedt, R. (eds), *Social Trust and the Management of Risk* (Earthscan 1999).

Miller, A., *The Assault on Privacy: Computers, Data Bases and Dossiers* (University of Michigan Press 1971).

Miller, A.R. and Tucker, C., 'Privacy Protection and Technology Diffusion: The Case of Electronic Medical Records' (2009) 55(7) *Management. Sci.* 1077, 1083.

Miller, R.H., 'Satisfying Patient-Consumer Principles for Health Information Exchange: Evidence From California Case Studies' (2012) 31(3) *Health Affairs* 537.

Mills, J.S., *On Liberty* (Longman, Roberts and Green 1869).

Milne, G.R. and Gordon, M.E., 'Direct Mail Privacy-Efficiency Trade-Offs within an Implied Social Contract Framework' (1993) 12 *J. Public Policy and Marketing* 206–215.

Ministry of Justice, Mandatory Minimum Measures for Protection of Personal Data, Annex to E of the Data Sharing Protocol. www.justice.gov.uk/downloads/information-accessrights/data-sharing/annex-e-mandatory-minimum-measures.pdf.

Miola, J., 'Owning Information – Anonymity, Confidentiality and Human Rights' (2008) 3(3) *Clinical Ethics* 116.

Moen, A. et al., 'eHealth in Europe – Status and Challenges' (2012) 8(1) *Eur. J. Biomedical Informatics* 2–7.

Moller, K., 'Two Conceptions of Positive Liberty: Towards an Autonomy-based Theory of Constitutional Rights' (2009) OJLS 757.

Moor, J., 'Towards a Theory of Privacy in the Information Age' (1997) 27 *Computers and Society* 3, 27.

Moore, A.D., 'Privacy: Its Meaning and Value' (2003) 40(3) *Am Philos. Q.* 215–217.

Moore, B., *Privacy: Studies in Social and Cultural History* (M E Sharpe 1984) 274.

Moore, I.N. et al., 'Confidentiality and Privacy in Health Care from the Patient's Perspective: Does HIPAA Help?' (2007) 17 *Health Matrix* 215, 219–227.

Morgan, J., 'Privacy in the House of Lords, Again' (2004) 120 *LQR* 563.

Mossialos et al. (eds), *Health Systems Governance in Europe: the Role of European Law and Policy* (CUP 2010).

Mulheron, R., 'A Potential Framework for Privacy? A Reply to Hello!' (2006) 69(5) *MLR* 679.

Mungamuru, B., Garcia-Molina, H., and Mitra, S., 'How To Safeguard Your Sensitive Data' in *Reliable Distributed Systems, SRDS 2006: 25th IEEE Symposium* (2–4 Oct. 2006), 199–211.

Mungamuru, B., Garcia-Molina, H. and Olston, C., *Configurations: Understanding Alternatives for Safeguarding Data* (Technical Report; Stanford 2005).

Murphy, R. 'Property Rights in Personal Information: An Economic Defence of Privacy' (1996) 84 *Geo. L. J.* 2381.

Nahra, K., 'Analysing the US HIPAA Legacy and Future Changes on the Horizon' (2013) 10(2) *DPL & P* 1–6.

National Information Board, 'Personalised Health and Care 2020 Using Data and Technology to Transform Outcomes for Patients and Citizens: A Framework for Action' (November 2014).

National Treatment Agency for Substance Misuse, 'Confidentiality and Information Sharing' (September 2003).

Ness, R.B., 'Influence of the HIPAA Privacy Rule on Health Research' (2007) 298(18) *JAMA* 2164–2170.

Newdick, C., 'NHS Governance after Bristol: Holding On, or Letting Go?' (2002) *MLR* 111.

——'Citizenship, Free Movement and Health Care: Cementing Individual Rights by Corroding Social Solidarity' (2006) 43 *CML Rev.* 1645.

Nguyen, L. et al., 'Electronic Health Records Implementation: An Evaluation of Information System Impact and Contingency Factors' (2014) 83(11) *Int. J. Med. Informatics* 779–796.

Nicholas, N. and Nicholas, S., 'Understanding Confidentiality and the Law on Access to Medical Records' (2010) 20 *Obstet. Gynaecol. Reprod. Med.* 161–163.

Nielsen, Claus D. et al., *Strategic Intelligence Monitor on Personal Health Systems: Country Study: Denmark*, Scientific and Policy Report by the Joint Research Centre of the European Commission (Publications Office of the European Union 2013).

Nissenbaum, H., 'Protecting Privacy in an Information Age: The Problem of Privacy in Public' (1998) 17 *Law and Philosophy* 559–596.

Noble, S., Donovan, J., Turner, E., Metcalfe, C., Lane, A., Rowlands, M.A., Neal, D., Hamdy, F., Ben-Shlomo, Y., Martin, R., 'Feasibility and Cost of Obtaining Informed Consent for Essential Review of Medical Records in Large-Scale Health Services Research' (2009) 14 *J. Health Serv. Res. Policy* 77–81.

Nordgren, A., 'Personal Health Monitoring: Ethical Considerations for Stakeholders' (2013) 11(3) *J. Information, Communication and Ethics in Society* 156–173.

OECD Working Party on Information Security and Privacy, 'The Evolving Privacy Landscape: 30 years after the OECD privacy guidelines' (April 2011).

Ohm, P., 'Broken Promises of Privacy: Responding to the Surprising Failure of Anonymization' (2010) 57 UCLA L. Rev. 1701.

Oliver, D. and Fedtke, J. (eds), *Human Rights and the Private Sphere* (Routledge-Cavendish 2007).

Oswald, M., 'Sealed Envelopes Briefing Paper: "Selective Alerting" Approach' (NHS 2006).

Ouellette, A. and Reider, J., 'Practical, State, and Federal Limits on the Scope of Compelled Disclosure of Health Records' (2007) 7 *Am. J. Bioethics* 46.

Ovey, C. and White, R., *The European Convention on Human Rights* (OUP 2006).

Pagliari, C., *Literature Review and Conceptual Map of the Area of e-Health* (NHS SDO 2005).

——Shand, T. and Fisher, B., 'Embedding Online Patient Record Access in UK Primary Care: A Survey of Stakeholder Experiences' (2012) 3(34) *J. R. Soc. Med.* Short Rep.

Parent, W., 'Privacy, Morality and the Law' (1983) 12(4) *Philosophy and Public Affairs* 269.

Parent, W.A., 'Recent Work on the Concept of Privacy' (1983) 20 *Am. Philos. Q.* 341–356.

Pasquale, F., 'Grand Bargains for Big Data: The Emerging Law of Health Information' (2013) 72 *Md. L. Rev.* 682–772.

Peel, D.C., 'Written Testimony Before the HIT Policy Committee, Electronic Privacy Information Center' (18 September 2009).

Perez-Carceles, M., Pereniguez, J., Osuna, E., and Luna, A., 'Balancing Confidentiality and the Information Provided to Families of Patients in Primary Care' (2005) 31(9) *J. Med. Ethics* 531–535.

Petkovic, M. and Ibraimi, L., 'Privacy and Security in E-Health Applications' in Carsten Röcker and Martina Ziefle' (eds), *E-Health, Assistive Technologies and Applications for Assisted Living: Challenges and Solutions* (IGI Global 2011).

Phillips, D.J., 'Privacy Policy and Pets: The Influence of Policy Regimes on the Development and Social Implications of Privacy Enhancing Technologies' (2004) 6(6) *New Media & Society* 691–706.

Pine, M., Sonneborn, M., Schindler, J., Stanek, M., Maeda, J.L., Hanlon, C., 'Harnessing the Power of Enhanced Data for Healthcare Quality Improvement: Lessons from a Minnesota Hospital Association Pilot Project' (2012) 57(6) *J. Healthcare Management* 406–420.

Pollio, M.C., 'The Inadequacy of HIPAA's Privacy Rule: The Plain Language Notice of Privacy Practices and Patient Understanding' (2004) 60 *NYU Ann. Surv. Am. L.* 579.

Porat, M.U. and Rubin, M.R. *The Information Economy* (Office of Telecommunications Special Publication 77-12, 9 Vols, US Department of Commerce, Washington DC 1977).

Posner, R.A., 'The Right of Privacy' (1978) 12 *Ga. L. Rev.* 393.

Post, R., 'The Social Foundations of Privacy: Community and Self in the Common Law Tort' (1989) 77 *Calif. L. Rev.* 957, 974.

Pritchett, S., 'Care.data – Why Should We Care?' (2014) 14(4) *P. & D.P.* 14–16.

Prosser, W., 'Privacy' (1960) 48 *Calif. L. Rev.* 383.

Pruski, C., 'e-crl: A Rule-based Language for Expressing Patient Electronic Consent' (International Conference on eHealth, Telemedicine, and Social Medicine 2010).

Quinn, P. and De Hert, P., 'The European Patients' Rights Directive: A Clarification and Codification of Individual Rights Relating to Cross Border Healthcare and Novel Initiatives aimed at Improving Pan-European Healthcare Co-operation' (2012) 12(1) *Med. L. Int.* 28–69.

Rachels, J., 'Why Privacy is Important' (1975) 4 *Philosophy and Public Affairs* 323.

Ram, N., 'Assigning Rights and Protecting Interests: Constructing Ethical and Efficient Rights in Human Tissue Research' (2009) 23(1) *Harv. J. L. & Tech.* 141.

Raman, A., 'Enforcing Privacy through Security in Remote Patient Monitoring Ecosystems' (6th International Special Topic Conference on Information Technology Applications in Biomedicine, Tokyo, Japan, 2007).

Regan, P., 'Privacy as a Common Good in the Digital World' (2002) 5(3) *Information, Communication and Society* 382–450.

Reid, E., 'Data Protection: the Right to be Forgotten' (2012) 114 *Human Rights Updater* 14.

Reid, J., Cheong, I., Henricken, M. and Smith, J., 'A Novel use of RBAC to Protect Privacy in Distributed Health Care Information Systems' in *ACISP 03: Proceedings of the 8th Australasian Conference on Information Security and Privacy* (Springer-Verlag, 2003), 406, 403–415.

Reiman, J.H., 'Privacy, Intimacy, and Personhood' (1976) 6(1) *Philosophy and Public Affairs* 26–44.

Rindfleisch, T.C., 'Privacy, Information Technology, and Health Care' (1997) 40(8) *Commun. ACM* 93–100.

Rodin, J., 'Control by Any Other Name: Definitions, Concepts and Processes' in J. Rodin, C. Schooler and K. Schaie (eds), *Self Directedness: Cause and Effects Throughout the Life Course* (Erlbaum 1990).

Rodrigues, R.J., 'Opportunities and Challenges in the Deployment of Global e-Health' (2003) 5(3/4/5) *Int. J. Healthcare Technology and Management* 348, 335–357.

——Torre, I. de la., Fernández, G., López-Coronado, M., 'Analysis of the Security and Privacy Requirements of Cloud-Based Electronic Health Records Systems' (2013) 15(8) *J. Med. Internet Res.* e186.

Rodwin, M.A., 'Patient Data: Property, Privacy & the Public Interest' (2010) 36 *AJLM* 586–618.

Roosendaal, A., 'Right to be Forgotten vs Need to be Remembered' (2012) 22(6) *Computers and Law* 10.

Rossler, B., *The Value of Privacy* (Polity Press 2005).

Rubenfeld, J., 'The Right to Privacy' (1989) 102 *Harv. L. Rev.* 737–807.

Ruebhausen, M. and Brim, O.G., 'Privacy and Behavioural Research' (1965) 65 *Colum. L. Rev.* 1184.

Safran, C. et al., 'Toward a National Framework for the Secondary Use of Health Data: An American Medical Informatics Association White Paper' (2007) 14(1) *J. Am. Med. Informatics Assoc.* 3.

Saltman, R.B. and Cahn, Z., 'Restructuring Health Systems for an Era of Prolonged Austerity' (2013) *BMJ* 346.

Samuelson, P., 'Privacy as Intellectual Property' (2000) 52 *Stan. L. Rev.* 1130–1131, 1125, 1170–1171.

Sandland, R., 'Case Comment: Freedom of the Press and the Confidentiality of Medical Records' (2007) *MLR* 405.

——'Freedom of the Press and the Confidentiality of Medical Records' (2007) *MLR* 400.

Sankar, P., Moran, S., Merz, J.F. and Jones, N.L., 'Patient Perspectives on Medical Confidentiality: A Review of the Literature' (2003) 18 *J. Gen. Intern. Med.* 659–669.

Sauter, W., 'The Impact of EU Competition Law on National Healthcare Systems' (2013) *E. L. Rev.* 459.

Saxon, L.A., 'Owning Your Health Information: An Inalienable Right', *The Huffington Post* (7 October 2009), www.huffingtonpost.com/leslie-a-saxon-md/owning-your-healthinform_b_312852.html.

Schoeman, F., *Privacy and Social Freedom* (CUP 1992).

Schwartz, P.M., 'Privacy and Democracy in Cyberspace' (1999) *52* Vand. L. Rev. 1607.

Scottish Government, 'A Scotland-wide Data Linkage Framework for Statistics and Research: Consultation Paper on the Aims and Guiding Principles' (March 2012).

——'Joined-up Data for Better Decisions: A Strategy for Improving Data Access and Analysis' (2012).

Señor, Inmaculada Carrión, Aleman, Jose Luis Fernández and Toval, Ambrosio, 'Personal Health Records: New Means to Safely Handle Health Data? (2012) 45(11) *Computer* 27–33.

Shah, S.G.S. et al., 'Accessing Personal Medical Records Online: A Means to What Ends?' (2015) 84(2) *Int. J. Med. Informatics* 111–118.

Shakespeare Review: An Independent Review of Public Sector Information (Department for Business, Innovation & Skills, May 2013).

Sheehan, K., 'Towards a Typology of Internet Users and Online Privacy Concerns' (2002) 18(1) *The Information Society* 21–32.

Sheikh, A., 'Confidentiality and Privacy of Patient Information and Records: A Need for Vigilance in Accessing, Storing and Discussing Patient Information' (2010) 16(1) *MLJI* 2, 5.

Silverman, D.L., 'Data Security Breaches: The State of Notification Laws' (2007) 19 *Intell. Prop. & Tech. L. J.* 5, 8.

Singh, R. and Strachan, J., 'Privacy Postponed' (2003) *EHRLR* 11, 19.

Singleton, P., Wadsworth, M., 'Consent for the Use of Personal Medical Data in Research' (2006) 333 *BMJ* 255–258.

——'Public and Professional Attitudes to Privacy of Healthcare Data: A Survey of the Literature' (General Medical Council 2007).

Sirc, N., 'Data Protection and the NHS: Putting Patients First?' (2005) 2(50) *D.P.L & P* 6–7.

Sparks, P., 'The Impact of the Human Rights Act for Patients and Accident Victims' (2008) *JPIL* 97.

Spencer, A.L., 'Responding to Challenging Aspects of HITECH's Modifications to HIPAA' in *Recent Developments with HIPAA: Leading Lawyers on Interpreting the New HIPAA Laws, Developing Effective Compliance Strategies, and Responding to Recent Enforcement Actions* (Aspatore Books 2010).

Spiekermann, S., 'Perceived Control: Scales for Privacy in Ubiquitous Computing' (10th International Conference on User Modelling, July 2005).

Stauch, M., Forgó, N. and Krügel, T., 'Using EHRs to Design Drug Repositioning Trials: A Devolved Approach to Data Protection (2014) 28(2) *Int. Rev. L.* 237–248.

Sterckx, S., 'The UK National Health Service's "Innovation Agenda": Lessons on Commercialisation and Trust' (2014) 22(2) *Med. L. Rev.* 221, 223.

Stigler, G.J., 'An Introduction to Privacy in Economics and Politics' (1980) 9 *JLS* 623.

Strahilevitz, L., 'Toward a Positive Theory of Privacy Law' (2013) 126 *Harv. L. Rev.* 2010.

Stroetmann, K.A., Artmann, J., Stroetmann, V., 'Developing National e-Health Infrastructures – Results and Lessons from Europe' (AMIA Annual Symposium Proceedings, 2011).

——Artmann, J., Stroetmann, V.N., 'European Countries on Their Journey Towards National e-Health Infrastructures: Final European Progress Report' (European Commission 2011).

——Artmann, J., Jos Dumortier, J. and Verhenneman, G., 'United in Diversity: Legal Challenges on the Road Towards Interoperable e-Health Solutions in Europe' (2012) 8(2) *Eur. J. Biomed. Informatics* 3–10.

——Jones, T., Dobrev, A. and Stroetmann, V.N. 'e-Health is worth it? The Economic Benefits of Implemented e-Health Solutions at Ten European Sites', E-Health IMPACT project study supported by the European Commission Information Society and Media Directorate-General

(Luxembourg Office for Official Publications of the European Community 2006).

Sutton, J., 'Of Information, Trust, and Ice Cream: A Recipe for a Different Perspective on the Privacy of Health Information' (2013) 55 *Ariz. L. Rev.* 1178.

Tavani, H.T., 'Privacy Security' in Langford, D. (ed.), *Internet Ethics* (Macmillan Press 2001).

——'Philosophical Theories of Privacy: Implications for an Adequate Online Privacy Policy' (2007) 38(1) *Metaphilosophy* 1–22.

——and Moor, J.H., 'Privacy Protection, Control of Information, and Privacy-Enhancing Technologies' (2001) *Computers and Society* 8.

Taylor, M.J., *Genetic Data and the Law: A Critical Perspective on Privacy Protection* (CUP 2012).

——and Grace, J., 'Disclosure of Confidential Patient Information and the Duty to Consult: The Role of the Health and Social Care Information Centre' (2013) *Med. L. Rev.* 1–33.

——and Taylor, N., 'Health Research Access to Personal Confidential Data in England and Wales: Assessing Any Gap in Public Attitude between Preferable and Acceptable Models of Consent' (2014) 10 *Life Sciences, Society and Policy* 1–24.

Taylor, R., 'Reversing the Retreat from Gillick? R (Axon) v Secretary of State for Health' (2007) 19(1) *CFLQ* 81-97.

Tene, O. and Polonetsky, J., 'Big Data for All: Privacy and User Control in the Age of Analytics' (2013) 11 *Nw. J. Tech. & Intell. Prop.* 260.

Thaler, R.H., 'Show us the Data. (It's Ours, After All)' *New York Times* (23 April 2011) at BU4.

The Academy of Medical Sciences, 'A New Pathway for the Regulation and Governance of Health Research' (Academy of Medical Sciences 2011).

The Care Record Guarantee, Our Guarantee for NHS Care Records in England (NIGB, January 2011).

Thomas, R., 'What Price Privacy: The Unlawful Trade in Confidential Personal Information' (ICO, May 2006).

——and Walport, M., 'Data Sharing Review' (2006).

——and Walport, M., 'Data Sharing Review Report' (Ministry of Justice, UK July 2008).

Thomson, J., 'The right to Privacy' (1975) 4(4) *Philosophy and Public Affairs* 295.

——*On Privacy* (Routledge 2011).

Toulson, R.G. and Phipps, C., *Confidentiality*(2nd edn, Sweet and Maxwell 2006).

Trueland, J., 'Patient Records: Too Much Information?' (2014) 123(6391) *Health Service J.* Suppl. 10–11.

Turnbull, G., 'Cancer Registries Say Informed Consent is Unworkable' (2001) 18(2) *Br. J. Healthcare Computing and Information Management* 11.

Turner, J., *Do Tesco Customers Exhibit a Social Type of Loyalty towards Tesco and Tesco Clubcard? A Critical Analysis of the Nature and Type of Tesco Customer Loyalty* (VDM Publishing 2011).

UK Administrative Data Research Network, 'Improving Access for Research and Policy' (Report from the Administrative Data Taskforce, December 2012).

Van de Gronden, J., 'Cross-border Health Care in the EU and the Organization of National Health Care Systems of the Member States: the Dynamics Resulting from the European Court of Justice's Decisions on Free Movement and Competition Law' (2009) 26 *Wisconsin Int. L. J.* 705.

Van Dijk, J., *The Network Society: Social Aspects of New Media* (Sage Publications 2006).

Varian, H.R., 'Theory of Markets and Privacy' in *Privacy and Self-Regulation in the Information Age* (Washington, DC: US Department of Commerce, June 1997).

Vedder, A.H., 'Medical Data, New Information Technologies, and the Need for Normative Principles other than Privacy Rules' in Freeman, M. and Lewis, A. (eds), *Law and Medicine: Current Legal Issues* (OUP 2000) 441–459.

——*Personal Information: Privacy and the Law* (Clarendon Press 1989).

——*Personal Information: Privacy and the* Law (Clarendon Press 1993 (Paperback)).

Wacks, R., 'Private facts: Is Naomi Campbell a Good Model?' (2004) 3(1) *SCRIPT-ed*, 460. www.law.ed.ac.uk/ahre/script-ed/issue3.wacks.asp.

Waller, A.A. and Alcantara, O.L., 'Ownership of Health Information in the Information Age' (1998) 69 *J. Am. Health Information Management Assoc.* 28.

Warren, C. and Laslett, B., 'Privacy and Secrecy: A Conceptual Comparison' (1977) 33 J. Social Issues 43.

Warren, S. and Brandeis, L., 'The Right to Privacy' (1890) 4 *Harv. L. Rev.* 193, 205–215.

Watson, B.L., 'Disclosure of Computerized Health Care Information: Provider Privacy Rights under Supply Side Competition' (1981) 7 *AJLM* 265, 269.

Weinstein, M.A. 'The Uses of Privacy in the Good Life' (1971) 13 *Nomos* XIII 88 in Pennock, J.R. and Chapman, J.W. (eds), *Privacy Nomos* XIII (New York: Atherton 1971).

Westin, A., *Privacy and Freedom* (New York: Atheneum 1970).

——*Computers, Health Records, and Citizen's Rights* (NBS Monograph 157, United States Department of Commerce 1976).

——'Social and Political Dimensions of Privacy' (2003) 59 *Journal of Social Issues* 431.

Wheeler, R., 'Gillick or Fraser? A Plea for Consistency over Competence in Children' (2006) 332 *BMJ* 807.

Willison. J. et al., 'Alternatives to Project-specific Consent for Access to Personal Information for Health Research: What Is the Opinion of the Canadian Public?' (2007) 14 *J. Am. Med. Informatics Assoc.* 706, 706–712.

Working Party on the Protection of Individuals with regard to the Processing of Personal Data, 'Article 29' Opinion on Consent. WP131 – Working Document on the Processing of Personal Data Relating to Health in Electronic Health Records (EHR) (WP 131, 2007), available at http://ec.europa.eu/justice policies/privacy/docs/wpdocs/2007/wp131_en.pdf.

World Economic Forum, 'Rethinking Personal Data: Strengthening Trust' (May 2012).

Zakaria, N. and Stanton, J.M., 'The Social Dynamic of Health Disclosure: Who Do Patients Tell and When?' (2008) 1(1) *Computer and Information Sci.* 72–80.

Index

www.ingramcontent.com/pod-product-compliance
Ingram Content Group UK Ltd.
Pitfield, Milton Keynes, MK11 3LW, UK
UKHW022021180926
475701UK00005B/969

* 9 7 8 0 3 6 7 5 9 7 3 1 3 *